Windows 3.1

by Joe Kraynak

alpha books

A Division of Macmillan Computer Publishing
201 W. 103rd Street, Indianapolis, Indiana 46290 USA

To the Youngstown Kraynak Clan, for all the great memories—keep them coming!

©1994 Alpha Books

All rights reserved. No part of this book shall be reproduced, stored in a retrieval system, or transmitted by any means, electronic, mechanical, photocopying, recording, or otherwise, without written permission from the publisher. No patent liability is assumed with respect to the use of the information contained herein. Although every precaution has been taken in the preparation of this book, the publisher and author assume no responsibility for errors or omissions. Neither is any liability assumed for damages resulting from the use of the information contained herein. For information, address Alpha Books, 201 W. 103rd Street, Indianapolis, Indiana 46290.

International Standard Book Number: 1-56761-491-4

Library of Congress Catalog Card Number: 94-70827

96 95 94   8 7 6 5 4 3 2

Interpretation of the printing code: the rightmost number of the first series of numbers is the year of the book's printing; the rightmost number of the second series of numbers is the number of the book's printing. For example, a printing code of 94-1 shows that the first printing of the book occurred in 1994.

Printed in the United States of America

Publisher   *Marie Butler-Knight*

Managing Editor   *Elizabeth Keaffaber*

Acquisitions Manager   *Barry Pruett*

Product Development Manager   *Faithe Wempen*

Development Editor   *Kelly Oliver, Seta Frantz*

Production Editor   *Phil Kitchel*

Copy Editor   *Barry Childs-Helton*

Cover Designer   *Tim Amrhein*

Designer   *Barbara Webster*

Indexer   *Bront Davis*

Production Team   *Gary Adair, Dan Caparo, Brad Chinn, Kim Cofer, Mark Enochs, Stephanie Gregory, Jenny Kucera, Chad Poore, Beth Rago, Bobbi Satterfield, Marc Shecter, Kris Simmons, Greg Simsic, SA Springer, Carol Stamile, Robert Wolf*

Special thanks to C. Herbert Feltner for ensuring the technical accuracy of this book.

Contents

Part 1 Windows Basics

Part 2 Working with Applications

Part 3 Using Accessories and Games

Part 5 Using the Windows Control Panel

Introduction

Windows is billed as the graphical, user-friendly interface of the '90s. It has a desktop on which you can spread all your work and flip from one project to the next by poking around with your mouse. When you start using Windows, however, things may not seem all that easy. Where do you poke with the mouse? How do you poke? Where did the document you were just working on disappear to, and how can you get it back?

As you grip your mouse tighter and tighter, the last thing you need is a book that's packed with fluff. You need a book that cuts through the drivel, presents the information you need, and lets you skip the details. You need the *Windows 3.1 Cheat Sheet*.

This Book Is Different

Most computer books on the market are designed to make you work. Interesting or significant details are buried under mounds of text you have to dig through to find what you need. The *Cheat Sheet* is different:

- **Headings** appear in the left-hand margin of each page, labeling each section. This makes it easy to find (and skip) information.

- **Step-by-step instructions** lead you through each task. You don't have to wade through paragraphs to figure out what to do next.

- **Lots of pictures** help you see what's going on as you perform a task, and act as checkpoints so you can be sure you've done things right.

- **Paragraphs** are used sparingly and are kept brief, so you don't have to dig through text to find the important points.

- **Highlighting** is used to call your attention to important information.

- **A Cheat Sheet** at the beginning of each chapter gives a quick rundown of the steps you follow to perform the essential tasks in the chapter.

- **Basic Survival** tasks are covered first in each chapter. That way, you can easily avoid the more advanced material.

- **Beyond Survival** sections at the end of each chapter cover advanced features that tell you how to use a feature more efficiently, or customize it for a specific use.

- **Hand-written tips** in the left-hand column provide quick ways of performing a task or call your attention to important text.

- Three tear-out **Cheat Sheets** at the back of this book contain the most important concepts, tips, and step-by-step instructions for working in Windows.

Something for Everyone

Sure, this book is easy to use, but don't think of it as just another beginner's Windows book. Every chapter of the *Windows 3.1 Cheat Sheet* contains advanced tips that give you more control and a deeper understanding of Windows. You'll learn about special switches you can use to start Windows, the advanced information-sharing capabilities of Windows 3.1, how to choose a wallpaper design for Windows, how to optimize your computer's memory, and much more.

In addition, this book contains a nine-chapter section at the end that's devoted exclusively to advanced features, tricks, and troubleshooting in Windows 3.1.

How to Use This Book

This book is designed for users who like to skip around, and who need to find information in a hurry. However, it also has an overall structure that allows you to concentrate on certain aspects of Windows:

- **To install Windows**, see the appendix at the back of the book. Because so many computers come with Windows pre-installed, we chose to put installation instructions in the back to keep them out of the way.

- **To master Windows basics**, such as how to start Windows, select commands from menus, get help, and run applications, see Part 1, "Windows Basics."

- **To install and set up applications**, skip to Part 2, "Working with Applications." In this part, you learn how to install Windows applications, set up DOS applications to run under Windows, and go to the DOS prompt.

- **To use the applications that come with Windows**, look to Part 3, "Using the Accessories and Games." You'll learn how to use Write (the word processor), Paintbrush (the graphics program), Cardfile (the address book), and much more. You'll even learn how to use the applications together.

- **To manage your disks, files, and directories**, skip to Part 4, "Managing Disks, Files, and Directories," to learn how to use the Windows File Manager. You'll learn how to format floppy disks, create directories on a disk, and copy files by dragging them with the mouse pointer from one disk to another.

- **To control the look and behavior of Windows**, see Part 5, "Using the Windows Control Panel." You'll learn how to change your screen colors, add fancy wallpaper backgrounds, and have Windows use your hard disk as memory. You'll even learn how to turn on Windows screen savers, and use a password to prevent unauthorized use of your computer.

- **To optimize your system, troubleshoot problems, or have fun,** turn to Part 6, "Tricks and Traps." You'll learn how to get stubborn DOS applications up and running, speed up Windows, solve printer problems, and even view a brief Windows animation sequence.

No matter which section you turn to, you'll find the information you need in the easily accessible Cheat Sheet format.

Acknowledgments

Many individuals contributed their knowledge and expertise to this book. Special thanks go to the Development Editors: Seta Frantz, who pointed me in the right direction with this book, and Kelly Oliver, who provided valuable ideas, insights, and funny hand-drawn sketches. Thanks to Barry Childs-Helton (Copy Editor), for his language expertise and timely reality checks; and Phil Kitchel (Production Editor), for carefully managing this production and having the best music in the hall. Thanks also to Herb Feltner (Technical Editor) for painstakingly stripping out any errors. Oh yeah, and thanks to my boss, Barry Pruett (Acquisitions Manager) for not being bossy.

Trademarks

Microsoft ®, MS ®, and MS-DOS ® are registered trademarks, and Windows ™ is a trademark of Microsoft Corporation.

TrueType ® is a registered trademark of Apple Computer, Inc.

Compaq ® is a registered trademark of Compaq Computer Corporation.

Terminal was developed for Microsoft by Future Soft Engineering, Inc.

Hayes ® is a registered trademark of Hayes Microcomputer Products, Inc.

DeskJet ® and LaserJet ® are registered trademarks of Hewlett-Packard Company.

IBM ® is a registered trademark of International Business Machines, Inc.

Recorder was developed for Microsoft by Softbridge Ltd.

Paintbrush ™ is a trademark of ZSoft Corporation.

PART 1

Windows Basics

Windows is billed as the friendly interface; it's friendly to anyone who has used Windows for awhile. But I've seen beginning users fumble around as much in Windows as they do in DOS. If you don't know what you're doing, you can get buried in a stack of Windows. In this part, you learn how to fly through Windows and master the following basics:

- Starting Windows

- Meeting the Program Manager

- Running and Using Applications

- Entering Commands in Windows

- Working with Windows

- Working with Icons

- Getting Help

- Exiting Windows

Cheat Sheet

Starting Windows

1. At the DOS prompt, type **c:** and press Enter.
2. Type **cd \windows** and press Enter.
3. Type **win**.
4. Press Enter.

Using a Mouse

- **Point**   Roll the mouse on your desk until the tip of the mouse pointer touches the desired object.
- **Click**   Press and release the left mouse button once without moving the mouse.
- **Double-click**   Press and release the left mouse button twice quickly without moving the mouse.
- **Drag**   Hold down the left mouse button while moving the mouse.

Finding the Program Manager

- Look at the top of your screen. If you see Program Manager, you've found it.
- Look in the lower left corner of your screen. If you see the Program Manager icon , double-click on it.

1

Starting Microsoft Windows

Before you can do anything in Windows, first you have to start the program. In this chapter, you learn the basic Windows startup procedure—and some fancy, time-saving ways to dazzle your friends.

Basic Survival

Starting Windows

Your computer may be set up to run Windows automatically. You turn on the power, and after all the beeps and grinds, you see the Windows Program Manager. If that's the case, you can skip all the preliminaries about starting Windows.

If you see the Program Manager,
Windows is already started.

Here's the menu bar
(you'll use it later).

If you start your computer and see the **C:\>** prompt or a similar prompt, you'll need to enter the WIN command to start Windows. Here's how you do it:

1. Make sure the **C:\>** prompt is displayed. (Some computers display a menu when you start them. Find the Exit or Quit command, and select it to return to the prompt.)

2. Type **win** and press Enter. Windows displays its advertising screen, and then displays the Program Manager.

Type win :
for no
Windows
advertisement
window

If you get a message that says **Bad command or filename**, try typing **cd\windows** and pressing Enter, and then repeat step 2. If that doesn't work, Windows may be on another drive. Try changing to drive D or E.

No Program Manager?

If you don't see the Program Manager window, it may be shrunk down to the size of an icon (a small picture that represents an application). Look for the icon in the lower left corner of the screen. To display the Program Manager, try one of the following steps:

Ctrl + Esc
displays a list
of running
applications.

- If you see the Program Manager icon , move the tip of the mouse pointer over it, and press and release the left mouse button twice quickly.

- Move the tip of the mouse pointer over the Program Manager icon, click the left mouse button (a small menu appears) and then click on Restore.

- Hold down the Ctrl key while pressing the Esc key (Ctrl+Esc), click on Program Manager, and click on the Switch To button.

When you press Ctrl+Esc, you get a list of running applications.

Task List
Write - (Untitled)
Program Manager

Switch To	End Task	Cancel
Cascade	Tile	Arrange Icons

Using Your Mouse

To do anything in Windows, you have to learn how to use your mouse. Here's a quick list of the basic mouse moves:

- **Point**   Roll the mouse around on your desk until the tip of the mouse pointer is over the desired object or command.

- **Click**   Press and release the mouse button (usually the left button) without moving the mouse. You usually click to highlight something.

- **Double-click**   Press and release the mouse button twice quickly without moving the mouse. You usually double-click on an icon (a small picture that represents an application or command) to run an application or execute a command.

- **Drag**   Hold down the left mouse button while moving the mouse. You usually drag to move an object or draw a line or shape.

Beyond Survival

Starting Another Program at Startup

You can start Windows and another program at the same time by typing a *path* to the directory that contains the program's files, followed by the command that runs the program. For example, to start Windows and start Word for Windows (assuming the program is installed on your computer), you might type the following command at the DOS prompt and press Enter:

win c:\winword\winword

Many applications set themselves up so they can run from any directory. If you can run your application from any directory, you don't need to type a path to the directory. For example, you can simply type **win winword** and press Enter.

Making Windows Run in a Specific Mode

Whenever you start Windows, it checks your system to determine which mode to run in (based on your computer hardware). If you have a 286 computer or a 386 with less than two megabytes of RAM, Windows starts in *Standard* mode. If you have a 386 or better, with at least two megabytes of RAM, Windows starts in *386 Enhanced* mode. To find out which mode you are in, click on the Help command on the Program Manager menu bar, and then click on About Program Manager.

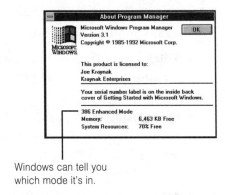

Windows can tell you
which mode it's in.

You can type a *switch* after the WIN command to force Windows to run in one mode or another. You can do this by starting Windows with one of the following commands:

- **win** /s   Forces Windows to run in Standard mode. If you run only Windows applications (not DOS applications), your applications will run faster in Standard mode. In Standard mode, however, Windows cannot use space on your hard disk as memory—and it may have trouble if you run DOS and Windows applications simultaneously.

- **win** /3   Forces Windows to run in Enhanced mode. In enhanced mode, Windows can use hard disk space as memory, allowing you to run more applications. Enhanced mode is also better for running Windows and DOS applications at the same time. Use this switch if you want to run in Enhanced mode *and* you have a 386 with less than two megabytes of RAM.

Making Windows Start Automatically

If your computer is not set up to run Windows automatically when you start (*boot*) your computer—and you want it to—type the **win** command at the end of your *AUTOEXEC.BAT file*. (This is a file containing commands that your computer executes on startup.) For details on how to edit AUTOEXEC.BAT and other system files, refer to Chapter 49, "Reading and Editing System Files."

Cheat Sheet

Windows Anatomy

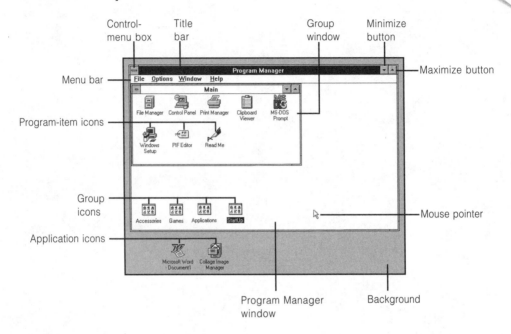

Control-menu box · Title bar · Group window · Minimize button

Maximize button

Menu bar

Program-item icons

Group icons

Mouse pointer

Application icons

Program Manager window

Background

Opening and Closing Group Windows

1. Double-click on the group window icon to expand it to window size.
2. Click on the group window's Minimize button ▼ to make it an icon again.

Meeting the Program Manager

When you start Windows, the first thing you see is the Program Manager, along with some small boxes (windows) and tiny pictures (icons). In order to proceed, you need to know what all the boxes and icons are for, and how to poke at them with your mouse to get them to do something. In this chapter, you learn how to get around in the Program Manager and do a couple of fancy tricks.

Basic Survival

Windows Anatomy

If you (or an overly zealous colleague) haven't messed around with your Windows setup, Windows should start with the Program Manager visible, and one additional window opened: the Main window.

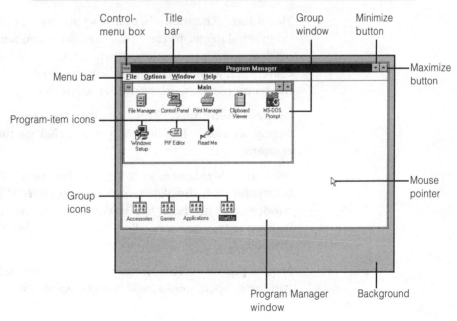

The labels in the picture don't tell you much. Here's a rundown of the items you see, and what each item is for:

Program Manager window   This is the head honcho, and you won't deal with it much. Most of the time, it works in the background, making sure your applications get along with each other.

Group window   The group window contains icons (small pictures) that represent applications. Each group window contains icons for one or more related applications. (Only one group window is shown in the picture.)

Group icons   A group icon is a miniaturized version of a group window. You can double-click on a group icon to transform it into a group window.

Program-item icons   These are icons that you select to run an application. Double-click on an icon to run its application.

Application icons   These icons represent currently running applications. If you run an application and then click on its Minimize button, the application shrinks down to the size of an icon, but remains running. You can double-click on the icon to restore it to window size.

Menu bar   The menu bar allows you to enter commands for the Program Manager to carry out. You can open a menu by clicking on its name, or by holding down the Alt key while typing the underlined letter in the menu's name. To close a menu, click on the menu name again, or press the Esc key.

Control-menu box   This box allows you to close a window, or change its size or location. When you click on the box, a menu appears.

Minimize, Maximize, and Restore buttons   The Minimize button lets you shrink a window to icon size. Maximize makes the window take up the entire screen. If you maximize a window, the Restore button appears, allowing you to return the window to its previous size.

Mouse pointer   The mouse pointer lets you select icons, resize windows, open menus, and select options on a menu.

Title bar A title bar appears at the top of every window. It usually indicates the application that's running in the window.

Background This is a shading that appears behind the Program Manager window. To change the look of the background, see Chapter 43, "Controlling Your Desktop."

Opening and Closing Group Windows

The group icons represent group windows. To transform a group icon into a group window, do one of the following:

- Double-click on the group icon.

- Click on the group icon, and then click on Restore.

To close a group window, double-click on its Control-menu box, or click on its Minimize button.

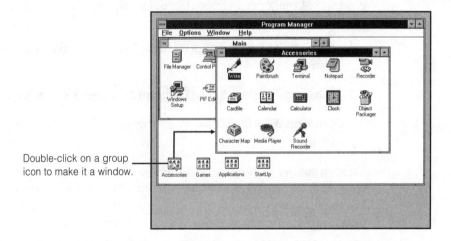

Double-click on a group icon to make it a window.

Viewing All the Icons in a Group

If a group window is too small to display all the program-item icons it contains, a scroll bar appears at the bottom or right of the window. You can view the remaining icons by doing one of the following:

- Click on the bottom or right arrow in the scroll bar.

- Click on the Maximize button ▲ in the upper right corner of the group window. (To restore the window to its previous size, click on the Restore button ↕.)

Click here to make the window big.

Scroll bar

Click here to see more icons.

Beyond Survival

Arranging Icons in a Window

Sometimes the program-item icons in a group window get stacked like pancakes, and you can't see the icon at the bottom. You can have the Program Manager rearrange the icons, by performing the following steps:

AuTo-arrange
icons =
Window
Arrange Icons

1. Display the group window that contains the icons you want to arrange.

2. Click on Window in the Program Manager's menu bar.

3. Click on Arrange Icons. The Program Manager arranges the icons for you.

To arrange the group icons in the Program Manager window, make sure all the group windows are shrunk down to icon size (click on the Minimize button in the upper right corner of each window). Then, open the Window menu and select Arrange Icons.

Finding Lost Windows and Icons

The Program Manager is like a big tablecloth that can hide all sorts of objects. If you can't find a group item, or you run an application and lose it, try the following techniques:

- Click on the Minimize button ▼ in the upper right corner of the Program Manager window. This shrinks the window to the size of an icon, revealing anything it may have been hiding.

- Click on the Restore button just to the right of the Minimize button. This returns the Program Manager window to its previous size. You can then drag the window's border to resize it, or drag the title bar to move it.

CTrl + Esc finds running applications.

- Click on Window in the menu bar. At the bottom of the menu are a list of group windows. Click on the desired group, or click on More Windows to view an extensive list.

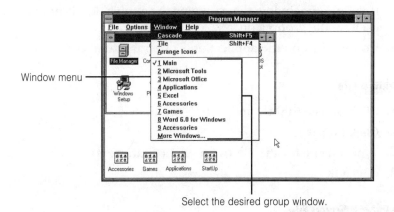

Window menu —

Select the desired group window.

Starting Like This Next Time

Windows is initially set up to save the Program Manager so it looks the same way when you start it up next time. To have Program Manager forget the changes you made, follow these steps:

1. Click on Options in the menu bar.

2. Click on Save Settings on Exit. A check mark next to the option means that the option is on. If you want to start with the same configuration next time, make sure there is a check mark next to this option.

To save your setup as it is now—and prevent it from changing in the future—turn off Save Settings on Exit. Set the screen as you want it to appear, then hold down the Shift key while opening the File menu and selecting Exit Windows. Windows saves your settings without exiting.

Cheat Sheet

Starting a Windows Application

1. If the group window that contains the application is not displayed, double-click on the group icon.
2. Double-click on the application's program-item icon.

Saving a File

1. Click on File in the application's menu bar.
2. Click on Save.
3. Type a name for the file (up to eight characters).
4. Click OK.

Opening a Saved File

1. Click on File in the application's menu bar.
2. Click on Open.
3. Click on the arrow to the right of the Drives option, and click on the letter of the drive that contains the file.
4. Double-click on the directory that contains the file in the Directories list.
5. Click on the name of the file you want to open.
6. Click OK.

Printing a File

1. Create or open the file you want to print.
2. Click on File in the menu bar.
3. Click on Print.
4. Click OK.

Exiting an Application

1. Click on File in the menu bar.
2. Click on Exit.

Running and Using Applications

Face it—you didn't buy Windows to play around with little pictures. You bought Windows so you could run *Windows applications*— programs that let you do something practical with your computer, like type a letter or balance your budget. In this chapter, you learn the basics of working with most Windows applications: how to run the application, save a file, print, and exit.

Basic Survival

Starting a Windows Application

Each group window on the Windows desktop contains one or more program-item icons that represent applications you can run. To run an application:

1. Open the group window that contains the application's icon. (Double-click on the group's icon, or select the window from the Program Manager's Window menu.)

2. Double-click on the icon.

Once opened, the application displays its own *application window* that allows you to start working.

Can select application by Typing first letter in name.

In a group window, you can quickly highlight a program-item icon by typing the first letter of the icon's title. If two or more icons start with the same letter, keep typing the beginning letter until the desired icon is highlighted. Then, press Enter to run the application.

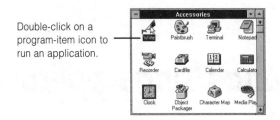

Double-click on a program-item icon to run an application.

Running a DOS Application

During the Windows installation, Windows may have created icons for your DOS applications. If that's the case, you can run a DOS application just as you would a Windows application: double-click on its icon. If your DOS application does not have an icon, you can skip ahead to Chapters 9 and 50 to learn how to make icons and get your DOS application up and running. Or, you can do the following to run the application right now:

1. Open the Program Manager's File menu. (If the Program Manager is not visible, press Ctrl+Esc, use the arrow keys to highlight Program Manager, and press Enter.)

2. Click on Run. The Run dialog box appears.

3. Click on the Browse button.

4. Click on the arrow to the right of the Drives option, and then click on the drive where the application is stored.

5. Double-click on the directory that contains the application's files in the Directories list.

6. Click on the name of the file that runs the application in the File Name list.

7. Click on OK. This returns you to the Run dialog box, and shows you the drive, directory, and file name of the file that runs the program.

Alt + Enter runs DOS program in window (not full-screen).

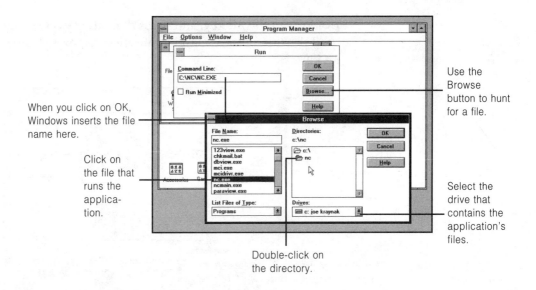

When you click on OK, Windows inserts the file name here.

Use the Browse button to hunt for a file.

Click on the file that runs the application.

Select the drive that contains the application's files.

Double-click on the directory.

8. Click on OK. Windows runs the program.

Beyond Survival

Running Two or More Applications

Windows is attractive to users partly because it lets you run two or more applications at the same time. If you are running Windows in 386 Enhanced mode (see Chapter 49, "Changing the 386 Enhanced Settings") you can be printing in one application while you're typing in another. To run another application, simply return to the Program Manager (Ctrl+Esc), and then run the second application. The following section explains how to switch from one application to another.

Switching Between Applications

When you run two or more applications, your application windows can get lost in the stack of windows. To switch to a specific application, do one of the following:

- Double-click on the application's icon (if you can see it).

- Press Ctrl+Esc, select the desired application, and press Enter.

- Click on the Control-menu box in the upper left corner of the current application window, and click on Switch To. Click on the desired application, and then click on the Switch To button.

Alt + Esc To cycle Through apps

• Hold down the Alt key, and press the Tab key one or more times until the title of the desired application appears. Then release the Alt key.

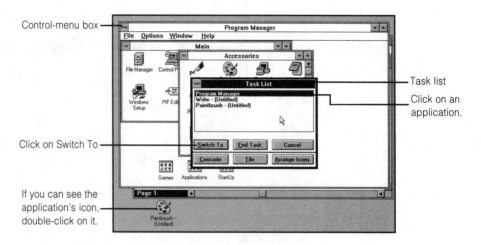

Control-menu box

Task list

Click on an application.

Click on Switch To

If you can see the application's icon, double-click on it.

Saving a File

In most applications, you create something, such as a picture or a business letter. You should save your work to disk early and often (at least every 10 minutes) to prevent it from getting obliterated when you quit the application, exit Windows, or lose power. The procedure for saving a file is the same in most Windows applications:

1. Click on File in the application's menu bar.

2. Click on Save.

Ctrl + S saves in most applications.

3. Type a name for the file (up to eight characters) in the File Name text box.

4. (Optional) To specify where you want the file saved, select a drive from the Drives list, and a directory from the Directories list.

5. Click on the OK button.

Opening a Saved File

If you saved and closed a file, and later decide you want to work with it, you have to run the application you used to create the file; then you can open it. Once the application is running, perform the following steps to open the file:

1. Click on File in the application's menu bar.

2. Click on Open. The Open File dialog box appears.

3. Click on the arrow to the right of the Drives option, and then click on the drive where the application is stored.

4. Click on the directory that contains the application's files in the Directories list.

5. Click on the name of the file that runs the application in the File Name list.

6. Click on the OK button. The application opens the file and displays it on-screen.

Some apps list recently opened files at bottom of File menu.

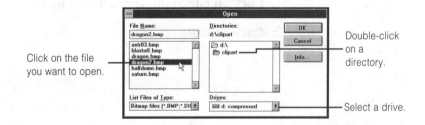

Click on the file you want to open.

Double-click on a directory.

Select a drive.

Printing a File

Once a file is opened and displayed on-screen, you can print it. To print in most applications, do the following:

1. Make sure your printer is turned on and has paper.

2. Click on File in the application's menu bar.

3. Click on Print. A Print dialog box appears.

4. Select your printing preferences.

5. Click on the OK button.

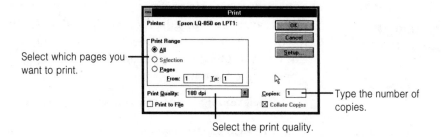

Select which pages you want to print.

Type the number of copies.

Select the print quality.

When you installed Windows, it asked you to pick a printer. If you changed printers—or Windows fails to print your document—refer to Chapter 47, "Setting Up and Selecting a Printer" and Chapter 48, "Using the Windows Print Manager".

Exiting an Application

When you're done working in an application, you should exit it properly to prevent losing any work. Most applications have safeguards that warn you if you are about to exit without saving your file. If you exit improperly (by turning off your computer, for instance), you bypass these safeguards. To exit an application, here's what you do:

1. Click on File in the application's menu bar.

2. Click on Exit.

ALT + F4 = EXIT, or double-click on Control- menu box (upper left corner).

Cheat Sheet

Selecting Commands from Pull-Down Menus

1. Click on the name of the menu you want to open in the menu bar.
2. Click on the desired option.
3. If a submenu opens, click on the desired submenu option.

Cancelling Menus

- Click anywhere outside the menu.
- Press Esc once or twice.

Responding to Dialog Boxes

Click on a tab to see a group of related options.

Type a setting or name in a text box.

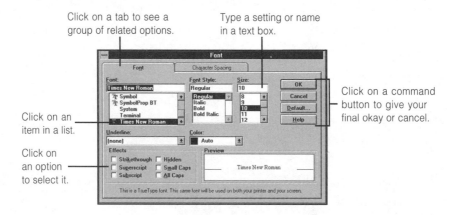

Click on an item in a list.

Click on an option to select it.

Click on a command button to give your final okay or cancel.

4

Entering Commands in Windows

In Windows, you enter commands not by typing them but by selecting them from *pull-down menus*. In this chapter, you learn how to select commands and how to respond to dialog boxes—boxes that request additional information.

Basic Survival

Selecting Commands from Pull-Down Menus

Just below the title bar of most windows is a *menu bar* that contains the names of several pull-down menus. Most menu bars include the following menus: File, Edit, Format, Window, and Help. Each menu contains several related commands. To enter a command, you can perform any one of the following steps:

- Click on the menu name, then click on the desired command.

- Move the mouse pointer over the menu name, hold down the mouse button while dragging over the desired command, and release the mouse button.

- Hold down the Alt key while typing the underlined letter in the menu's name, release the Alt key, and type the underlined letter in the name of the command or option you want to select.

Shortcut Keys To bypass menus

Many menu options have corresponding *shortcut keys* that enable you to bypass the menu system. These shortcut key combinations are listed on the menus, so you can wean yourself from the menus.

You can drag over an option's
name and release the mouse button.

You may notice that not all the options on the menu appear the same. Some options are followed by an arrow or a series of dots (...). Other options appear light gray instead of black. Following is a rundown of some of the variations you may encounter:

Light gray options are unavailable for what you are currently doing. For example, if you want to copy a chunk of text, and you have not yet marked the text, the Copy command will not be available.

Options with an arrow open a *submenu* that requires you to select another option.

Options with a check mark indicate that an option is currently active. To turn the option off, select it. This removes the check mark.

Options followed by a series of dots (...) open a *dialog box* that requests additional information. You'll learn how to respond to dialog boxes later.

Cancelling Menus

If you open a menu, and then decide that you do not want to select an option, you have several choices:

- Click on the menu name (or anywhere outside the menu) to close it.

Press Esc To cancel menu

- **Press the Alt key or F10.**

- **Press Esc** to back out of the menu. You may have to press it two or more times to deactivate the menu bar.

• Use the ← key to open the menu to the left, or the → key to open the menu to the right.

Responding to Dialog Boxes

If you choose a command that is followed by a series of dots (...), the application will display a *dialog box* that requests additional information.

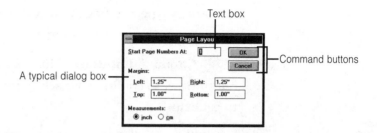

Text box

A typical dialog box

Command buttons

Dialog boxes are chock-full of all sorts of interesting objects. Here's a list of all the items you might encounter, though you'll see only two or three items in any given dialog box:

Tabs   Each tab has a group of related options. To switch to a set of options, click on its tab.

Text boxes   A text box stands for "fill in the blank." It enables you to type text, such as the name of a file. To replace an entry in a text box, double-click inside it and then type your entry. To edit an entry, click inside the text box, use the arrow keys to move the insertion point, and type your correction.

Option buttons   Option buttons look like Cheerios. You click on a button to turn it on. You can turn on only one option in a group.

Check boxes   Check boxes allow you to turn an option on or off. Click inside a check box to turn it on if it's off, or off if it's on. You can select more than one check box in a group.

List box   A list box presents two or more options. Click on the option you want. If the list is long, you'll see a *scroll bar*. Click on the scroll bar arrows to move up or down in the list.

25

ATT + ↓
opens
drop-down
list

Auto ▼ **Drop-down list box** This list box has only one item in it. It hides the rest of the items. Click on the arrow to the right of the box to display the rest of the list, and then click on the item you want.

1 pt ⬍ **Spin box** A spin box is a text box with controls. You can usually type a setting in the text box or use the up or down arrow key to change the setting.

OK **Cancel** **Command buttons** Most dialog boxes have at least three buttons: OK to confirm your selections, Cancel to quit, and Help to get help.

Press Tab To
move around
a dialog box.

To get around in a dialog box, you can click on items with the mouse, use the Tab key to move from item to item (Shift+Tab to move back), or hold down the Alt key while typing the underlined letter in the option's name.

Beyond Survival

Finding a File in a Dialog Box

One of the most common (and confusing) dialog boxes you will encounter is the one you get when you enter the File Save or File Open command.

Select the desired drive, directory, and file name.

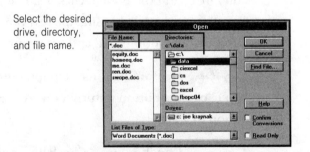

To respond to such a dialog box, take the following steps:

1. Click on the arrow to the right of the Drives list, and then click on the letter of the desired drive.

2. In the Directories list, double-click on the desired directory. (To move up the directory tree, double-click on the drive letter or directory name at the top of the list.)

3. To view the names of only those files that end with a specific extension, click on the arrow to the right of the List Files of Type list, and click on the desired file type.

4. Perform one of the following steps:

  • If you are saving a file, click inside the File Name text box, and type the name you want to use for the file (up to eight characters).

  • If you are selecting an existing file, click on the desired file in the File Name list, or type its name in the text box.

5. Click on the OK button.

Moving a Dialog Box

Sometimes a dialog box blocks your view, preventing you from seeing an important message or an object that's behind it. In such cases, you can move the dialog box by *dragging* its title bar. Simply move the mouse pointer inside the dialog box title bar, and hold down the mouse button while moving the mouse.

Selecting Multiple Items in a List

Some dialog box lists enable you to select more than one item at a time. To select two or more items, do one of the following:

  • To select neighboring items in the list, click on the first item you want to select, and then hold down the Shift key while clicking on the last item.

  • To select non-neighboring items, hold down the Ctrl key while clicking on each desired item.

Using Toolbars (in Some Applications)

Many applications include *toolbars* that are usually just below the menu bar or on the left or right side of the application's window. These toolbars provide a quick way to enter commonly used commands. For example, instead of opening the File menu and selecting Print, you can simply click on a toolbar button.

In most applications, if you move the mouse pointer over a button, a description of the button appears in the lower left corner of the window. Some applications also display the name of the button near the mouse pointer.

Click on a tool to bypass
the menu system.

Toolbars offer
quick
commands.

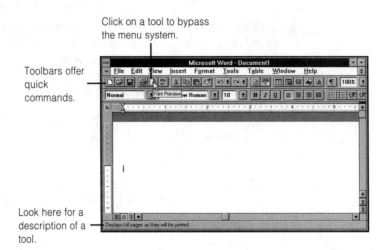

Look here for a
description of a
tool.

Using Pop-Up Menus (in Some Applications)

If you're wondering what the right mouse button is for, some applications use it to bring up a *pop-up menu* that contains several options for a specific object. For example, if you right-click on a toolbar, you might get a menu that shows all the available toolbars and enables you to turn them on or off.

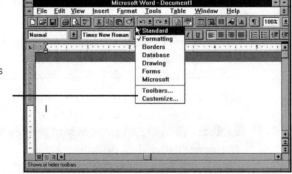

Some applications
display a pop-up
menu when you
right-click on an
item.

Cheat Sheet

Opening and Closing Windows

1. Double-click on an icon to expand it into a window.
2. Double-click on the Control-menu box to close a window.

Arranging Windows

1. Click on Window in the menu bar.
2. Select Cascade (to view overlapping windows) or Tiled (to view windows side-by-side).

Sizing Windows

1. Move the mouse pointer over any of the window's borders until the pointer turns into a double-headed arrow.
2. Hold down the mouse button, while moving the mouse until the window is the desired size and dimensions.
3. Release the mouse button.

Quick Sizing Options

- Click on the Maximize button ▲ to make the window full-screen size.
- Click on the Minimize button ▼ to make the window into an icon.
- Click on the Restore button � to return a maximized window to its previous size.

Moving Windows

1. Move the mouse pointer inside the window's title bar.
2. Hold down the mouse button while moving the mouse until the window is in the desired position.
3. Release the mouse button.

5

Working with Windows

Working with Windows is like working with a deck of cards. Whenever you run an application, open a group window, or create a file, you open another window that may hide an existing window. In order to manage all these windows, you need to know how to move, size, and arrange the windows to your liking. You learn all you need to know in this chapter.

Basic Survival

Types of Windows

Windows uses two types of windows: *application* windows and *document* windows. An application window contains a running application. For example, if you run Word for Windows, an application window opens. (Program Manager is an application window as well.) A document window contains a file you opened or created in the application. For example, you type text in Word for Windows in a document window. Group windows in the Program Manager are also considered document windows.

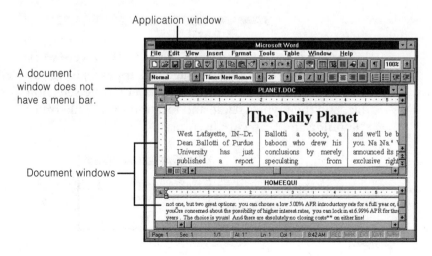

Application window

A document window does not have a menu bar.

Document windows

Opening and Closing Windows

You can open windows in various ways. If you double-click on a program-item icon, an application window appears. Double-click on a group icon, and a group window appears. Open a file in an application window, and a document window appears inside the application window. To close any of these windows, perform one of the following steps:

- To close an application window (exit the application), open the File menu and select Exit, or press Alt+F4.

- To close a document window without exiting the application (in some applications), open the File menu and select Close.

- To close any window (document or application), click on the Control-menu box in the upper left corner of the window, and select Close.

- To close any window (document or application), double-click on the Control-menu box in the upper left corner of the window.

ATT ≠ 4 = EXiT applica-Tion

Control-menu box ⎯⎯

Control menu ⎯⎯

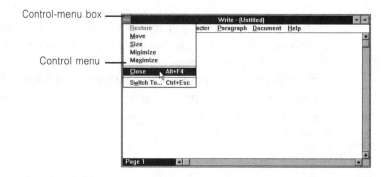

If you close a window that contains a file you were working on—but did not save—a warning message will appear, giving you a chance to save the file. Click on the Yes button, enter the selection to name the file, and then type a name and location for the file (refer to Chapter 3, "Running and Using Applications").

If you exit without saving, you are warned. ⎯⎯

Arranging Windows

Windows knows how easy it is to lose a window in a stack, so it gives you two possible arrangements: tiled or cascading windows. Tiled places the windows side-by-side. Cascade overlaps the windows, showing a portion of each window. To choose an arrangement for your windows, open the Window menu and choose Tiled or Cascade.

ShiET ≠ F5
= Cascade

ShiET ≠ F4
= Tiled

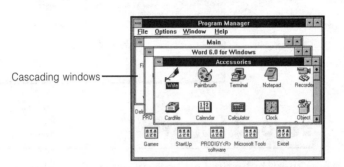

Cascading windows

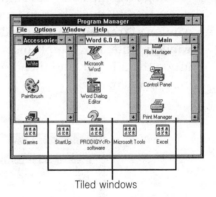

Tiled windows

The tiled and cascading arrangements make it easy to change from one window to another. You simply click on the desired window, and it jumps to the front of the stack. If you cannot see a portion of a window, you can change to it by opening the Window menu and clicking on the desired window (the names of the windows are listed at the bottom of the Window menu).

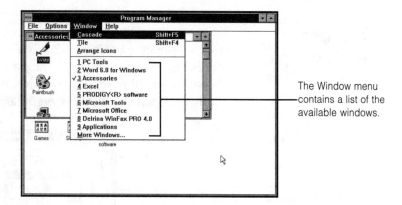

The Window menu contains a list of the available windows.

Beyond Survival

Moving Windows

Although the tiled and cascading windows allow you to arrange windows quickly, they give you little control over the actual position of the windows. You can move a window more precisely by dragging the window's title bar. Simply move the tip of the mouse pointer anywhere inside the title bar, and then hold down the mouse button while moving the mouse.

Drag a window's title bar to move it.

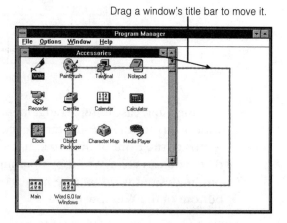

Sizing Windows

While you're rearranging your windows, you may want to resize them. The easiest way to resize a window is to move the mouse pointer over one of the window's borders, then hold down the mouse button while dragging the border.

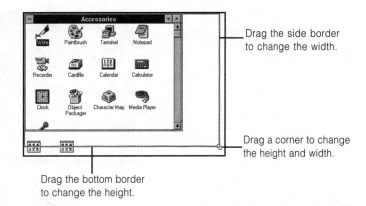

Drag the side border
to change the width.

Drag a corner to change
the height and width.

Drag the bottom border
to change the height.

For a fast-and-loose resize job, use the following buttons in the upper right corner of the window:

The **Maximize button** makes the window full-screen size.

The Maximize button is then replaced by the Restore button.

The **Minimize button** reduces the window to icon size. You can restore the window by double-clicking on the icon, or by clicking on it and selecting Restore.

The **restore button** returns a maximized window to the size it was before you clicked on the Maximize button.

If the Program Manager window is maximized, it will hide any application icons (minimized applications). Click on the Program Manager's restore button, and then drag the bottom border up an inch or two to reveal any icons it may be hiding.

Minimize
Program
Manager
Window To
Keep iT ouT
of The way

Window Panes (in Some Applications)

Some applications (not many), use window *panes* to separate a window into two or more sections. You can drag the pane borders, just as you can drag window borders to change the relative size of the sections.

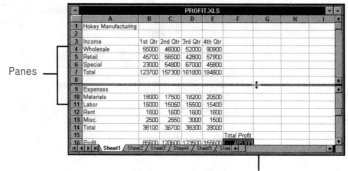

Panes

Drag the dividing line to change
the relative size of the sections.

Controlling Window Placement

As you drag a window across the screen, it moves smoothly into its new position. You can place it anywhere. You can change this to have the windows snap into place using an invisible grid. By using this invisible grid, you can easily align the edges of two or more windows or icons. Here's what you do:

1. Change to the Program Manager window.

2. Double-click on the Main icon to display the Main group window.

3. Double-click on the Control Panel icon to display the Control Panel group.

4. Double-click on the Desktop icon . The Desktop dialog box appears.

5. Use the Granularity spin box to set the granularity to 1 or 2. One sets the grid at 8 pixels. Two sets it at 16 pixels. (A pixel is an on-screen dot, whose size may vary depending on your monitor.)

6. Click on the OK button when you're done.

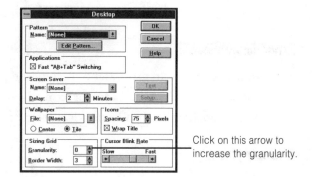

Click on this arrow to increase the granularity.

Changing the Border Width

If your window borders are too narrow or too thick for your liking, you can change the border thickness. Perform steps 1–4 in the previous section to display the Desktop dialog box. Then, use the Border Width spin box (just below the Granularity spin box), to set the border width. In general, use a lower setting for low-resolution (VGA) monitors (640-by-480), and a higher setting for higher-resolution (SVGA, Super VGA) monitors (1024-by-768).

Display mode? In Main group, double-click on Windows SeTup icon

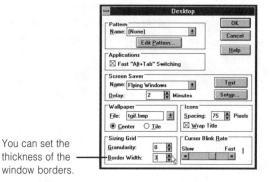

You can set the thickness of the window borders.

37

Cheat Sheet

Expanding an Icon

- Double-click on an group icon to view the program-item icons in the group.
- Double-click on a program-item icon to run an application.
- Double-click on an application icon to restore the application window.

Arranging Icons

1. Click anywhere inside the window that has the icons you want to rearrange.
2. Click on Window in the menu bar.
3. Click on Arrange Icons.

Moving an Icon

1. Move the tip of the mouse pointer over the icon you want to move.
2. Hold down the left mouse button, and drag the icon to its new position.

Copying an Icon

1. Move the tip of the mouse pointer over the icon you want to copy.
2. Hold down the left mouse button and the Ctrl key, while dragging the icon to another group window.

6

Working with Icons

As you work with Windows, you'll notice all sorts of tiny pictures, called *icons*, that pepper the screen. In this chapter, you learn how to control the size, position, and appearance of these icons.

Basic Survival

Types of Icons

Windows comes with four basic types of icons: group icons, program-item icons, application icons, and document icons. To expand an icon to window size, here's what you do:

Group icon   Double-click on the icon, or click on it and then click on Restore. A group window appears, showing the program-item icons in the group.

Program-item icon   Double-click on a program-item icon to run the corresponding application.

Application icon   Double-click on the icon, or click on it and then click on Restore to return it to window size. (An application icon is an application window that has been minimized, reduced to icon size.)

Document icon   Double-click on the icon, or click on it and then click on Restore to return it to window size. (A document icon is a document window that has been minimized.)

Program-item icons allow you to run applications.

Group icons
represent group
windows.

Application icons represent
currently running applications.

*Minimize
groups &
applications
when not
using Them*

Windows uses memory to display icons and windows. To free up this memory for use by applications, try to keep group windows and application windows minimized when you are not using them.

Arranging Icons

Like windows themselves, icons can overlap, causing some icons to get lost in the stack. If this happens, do the following steps to have Windows arrange the icons for you:

1. Click anywhere inside the window that contains the icons.

2. Click on Window in the menu bar.

3. Click on Arrange Icons.

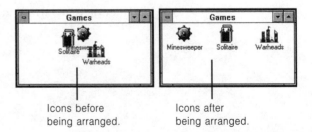

Icons before
being arranged.

Icons after
being arranged.

Beyond Survival

Moving and Copying Icons

You can move an icon inside a group window or from one group window to another. You can also copy icons. Here's what you do:

1. If you want to move or copy an icon from one group window to another, make sure both group windows are displayed.

2. Move the mouse pointer over the icon you want to copy or move.

Hold down Ctrl To copy an icon

3. To copy the icon, hold down the Ctrl key while performing the next step.

4. Hold down the left mouse button, and drag the icon where you want it.

5. If the icon overlaps another icon, you can arrange the icons, as explained in the previous section.

To have Windows rearrange the program-item icons for you whenever you move icons or resize a group window, open the Program Manager's Options menu, and select Auto Arrange.

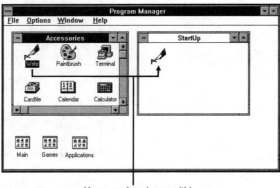

You can drag icons within a window or from one group window to another.

Changing the Spacing Between Icons

When Windows arranges the icons, it spaces them 75 pixels apart, and wraps the icon name, so the name does not overlap other icon names. To change either of these settings, do the following:

1. Change to the Program Manager window.

2. Double-click on the Main icon 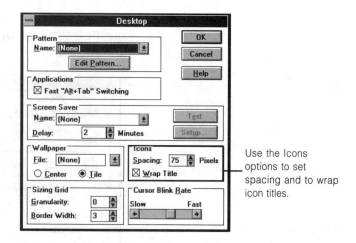 to display the Main group window.

3. Double-click on the Control Panel icon to display the Control Panel group.

4. Double-click on the Desktop icon . The Desktop dialog box appears.

5. To change the spacing between icons, use the Spacing spin box.

6. To prevent the icon name from wrapping, click on the Wrap Title option to turn it off.

7. Click on the OK button when you're done.

Use the Icons options to set spacing and to wrap icon titles.

Selecting a Different Icon

If you don't like the look of a particular icon, you may be able to change it. Many applications come with several icons; some applications have only one. Here's what you do:

1. Click on the icon whose look you want to change.

2. Open the Program Manager's File menu and click on Properties.

3. Click on the Change Icon button.

4. Click on the icon you want to use.

5. Click on the OK button.

moricons.dll
has more
icons.

If the selection of icons is limited, click on the Change Icon button, click on the Browse button, type c:\windows\moricons.dll in the File Name text box, and press Enter. PROGMAN.EXE also contains additional icons. Perform the same steps to browse for an icon, and then type c:\windows\progman.exe in the File Name text box and press Enter.

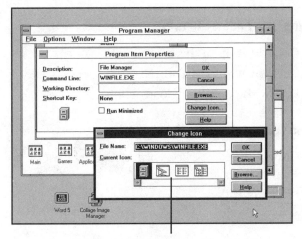

You may be able to select a different icon.

Cheat Sheet

Selecting a Help Topic

1. Click on Help in the menu bar.
2. Click on Contents.
3. Click on the desired help topic (topics are green and underlined).

Jumping Around in the Help System

- Click on a solid-underlined topic to display information about the topic.
- Click on a dotted-underlined term to display a pop-up box with a definition.

Running the Windows Tutorial

1. Click on Help in the menu bar.
2. Click on Windows Tutorial.
3. Follow the on-screen instructions.

Getting Context-Sensitive Help

1. Display the dialog box (or highlight the menu command) for which you want help.
2. Press the F1 key.

7

Getting Help

Windows contains an online help system that can answer most of your questions. It offers a table of contents, index, beginner's tutorial, and even explanations that tell you how to use the help system. In this chapter, you get a crash course on using the help system.

Basic Survival

Selecting a Help Topic

The easiest way to get help for using Windows is to use the Help Table of Contents. Here's how:

1. Click on Help in the Program Manager's menu bar.

2. Select the Contents option. This displays a list of topics for which you can get help.

3. Click on the desired topic.

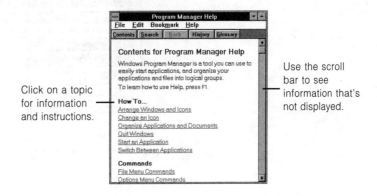

Click on a topic for information and instructions.

Use the scroll bar to see information that's not displayed.

Fl = Help Contents Fl again To view instructions on how To use help

To close a help window, open the File menu and select Exit, or click on the Control-menu box, and select Close.

Jumping Around in the Help System

Most help windows contain green underlined items called *jumps* that you can click on to get additional information. If the jump has a dotted underline, clicking on it displays a pop-up window that contains a definition of the term. If the jump has a solid underline, information for that topic is displayed in the help window.

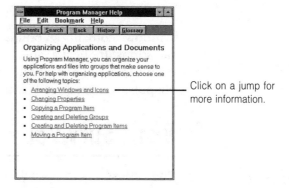

Click on a jump for more information.

In addition to using jumps to skip around in the help system, you can use the Back and History buttons. The Back button displays the previous help topic. The History button displays a list of the help topics you've accessed; you can click on a topic to go back to it.

Click on Back to view the previous topic.

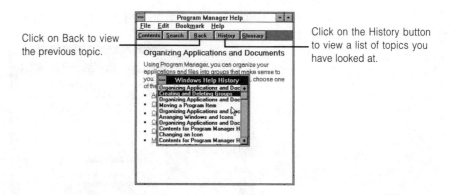

Click on the History button to view a list of topics you have looked at.

Beyond Survival

Running the Windows Tutorial

Windows contains a hands-on tutorial that can help you learn and practice some Windows basics, such as maximizing windows, running applications, and using a mouse. If you have a VGA monitor or better, you can run the tutorial. Here's how:

1. Click on the Help menu in the Program Manager's menu bar.

2. Select the Windows Tutorial command.

File Run:
Type
WinTUTor,
press Enter

3. Follow the on-screen instructions to continue.

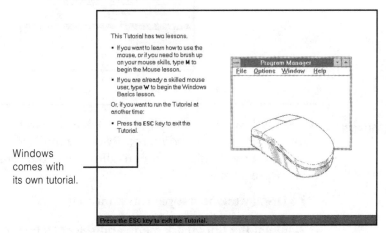

Windows comes with its own tutorial.

Getting Context-Sensitive Help

If you want specific help for a menu option or a specific dialog box, follow these steps:

1. Highlight the menu option or display the dialog box you want help with.

2. Press the F1 key. Windows displays a help window that contains information pertaining to that menu option or dialog box.

Searching for Help

If you know the name of the topic for which you want help, you can search specifically for that topic. Here's what you do:

1. Open the Help menu and choose Search for Help on. This opens the search dialog box.

2. Start typing the name of the topic. As you type, a list of available topics that match what you type scrolls into view.

3. When you see the desired topic, double-click on it. A list of subtopics appears.

4. Double-click on the desired subtopic.

You can search for a specific topic.

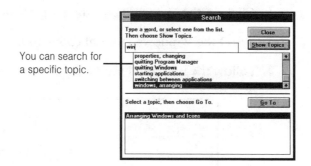

Using Bookmarks

If you think you might need to go back to a help topic later, you may want to flag it with a *bookmark*. By doing this, the bookmark name appears on the Bookmark menu, allowing you to quickly return to the topic. Here's what you do:

1. Display the help topic you want to flag.

2. Open the Bookmark menu and select Define. A dialog box appears, asking you for a name.

3. Type a descriptive name for the bookmark, and press Enter.

4. To return to the topic, display any help window, open the Bookmark menu, and select your bookmark.

Use a bookmark to return quickly to a topic.

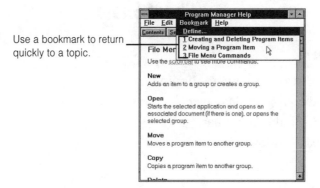

Once you have created a bookmark, you can delete it by doing the following:

1. Open the Bookmark menu and select Define. A dialog box appears, showing the names of existing bookmarks.

2. Click on the bookmark you want to delete.

3. Click on the Delete button.

Cheat Sheet

Exiting Windows

1. Exit any applications you are running.
2. Return to the Program Manager.
3. Click on File in the menu bar.
4. Click on Exit Windows.
5. Click OK.

Quick Exit Options

- Press Alt+F4.
- Double-click on the Control-menu box in the upper left corner of the Program Manager window.

When Your System Locks Up

1. Press Ctrl+Alt+Del.
2. Press Esc to return to the application.

   or

   Press Enter to end the application.

   or

   Press Ctrl+Alt+Del to reboot. (Be careful about doing this.)

8

Exiting Windows

When you are done working in Windows, don't just turn your computer off. This could cause you to lose some work. You should exit any applications you were running, and *then* exit Windows. In this chapter, you learn how to exit Windows properly.

Basic Survival

Properly Exiting Windows

During a Windows work session, Windows does a lot behind the scenes, including opening *temporary files*. If you exit by flipping the power switch on your system unit, these temporary files can get scattered, and you can lose the work you've done during the session. To exit Windows properly and avoid this mess, do the following:

1. Use the File Exit command in any applications you are running to exit those applications.

2. Display the Program Manager window.

3. Click on File in the menu bar.

Open the File menu and select Exit Windows.

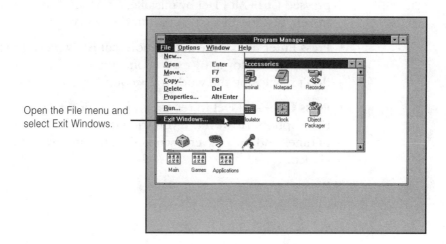

4. Click on Exit Windows. The Exit Windows dialog box appears, asking for your confirmation.

The Exit Windows dialog box

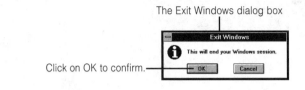

Click on OK to confirm.

ALT + F4 or double-click on Program Manager Control-menu box To Exit.

5. Click on OK. If you have any DOS applications open or you have work that you haven't saved, Windows will display a warning message.

6. Follow the on-screen instructions to exit Windows.

Beyond Survival

When Your System Locks Up

Windows is a bit temperamental. If it doesn't get along with a particular application—or if it doesn't like a command you entered—your system can freeze. You won't be able to open any menus or select any options. Even the shortcut keys won't work. Luckily, Windows provides some help. If you press Ctrl+Alt+Del to reboot your computer, Windows 3.1 displays a message that indicates which application is causing problems, and gives you some options. Usually the following options are available:

- **Press Esc to return to the application.** This option is good if you pressed Ctrl+Alt+Del by mistake, or if Windows is busy (not frozen, just too busy to get around to you).

- **Press Enter to exit the application that is giving you problems and return to Windows.** By exiting only the problem application, you don't risk losing the work you've done in other applications.

- **Press Ctrl+Alt+Del to reboot your computer.** This is the most risky option. However, if you tried the other two options a couple of times and they haven't worked, you don't have much of a choice.

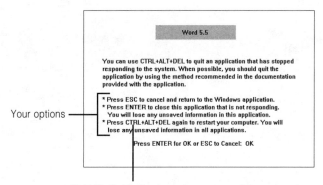

Your options ──

Ctrl+Alt+Del is the most dangerous option.

53

PART 2

Working with Applications

In the previous part, you learned how easy it is to run applications in Windows. You simply double-click on the application's program-item icon, and you're up and running. However, there's more to running applications than just double-clicking on an icon. You should know how to install applications, work with DOS applications in Windows, and customize group windows and program-item icons for your own convenience. In this part, you get some hands-on experience with the following tasks:

- Setting Up Applications
- Working with Group Windows
- Going to the DOS Prompt

Cheat Sheet

Installing a Windows Application

1. Exit all other Windows applications, and return to the Program Manager.
2. Write-protect your application disks.
3. Insert your application disk 1 into drive A or B.
4. Open the File menu and select Run.
5. Type **a:** if disk 1 is in drive A, or **b:** if disk 1 is in drive B.
6. Click on the Browse button.
7. Click on the Install or Setup file in the File Name list.
8. Click OK.
9. Click OK.
10. Follow the installation instructions that appear on-screen.

Setting Up DOS Applications with Windows Setup

1. If the DOS application is not installed, follow the installation instructions to install it from the DOS prompt.
2. Go to the Main group window.
3. Double-click on the Windows Setup icon.
4. Open the Options menu and select Set Up Applications.
5. Click on Search for applications, then click on OK.
6. Click on each drive to search, then click on the Search Now button.
7. Follow the on-screen instructions until the search is complete.
8. In the Applications found on hard disk(s) list, click on each application to set up.
9. Click on the Add button.
10. Click OK.

Setting Up Applications

Before you can use any application, you have to install it. The installation process consists of copying the program files from floppy disks to your hard disk, and (usually) decompressing the files to make them usable. Most applications come with an Install or Setup program that does everything for you. In this chapter, you learn how to run the Install or Setup program in Windows, and how to set up DOS programs to run in Windows.

Basic Survival

Installing a Windows Application

*File Run
To run
installation
program*

Whenever you get a new Windows application, you must install it before you can use it. Most applications come with a setup or install program that copies the program files to a directory on your hard disk, prepares the files for use, and creates the group window and program-item icons you need to run the application. Take the following steps to start the installation program for most Windows applications:

1. Exit all other Windows applications, and return to the Program Manager.

2. Write-protect your application disks. (For 3.5-inch disks, slide the write-protect tab so you can see through the "window." For 5.25-inch disks, place a write-protect sticker over the notch in the side of the disk.)

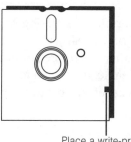

Place a write-protect
sticker over the notch.

Slide the write-protect tab so
you can see through the hole.

3. Insert your application disk 1 into drive A or B, and close the drive door, if it has one.

4. Open the File menu and select Run. The Run dialog box appears.

5. Type **a:** if disk 1 is in drive A, or **b:** if disk 1 is in drive B.

Click on Browse To look for files.

6. Click on the Browse button. The Browse dialog box appears, showing the *executable files* (the files you can run) on the disk.

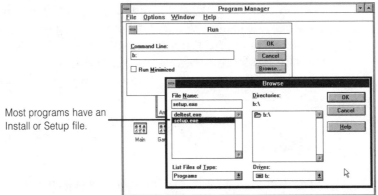

Most programs have an Install or Setup file.

7. Click on the Install or Setup file in the File Name list. The names of these files usually end with an .EXE or .BAT extension.

8. Click on the OK button. You are returned to the Run dialog box, and the name of the file you selected is inserted into the Command Line text box.

9. Click on the OK button. Windows runs the Setup or Install program, and displays its initial screen.

10. To complete the installation process, follow the installation instructions that appear on-screen.

Setting Up DOS Applications with Windows Setup

In Lesson 3, "Running and Using Applications," you learned how to run a DOS application by using the Program Manager's File Run command. However, if you have trouble running an application, or you want to run it by double-clicking on an icon, you should use Windows Setup to install the DOS application properly.

Windows Setup in The Main group

Windows Setup does two things. First, it creates a PIF (*program information file*) that tells Windows how to run the program most efficiently. Second, it assigns a program-item icon to the application, so you can run the application by double-clicking on its icon. If you have only one DOS application you want to set up (and you know where it is), skip ahead to the next section. If you have two or more applications to set up (or if you don't know where the application is), do the following:

1. If the DOS application is not installed, follow the installation instructions to install it from the DOS prompt. (The DOS program must be installed before you can set it up in Windows.)

2. Go to the Main group window.

3. Double-click on the Windows Setup icon. The Windows Setup window appears.

4. Open the Options menu, and select Set Up Applications. The Set Up Applications dialog box appears.

5. Click on Search for applications, and click on OK. A dialog box appears, prompting you to specify which drives you want to search for applications.

Path searches the drives and directories in AUTOEXEC.BAT's path statement.

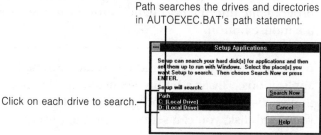

Click on each drive to search.

6. Click on each drive you want to search, and then click on the Search Now button. (The Path option searches only the drives and directories that are in the Path statement in your AUTOEXEC.BAT file. The Path statement tells your computer where to look for files. See Chapter 49, "Reading and Editing System Files," for details.)

7. Follow the on-screen instructions until the search is complete.

8. In the Applications found on hard disk(s) list, click on each application you want to set up. (If the application you want to set up is not in the list, Windows Setup cannot handle it. Skip ahead to the section called "Setting Up a DOS Application with the Program Manager.")

Click on each application you want to set up.

9. Click on the Add button.

10. Click on the OK button. Program Manager creates the icons, and places them in the Applications group.

Quick icons with File Manager

You can use File Manager (discussed in Part 4) to create program-item icons quickly. Run File Manager (Chapter 26). Change to the drive and directory that contains the program files (Chapter 27), and select the file that runs the program (Chapter 30). Change the size of the File Manager window so you can see the group window or icon in which you want the new program-item icon created. Drag the executable program file into the destination group window or icon, and release the mouse button.

Setting Up a Single Application with Windows Setup

In the previous section, Windows Setup searched your disk drive(s) for applications. This is a bit time-consuming. If you know which application you want to set up, and you know where its files are located on your hard disk, you can set up a single application. Here's what you do:

1. If the DOS application is not installed, follow the installation instructions to install it from the DOS prompt.

2. Double-click on the Main group icon. The Main group window appears.

3. Double-click on the Windows Setup icon. The Windows Setup window appears.

4. Open the Options menu and select Set Up Applications. The Set Up Applications dialog box appears.

Click here to set up a
specific application.

5. Click on Ask you to specify an application, and click on OK. A
   dialog box appears, asking you to specify the name of the file that
   runs the program and the name of the group window in which
   you want the icon to appear.

6. Click on the Browse button. The Setup Applications dialog box
   appears, prompting you to select the drive, directory, and name of
   the file that runs the program. (Any file that ends in .BAT, .COM,
   .EXE, or .PIF can run a program.)

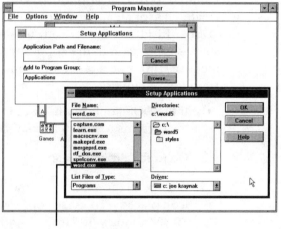

Select the file that runs the application.

Executable
files end in
.BAT,
.COM,
.EXE, or .PIF

7. Click on the arrow to the right of the Drives option, and click on
   the letter of the drive that contains the application's files.

8. Double-click on the directory that contains the application. (To
   move up in the directory tree, double-click on the topmost directory or drive letter.)

9. Click on the name of the file that runs the application in the File
   Name list.

10. Click on the OK button.

11. From the Add to Program Group drop-down list, click on the program group in which you want the icon to appear.

12. Click on the OK button. If all goes as planned, Windows creates a program information file for the application, assigns it an icon, and places the icon in the Applications group.

If you get a message indicating that Setup cannot set up this application, skip ahead to the following section to assign an icon to the application.

Beyond Survival

Setting Up a DOS Application with the Program Manager

The best way to set up a DOS application is to use the Windows Setup program, as explained previously. That way, Windows creates the PIF required to run the application correctly. However, Windows cannot create PIFs for all applications. In that case, Windows uses a file called _DEFAULT.PIF whenever you run the application. However, you can still assign an icon to the application's executable file (the file that runs the program), to make it more convenient to run the application. Here's what you do:

Do This only if Windows Setup doesn't work.

1. If the DOS application is not installed, follow the installation instructions to install it from the DOS prompt.

2. Go to the Program Manager.

3. Change to the group window in which you want the program-item icon placed. (To make your own group window, refer to Chapter 10, "Working with Group Windows.")

4. Open the File menu and select New. The New Program Object dialog box appears.

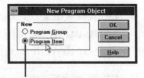

Select Program Item to make an icon.

5. Make sure Program Item is selected, and then click on OK.

6. Type a description of the program as you want it to appear under the program-item icon in the Description text box.

This description appears under the icon.

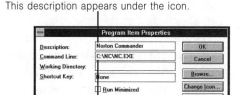

The drive, directory, and file name of the file that executes the program.

7. Click inside the Command Line text box.

8. Click on the Browse button. The Browse dialog box appears.

Double-click on a directory.

Click on the file.

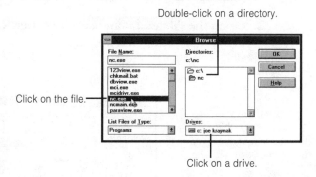

Click on a drive.

9. Click on the arrow to the right of the Drives option, and click on the letter of the drive that contains the application's files.

10. Double-click on the directory that contains the application. (To move up in the directory tree, double-click on the topmost directory or drive letter.)

Click on Change Icon To choose an icon.

11. Click on the name of the file that runs the application in the File Name list.

12. Click on the OK button. You are returned to the Program Item Properties dialog box, and the name and location of the selected file are inserted in the Command Line text box.

13. Click on the OK button. Program Manager assigns an icon to the application, and inserts the icon in the active group window. To change the icon, refer to the next section.

If you have trouble running the application, the _DEFAULT.PIF file may contain incorrect settings for this file, or the application may not be able to run under Windows (this happens mostly with game applications). Skip ahead to Chapter 50, "Editing PIFs for Stubborn DOS Applications," to learn how to create and edit PIF files.

Editing a Program-Item Icon

No matter how you create a program-item icon (by installing a Windows program, using Windows Setup, or using the Program Manager), you can edit the icon to change its title, assign it a shortcut key, change its icon, or specify that it run minimized when you start it. To edit a program-item icon, here's what you do:

Zoom To application: assign iT a shorTcuT Key

1. Click on the program-item icon you want to edit.

2. Open the File menu and select Properties. The Program Item Properties dialog box appears.

You can change the description.

The working directory tells the program which directory to use for the files you create.

Program Item Properties	
Description:	Microsoft Word 5.0
Command Line:	WORD.PIF
Working Directory:	
Shortcut Key:	None
	☐ Run Minimized

OK
Cancel
Browse...
Change Icon...
Help

Click here to change the icon.

You can assign a shortcut key. Click here to run the application minimized.

3. To change the icon's title, type a new title in the Description text box.

4. To specify the directory you want to use for the files you create, type a path to the directory in the Working Directory text box. (The path includes the drive letter and all directory names that lead up to the desired directory. For example, **c:\data\letters** tells the program to store files in the LETTERS directory.)

5. To assign a shortcut key to the application (so you can quickly switch to it when it is running), click inside the Shortcut Key text box, and then do one of the following:

- Hold down the Ctrl key and type the character you want to use. For example, hold down Ctrl while typing **W** to create the Ctrl+Alt+W shortcut combination.

- Hold down the Ctrl and Shift keys while typing the character you want to use. For example, hold down Ctrl+Shift while typing **W** to create the Ctrl+Shift+W shortcut combination.

- Hold down the Shift key while typing the character you want to use. For example, hold down Shift while typing **W** to create the Ctrl+Shift+Alt+W shortcut combination.

More icons—
Type
c:\windows
\moricons.dll
in The File
Name Text
box and
press Enter.

6. To have the application appear as an icon when you start it, click on the Run Minimized option.

7. To select a different icon for the application, click on the Change Icon button, click on the icon you want to use, and then click on OK.

8. Click on the OK button to put your changes into effect.

To delete a program-item icon, click on it and press the Del key.

Cheat Sheet

Making Group Windows

1. Go to the Program Manager.
2. Open the File menu and select New.
3. Select Program Group and click OK.
4. Type a name for the group, and press Enter.

Deleting Group Windows

1. Make sure you want to delete the group window and all of its program-item icons.
2. Click on the group window's Minimize button.
3. Click on the group icon you want to delete.
4. Open the File menu and select Delete.
5. Click on Yes.

Changing a Group Window's Title

1. Click on the group window's Minimize button.
2. Click on the group icon whose title you want to change.
3. Open the File menu and select Properties.
4. Type a new name in the Description text box.
5. Click OK.

Setting Up Applications to Run Automatically

1. Open the group window that contains the program-item icon(s).
2. Make sure the StartUp group window or icon is visible.
3. Hold down the Ctrl key while dragging the program-item icon from its group window to the StartUp window or icon.
4. Release the mouse button and Ctrl key.

10

Working with Group Windows

Your Program Manager contains several windows, including the Main and Accessories windows that came with Windows, and group windows for any applications you may have installed. Most users choose to live with whatever windows they have. However, this chapter shows you several ways you can use group windows to place the applications you use most at your fingertips.

Basic Survival

Making Group Windows

Whenever you want to start an application, you have to open the group window that contains the application's icon, and then double-click on the icon. To save steps, you can create your own group window, and then copy or move the program-item icons you use most often into that group window. Here's what you do:

Make a group for each user.

1. Go to the Program Manager.

2. Open the File menu and select New.

3. Select Program Group and click on the OK button. The Program Group Properties dialog box appears.

Type the window's title here.

Program Group Properties		
Description: My Work Group		OK
Group File:		Cancel
		Help

4. Type a name for the group window in the Description text box (for example, type **My Work Group**). Don't worry about the Group File text box. Windows will name the group file for you, and store it in the Windows directory.

5. Click on the OK button. The new (empty) window appears.

Now that you have a window, you can copy or move program-item icons into it. Refer to Chapter 6, "Working with Icons," for details.

Deleting Group Windows

Each group window and icon requires a tiny bit of memory, memory that other applications could make use of. If you have an empty group window, or a group window that you never use, you should delete it to free up that memory. To delete an empty window, simply click on the window and press the Del key. To delete a group window—and all its program-item icons—do the following:

1. Make sure you want to delete the group window and all its program-item icons.

2. Click on the group window's Minimize button. This shrinks the window down to icon size.

3. Click on the group icon you want to delete. The icon's control menu pops up; ignore it.

Press Del instead of File Delete

4. Open the File menu and select Delete. A confirmation dialog box appears.

This warning message asks for confirmation.

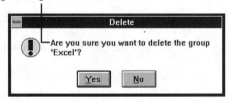

5. Click on Yes.

Recover with SETUP /P

If you delete a Windows program group by mistake (Accessories, SetUp, Main, or Games), you can get it back. Open the File menu and select Run. Type **c:\windows\setup /p** and press Enter. Windows Setup returns all the Windows program groups and icons to the desktop.

Changing a Group Window's Title

Each group window and icon has a title. You may want to edit a title to make it more descriptive. Here's what you do:

1. Click on the group window's Minimize button. The window must be minimized. Otherwise, Program Manager assumes you want to rename the highlighted program-item icon inside the window.

2. Click on the group icon for the window you just minimized.

3. Open the File menu and select Properties. The Program Group Properties dialog box appears.

Type a new title here.

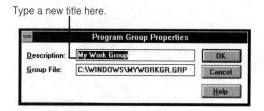

4. Type a new name in the Description text box.

5. Click on OK.

Beyond Survival

Setting Up Applications to Run Automatically

Windows 3.1 contains a StartUp group window that runs any applications automatically when you start Windows. You simply copy the program-item icons for the applications you want to run to the StartUp group window. Here's how you do it:

1. Open the group window that contains the program-item icon(s) for the application(s) you want to run when you start Windows.

2. Make sure the StartUp group window or icon is visible. You can drag an icon into a group window or icon.

3. Hold down the Ctrl key while dragging the program-item icon from its group window to the StartUp window or icon.

Prevent apps from running: hold down Shift when starting Windows

Hold down the Ctrl key while dragging the program-item icon to the StartUp window or icon.

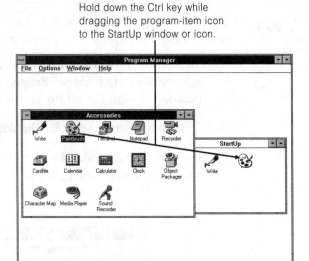

4. Release the mouse button and Ctrl key.

Cheat Sheet

Going to the DOS Prompt

1. Display the Main group window.
2. Double-click on the MS-DOS icon.

Running Applications at the Prompt

- To run an application at the DOS prompt, change to the drive and directory that contains the program's files, type the required command, and press Enter.
- To return to Windows or switch to another application, press Ctrl+Esc, click on the desired application, and click on Switch To.
- To run a DOS program in a window, press Alt+Enter.
- Some applications do not run properly under Windows. These include disk optimization utilities, DOS CHKDSK (when used with the /F switch), and undelete programs. To run these programs, quit Windows first.

Exiting the DOS Prompt

1. Quit any DOS applications you ran from the prompt.
2. Type **exit**.
3. Press Enter.

11

Going to the DOS Prompt

If you are having trouble with the concept of totally abandoning DOS, Windows provides a way of going out to the DOS prompt. That way, you can run applications and perform other tasks at the DOS prompt, just as you could before you ran Windows. In this chapter, you learn how to display the DOS prompt, run applications, and return to Windows.

Basic Survival

Displaying the DOS Prompt

To go to the DOS prompt, here's what you do:

1. Display the Main group window.

2. Double-click on the MS-DOS icon. Windows kicks you out to the DOS prompt.

Windows tells you how to get back later.

```
  ▪ Type EXIT and press ENTER to quit this MS-DOS prompt and
    return to Windows.
  ▪ Press ALT+TAB to switch to Windows or another application.
  ▪ Press ALT+ENTER to switch this MS-DOS Prompt between a
    window and full screen.

Microsoft(R) MS-DOS(R) Version 6.20
            (C)Copyright Microsoft Corp 1981-1993.

C:\WINDOWS>_
```

The DOS prompt

Running Applications at the Prompt

Before you run applications at the DOS prompt, you should consider a couple of factors. First, if the application has a PIF file (see Chapter 50, "Editing PIFs for Stubborn DOS Applications"), you should run the application from Windows (by double-clicking on its icon). Otherwise, Windows uses the DOSPRMPT.PIF (a generic PIF) when it runs the application, and you may encounter problems.

It's better to run applications from Windows.

Secondly, some applications and utilities are not designed to run under Windows. Examples include defragmentation programs, disk optimization utilities, DOS-file undelete programs, and most programs that will change your system settings. For example, if you want to use the DOS DEFRAG program to eliminate file fragmentation on your hard disk, you should exit Windows before running the program.

Once you've decided to run an application at the DOS prompt, perform the following steps:

1. Change to the drive that contains the program's files. For example, type **c:** and press Enter to change to drive C.

2. Change to the directory that contains the program's files. For example, type **cd\word** and press Enter to change to the \WORD directory.

3. Type the command required to run the program, and press Enter. This starts the program.

Exiting the DOS Prompt

You can go back to the Windows Program Manager, or switch from your DOS application to a running Windows application, just as you can with any other application. Press Ctrl+Esc, select the desired application from the Task List, and click on the Switch To button. If you want to quit the DOS prompt entirely, here's what you do:

1. Quit any DOS applications you ran from the prompt.

2. Type **exit**.

Switch apps: Hold down Alt while pressing Tab

Type exit and press Enter.

```
C:\WORD5>exit
```

3. Press Enter.

Beyond Survival

Running a DOS Application in a Window

Alt + Enter = DOS in a window

When you run a DOS application from the DOS prompt, it starts in full-screen mode, not in a window. However, you can run the application in a window by pressing Alt+Enter. This makes it easier for you to work with other Windows applications, and it gives you a Control-menu box you can click on for access to Windows commands. To return the Window to full-screen view, press Alt+Enter again.

Click here to open the Control menu.   Word 5.0 in a window.

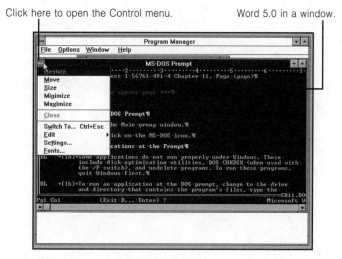

The Control menu has a Fonts command that lets you change the size of the text displayed in the window. If the window is too small, and you can't maximize it, try selecting a larger font.

PART 3

Using Accessories and Games

When you purchase Windows, you not only get the most popular operating system on the market, you also get a collection of applications that you can use to type documents, draw pictures, keep an address book, record sounds, and perform basic calculations. You even get a couple very addictive games that you can play while on break. In this part, you learn how to use these applications, and perform the following tasks:

- Typing and Printing with Write
- Editing and Formatting Your Write Document
- Making Pictures with Paintbrush
- Moving, Copying, and Sharing Information
- Making an Address Book with the Cardfile
- Keeping Appointments with the Calendar
- Go Figure with the Calculator
- Tracking Time with the Clock
- Editing Text with the Notepad
- Playing the Windows Games
- Dialing Out with the Terminal
- Recording Sounds with the Sound Recorder
- Automating Windows with the Recorder
- Inserting Characters and Symbols with the Character Map

Cheat Sheet

Starting Write

1. Open the Accessories group window.
2. Double-click on the Write icon.

Typing Your Document

- Start typing.
- Press Enter only to end a paragraph. Do not press Enter at the end of each line.
- To move the insertion point, click where you want it, or use the arrow keys.
- Use the Page Up or Page Down keys, or the scroll bar, to move up or down a page in the document.

Printing Your Document

1. Open the File menu and select Print.
2. Click OK.

Saving Your Work

1. Open the File menu and select Save.
2. Type a name for the file (up to eight characters).
3. Click OK.

Opening a Saved File

1. Open the File menu and select Open.
2. Select the drive and directory that contains the file.
3. Click on the name of the file in the File Name list.
4. Click OK.

12

Typing and Printing with Write

Write is a basic *word processing* program that allows you to type and print letters, articles, stories, and any other simple documents you want to create. Write provides *editing* tools that allow you to cut and paste text, *formatting* tools for styling your text and paragraphs, and *page layout* tools for setting margins. In this chapter, you learn how to type, save, open, and print a document. In Chapter 13, you will learn how to change the look and layout of a document.

Basic Survival

**Starting Write:
What You'll See**

To start Write, perform the following steps:

1. **Display the Accessories group window.** You may have to double-click on its icon or select it from the Program Manager's Window menu.

2. **Double-click on the Write icon** 📝. The Write application window appears.

Click on The Maximize buTTon for full-screen window

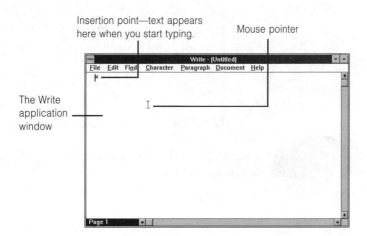

Insertion point—text appears here when you start typing.

Mouse pointer

The Write application window

Typing Your Document

If you have already done some typing in a word processing application, you know what to do: start typing. If you have no experience with word processors, here are a few tips:

- Press Enter only to end a paragraph. The program *wraps* text automatically from one line to the next as you type.

- You can't move down if there is no text to move down to. Pressing the Enter key will move the insertion point down by creating new paragraphs.

- Text that floats off the top of the screen is NOT gone. Use the Page Up key or the scroll bar to view the text.

- To delete text, drag the mouse pointer over the text you want to delete, and then press the Del key. If you don't select text, press Del to delete one character to the right, or use Backspace to delete characters to the left.

- To move the insertion point, click where you want it, or use the up, down, left, or right arrow keys to move.

Press Enter to end a paragraph or insert a blank line.

Drag over text to select it.

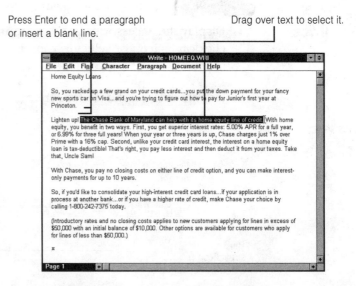

ATT + F4 = EXIT

To exit Write, open the File menu and select Exit, or double-click on the Control-menu box.

Printing Your Document

You can print your document at any stage in the process of creating a document. Here's how you do it:

1. Make sure the document you want to print is displayed.

2. Open the File menu and select Print. The Print dialog box appears.

Select your print options. ——

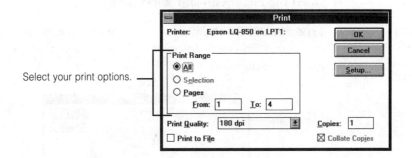

3. In the Print Range section, select one of the following options:

All prints the entire document.

Selection prints only the selected portion of the document, assuming you dragged over some text before selecting the Print command.

Pages prints only the specified pages. If you select this option, type entries in the From and To boxes to specify which pages you want to print.

4. Click on the arrow to the right of the Print Quality option, and select the desired quality. (High prints sharp but slow. Low prints faint but fast.)

5. To print more than one copy of the document, type the desired number of copies in the Copies text box.

6. Click OK.

If you have trouble printing, refer to Chapters 47, 48, and 55 which explain how to set up a printer and use the Print Manager.

Beyond Survival

Saving Your Work

As you type, your typing is saved only in your computer's electronic memory (RAM). If the power goes off (even for an instant), you will lose your work. To avoid losing work, you should save it early (and often). Here's what you do the first time you save the file:

1. Open the File menu and select Save.

Save files every 10 minutes

2. Type a name for the file (up to eight characters) in the File Name text box. (Write will automatically add the extension .WRI to the end of the filename.)

Type a file name here. →

3. (Optional) To specify where you want the file saved, **select a drive from the Drives list and a directory from the Directories list.** (If you do not select a drive and directory, Windows uses the current drive and directory, usually C:\WINDOWS.)

Click on Backup for an extra copy of the file

4. Click OK.

File Save As makes a copy of the file

The next time you save your file, all you have to do is open the File menu and select Save. Write "remembers" the name and location of the file, so you don't have to retype it.

You can also use the File Save As command to save a file. This allows you to save the file under another name, or to a different drive and directory. You can then edit the new file you created without changing the original.

Opening a Saved File

Whenever you start Write, it displays a blank window in which you can start typing. To work on a file you already created and saved, you must open it. Here's how you open a file:

1. Open the File menu and select Open. The Open dialog box appears.

2. Click on the arrow to the right of the Drives option, then click on the drive where the application is stored.

3. Double-click on the directory that contains the application's files in the Directories list. (To move up the directory tree, double-click on the drive letter or directory name at the top of the list.)

4. Click on the name of the file you want to open in the File Name list.

5. Click on the OK button. Write opens the file and displays it on-screen.

Work on 2 Docs—Run WriTe Twice; open a document in each WriTe Window

Double-click on a directory.

Click on the file you want to open.

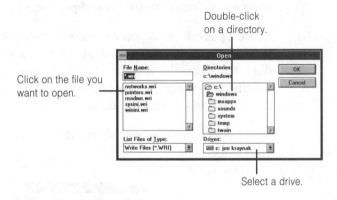

Select a drive.

Inserting Pictures and Other Data

As you create a document, keep in mind that you can copy and paste text and pictures from other applications. For example, you can create a picture in Paintbrush (see Chapter 14), copy it (or a portion of it), and then paste it into your document. Here's what you do:

1. Change to the application you need to open the file or enter the data you want to copy. For example, to paste a picture from Paintbrush, run Paintbrush.

2. Select the data you want to copy.

3. Open the Edit menu and choose Copy. The selected data is placed on the Windows Clipboard (see Chapter 15).

Ctrl + C =
Copy
Ctrl + V =
Paste

4. Switch back to Write, and open the document into which you want the copied data inserted.

5. Move the insertion point where you want the copied data pasted.

6. Open the Edit menu and select one of the following options:

Paste   Pastes the copied data from the Clipboard into the document.

Paste Link   Pastes the copied data from the Clipboard into the document, and creates a link between the pasted data and the file that contains the data. If you change the file that contains the pasted data, the pasted data is automatically updated. For example, if you edit a picture that you created in Paintbrush, those changes are made to the pasted picture in your Write document.

Paste Special   Lets you choose whether you want to Paste or Paste Link, and allows you to specify the format for the pasted data. For example, you can choose to paste a Paintbrush file as a Paintbrush object, or in Bitmapped format. Make your selections, then click on the Paste button.

Whichever command you selected, the copied data is inserted into your document.

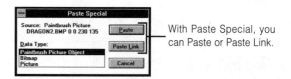

With Paste Special, you can Paste or Paste Link.

Another way to insert data into your document is to use the Edit Insert Object command. This command lets you run an application that you can use to open a file or create an object. When you exit the application, the object you created is inserted in the Write document. For more information, refer to the end of Chapter 15, in the section called "Dynamic Data Sharing."

Cheat Sheet

Cutting, Copying, and Pasting Text

1. Drag over the text you want to cut or copy.
2. Open the Edit menu and select Cut or Copy.
3. Move the insertion point where you want the text inserted.
4. Open the Edit menu and select Paste.

Changing the Document Margins

1. Open the Document menu and select Page Layout.
2. Tab to the margin setting you want to change.
3. Type the desired setting.
4. Repeat steps 2 and 3 for each margin setting you want to change.
5. Click OK.

Aligning Text

1. Move the insertion point inside the paragraph you want to align.
2. Open the Paragraph menu.
3. Select Left, Centered, Right, or Justified.

Formatting Text

1. Drag over the text you want to format.
2. Open the Character menu.
3. Select the desired format.
4. Repeat steps 2 and 3 to apply additional formats.

13

Editing and Formatting Your Document

In the previous chapter, you learned how to create and print a document, and how to save and open document files. In this chapter, you learn how to cut and paste text in a document and how to control the look and layout of your text. You learn how to change margins, make text bold and italic, change the text size, and change the tab settings.

Basic Survival

Selecting Text in a Document

Several tasks in this chapter require you to select text. To cut or copy text, you must first select it. To make a word or sentence bold, you must select it. The following list explains various ways to select text:

Select text	Move the mouse pointer to the first character you want in the selection, and hold down the mouse button while dragging over additional text.
A single line	Click inside the selection area to the left of the line you want to select.
Several lines	Move the mouse pointer inside the selection area to the left of the first line you want to select, and then hold down the mouse button while dragging up or down.
One paragraph	Double-click inside the selection area to the left of the paragraph you want to select.
Several paragraphs	Double-click inside the selection area to the left of the first paragraph. On the second click, hold down the mouse button, and drag the pointer up or down.

Select word = double-click on it

87

Range of text	Click inside the selection area to the left of the first line in the desired range. Hold down the Shift key while clicking on the last line in the desired range.
Entire document	Hold down the Ctrl key while clicking anywhere inside the selection area.

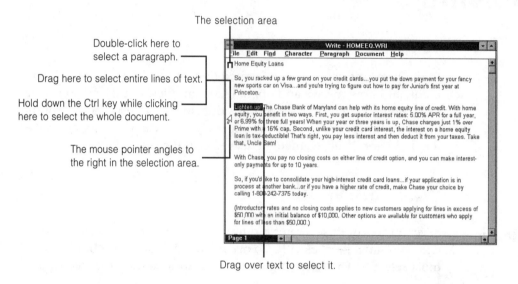

The selection area

Double-click here to select a paragraph.

Drag here to select entire lines of text.

Hold down the Ctrl key while clicking here to select the whole document.

The mouse pointer angles to the right in the selection area.

Drag over text to select it.

Cutting, Copying, and Pasting Text

As you edit your document, you may want to cut and paste text (to move it) or copy and paste text that you want to use in two or more places (for example, a list of numbers). To cut or copy and then paste text, do the following:

1. Select the text you want to cut or copy.

2. Open the Edit menu and select Cut or Copy. Cut removes the text and places it on the Clipboard, so you can paste it somewhere else. Copy leaves the original text in place, and sticks a copy of it on the Clipboard.

Copy, Cut, and Paste are on the Edit menu.

Write - HOMEEQ.WRI

File Edit Find Character Paragraph Document Help

Undo Editing   Ctrl+Z

Cut   Ctrl+X
Copy   Ctrl+C
Paste   Ctrl+V
Paste Special...
Paste Link

Links...
Object
Insert Object...

Move Picture
Size Picture

With Chase, you pay no closing costs on either line of credit option, and you can make interest-only payments for up to 10 years.

So, if you'd like to consolidate your high-interest credit card loans...if your application is in process at another bank...or if you have a higher rate of credit, make Chase your choice by calling 1-800-242-7375 today.

(Introductory rates and no closing costs applies to new customers applying for lines in excess of $50,000 with an initial balance of $10,000. Other options are available for customers who apply for lines of less than $50,000.)

Page 1

Ctrl + C =
    Copy

Ctrl + X =
    Cut

Ctrl + V =
    Paste

3. Move the insertion point to where you want the text inserted.

4. Open the Edit menu and select Paste. The text is inserted.

For more details about cutting and pasting data using the Windows Clipboard and to learn about other ways to share data between applications, see Chapter 15, "Moving, Copying, and Sharing Information."

Changing the Document Margins

The first thing you might want to do when creating a document is to change the margins. The left and right margins are initially set at 1.25 inches. The top and bottom margins are set at 1 inch. You can change margins before you start typing, or at any time during the typing or editing stages. To change the margins, here's what you do:

1. Open the Document menu and select Page Layout. The Page Layout dialog box appears.

Click inside a text box and edit the setting, or tab to it and type over the setting.

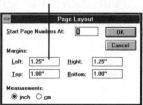

Page Layout

Start Page Numbers At: [0]   OK
                                   Cancel
Margins:
Left: 1.25"   Right: 1.25"
Top: 1.00"   Bottom: 1.00"

Measurements:
● inch ○ cm

2. Tab to the margin setting you want to change.

3. Type the desired setting. When you start typing, the original setting is deleted.

4. Repeat steps 2 and 3 for each margin setting you want to change.

Ctrl + Z = Undo

5. Click on the OK button.

Beyond Survival

Changing the Look of Your Text

You can change the look of your text by changing its font (type style and size) or by adding an enhancement, such as bold or italic. Here's what you do:

1. Drag the mouse pointer over the text whose look you want to change.

2. Open the Character menu and select Fonts. The Font dialog box appears.

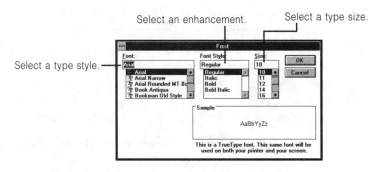

Select an enhancement.

Select a type size.

Select a type style.

3. Enter your settings for the following options:

Ctrl + B = Bold

Font   Select the desired type style from the list. The Sample area shows what you'll get.

Ctrl + U = Underlined

Font Style   Select the desired enhancement (if any): bold or italic.

Ctrl + I = Italic

Size   Select the desired type size. Size is measured in points. There are 72 points in an inch.

F5 = Normal

4. Click on the OK button.

You may have noticed that some type styles in the Font list have a TT next to them. TT stands for TrueType fonts. These are special fonts that allow you to change the type size by a single point. Instead of selecting a type size from the Size list, you can type the precise size in the Size text box. Non-TrueType fonts usually allow you to select from a limited list of sizes. For information about installing fonts, see Chapter 41.

Formatting Your Paragraphs

You can apply paragraph formatting to any selected paragraphs to control their alignment (left, center, right), line spacing (single or double), or to indent the paragraphs from the margins. Here's what you do:

1. Drag over all the paragraphs you want to format. (To change the formatting for the entire document, hold down the Ctrl key while clicking in the selection area—the area to the left of the paragraphs.)

Paragraph Normal To remove paragraph formatting

2. To change the paragraph alignment, open the Paragraph menu, and select one of the following options:

   Left places the paragraph against the left margin.

   Centered centers the paragraph between the left and right margins.

   Right shoves the right side of the paragraph against the right margin, leaving the left side of the paragraph uneven.

   Justified spreads each line of the paragraph between the left and right margins, making both sides of the paragraph even.

3. To change the line spacing of the paragraphs, open the Paragraph menu and select the desired spacing: Single Space, 1 1/2 Space, or Double Space.

4. To indent the paragraphs from the left or right margins, open the Paragraph menu, select Indents (the Indent dialog box appears), enter the following indent settings, and click on OK:

   Left Indent indents the left side of the paragraph from the left margin. For example, if you type **.5**, the left side of the paragraph will be indented one half inch.

First Line indents the first line of the paragraph from the left margin, leaving remaining lines pressed against the left margin.

Right Indent indents the right side of the paragraph from the right margin.

Type indent settings (in inches).

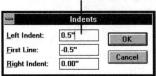

You can use the Left Indent and First Line Indent settings to create a hanging indent, for a bulleted or numbered list. For example, you can set the left indent at **.5** and the first line indent at **–.5** to have the first line start at the left margin, and have all following lines indented .5 inches from the left margin.

Setting Tabs

Write is set up so that if you press the Tab key, the insertion point (and any text to the right of it) moves .5 inch to the right. This allows you to indent the first line of a paragraph or create columns of text. If you want to change the tab settings, perform the following steps:

1. Open the Document menu and select Tabs. The Tabs dialog box appears.

Type the desired settings here.

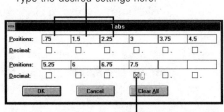

To align a column on decimal points (periods), turn on the Decimal option for the tab stop.

2. Type a tab stop position in inches.

3. To enter another tab stop setting, tab to or click inside the next Position text box.

4. Repeat steps 2 and 3 for each tab stop setting you want to enter.

5. To have any of the tab stops act as decimal tabs (for example, to align a column of dollar figures on their decimal points), **click inside the Decimal check box for those tab stops.**

6. Click on the OK button.

Quick Formatting with the Ruler

Write has a formatting ruler that you can use to set tabs and margins quickly, and select paragraph alignment and line spacing.

- To turn the ruler on, open the Document menu and select Ruler On.

- To turn it off, open the Document menu and select Ruler Off.

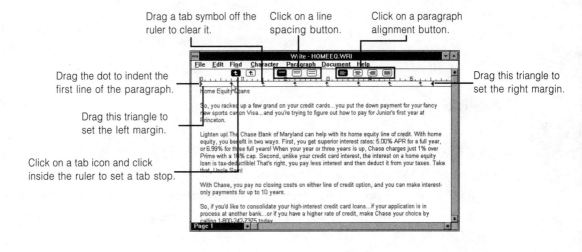

Drag a tab symbol off the ruler to clear it.

Click on a line spacing button.

Click on a paragraph alignment button.

Drag the dot to indent the first line of the paragraph.

Drag this triangle to set the right margin.

Drag this triangle to set the left margin.

Click on a tab icon and click inside the ruler to set a tab stop.

Cheat Sheet

Starting Paintbrush

1. Go to the Accessories group window.
2. Double-click on the Paintbrush icon.

Using the Paintbrush Tools

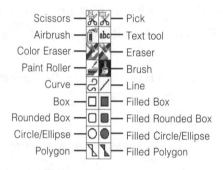

Scissors	Pick
Airbrush	Text tool
Color Eraser	Eraser
Paint Roller	Brush
Curve	Line
Box	Filled Box
Rounded Box	Filled Rounded Box
Circle/Ellipse	Filled Circle/Ellipse
Polygon	Filled Polygon

Drawing Objects

1. Click on the desired line thickness.
2. Click on the desired color or pattern.
3. Click on the shape you want to draw.
4. Move the mouse pointer to where you want one end of the object to appear.
5. Hold mouse button and drag mouse pointer to where you want the opposite end of the object to appear.
6. Release the mouse button.

14

Making Pictures with Paintbrush

With Paintbrush, you can create color or black-and-white drawings by "painting" your screen. Paintbrush comes with a collection of basic shapes that you can assemble and fill to create simple or complex illustrations. Additional tools allow you to add text to your drawings; cut, copy, and paste objects; and even zoom in for detailed work. In this chapter, you learn how to use these tools to create and edit your own pictures.

Basic Survival

Starting Paintbrush: What You'll See

To start Paintbrush, display the Accessories group window, and then double-click on the Paintbrush icon. The Paintbrush application window appears.

Click on The Maximize buTTon for full-screen window

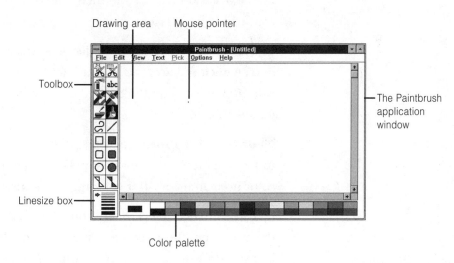

Drawing area   Mouse pointer

Toolbox

The Paintbrush application window

Linesize box

Color palette

Using the Paintbrush Tools

The Paintbrush Toolbox (on the left side of the screen), contains several tools that allow you to paint your screen, create basic lines and shapes, and edit your drawing. Following is a list of the tools and what they do:

Scissors and Pick   Click on the Scissors tool, and drag the mouse pointer around a section of the drawing to select it for cutting or copying. The Scissors tool allows you to select an irregular area. The Pick lets you select a rectangular area.

Airbrush   Click on the Airbrush tool and drag the mouse pointer across the screen to "spray-paint" your screen. Drag slowly to make the ribbon dark or quickly to make it light.

Text tool   Click on the text tool, and click where you want to type your text. Start typing. This is useful for labeling a picture.

Erasers   The Color Eraser tool (on the left) erases only the color that's currently selected in the palette (bottom of the window). The Eraser tool (on the right) erases everything. Select the Eraser you want to use, and then drag over the portion of the picture you want to erase.

Paint Roller   The Paint Roller lets you pour color or shading into an enclosed area. So, if you draw a box, you can click on the Paint Roller, click on the desired color, and click inside the box to fill it with color.

Brush   The Brush lets you stroke color onto the screen. Unlike the Airbrush, the Brush puts down a uniform ribbon of color no matter how fast you drag the mouse pointer.

Assemble
shapes
To create
illustrations

Curve   This tool is tricky. You click on the tool and then drag the mouse pointer to create a straight line. Then, you drag the line you drew to one side or the other to make it curve.

Line   The Line tool lets you drag a straight line on the screen.

Boxes   The Box tool on the left creates a rectangle that has no color or shading inside. The Filled Box (on the right) creates a box that's filled with the selected color.

Rounded Boxes   The Rounded Box tools are similar to the Box tools. However, these boxes have rounded corners.

Circle/Ellipse   The Circle/Ellipse tool (on the left) lets you draw circles or ovals. The Filled Circle/Ellipse tool creates circles or ovals that are filled with the selected color.

Polygons   The Polygon tools allow you to create an object that's made up of several straight lines. Select the tool, drag your first line segment, release the mouse button, and drag the next line. Continue until the object is complete, and then double-click where you want the last line to end.

Drawing Objects

RighT-click To cancel drawing

Although each drawing tool creates a different type of object, the procedure for drawing objects is generally the same:

1. In the Toolbox, click on the drawing tool you want to use.

2. In the Linesize box, click on the desired line thickness.

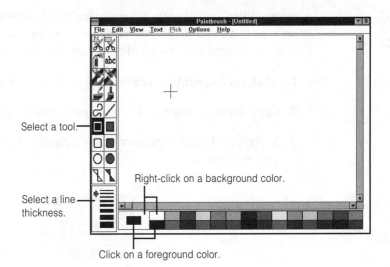

Select a tool.

Select a line thickness.

Right-click on a background color.

Click on a foreground color.

3. In the Color Palette, click on the color you want to use as the object's foreground color, and then right-click on the color you want to use as the background color. In an *unfilled* object (a line, curve, or unfilled shape), the foreground color is the color of the line that defines the shape. In a *filled* object, the foreground color is the color that fills the object; the background color is the line that defines the object.

4. Move the mouse pointer where you want one end or corner of the object to appear.

5. Hold down the mouse button, and drag to where you want the other end or corner of the object to appear.

For uniform
dimensions:
hold down
Shift while
dragging

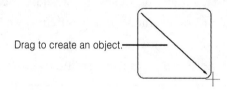

Drag to create an object.

6. Release the mouse button.

Beyond Survival

Filling Objects with Color

You can fill an object with color or shading in two ways: draw a filled object, as explained in the previous section, or use the Paint Roller to "pour" paint into the object. Here's how you use the Paint Roller:

1. Click on the Paint Roller tool [icon] in the toolbox.

2. Click on the color you want to use in the color palette.

3. Move tip of mouse pointer (now a paint roller) inside the object you want to fill.

Click outside
of object to
fill the
background

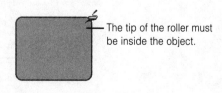

The tip of the roller must be inside the object.

4. Click the left mouse button.

Adding Text

If you want to add a label or title to your picture, you can do it with the text tool. Here's what you do:

1. Click on the text tool |abc| in the toolbox.

2. Click where you want to start typing the text. An insertion point appears.

3. Open the Text menu and select the desired look for your text, or select Fonts, and use the Font dialog box (as shown) to style the text.

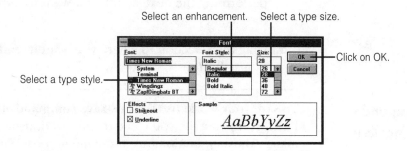

4. To change the text color, click on the desired color in the palette.

5. Type your text. The text appears in the style, size, and color you selected in steps 3 and 4.

You can change fonts before you type or immediately after typing text. However, if you click somewhere else or create a different object, you can't go back and style the text. In such a case, you have to cut the text and start over.

Cutting, Copying, and Pasting Selected Areas

In Paintbrush, you cannot select text by dragging over it, or select an object (such as a circle or square) by clicking on it. Instead, you must use the *selection tool* to mark an area of the picture that might contain one or more objects.

Once you mark an area, you can cut, copy, and paste the selection. Cutting removes the selection and places it on the Windows Clipboard. Copying leaves the selection where it is, and places a copy of it on the Clipboard. Pasting inserts the copied or cut selection from the Clipboard onto the work area. For more details, see Chapter 15. To cut (or copy) and paste a selection, perform the following steps:

1. Click on the Scissors or Pick tool. Use Scissors to select an irregular area. Use the Pick to select a rectangular area.

2. Drag the mouse pointer to select the portion of the drawing you want to cut or copy. With Scissors, you must drag a circle around the area. With Pick, you drag a box around the area just as if you were drawing a rectangle.

3. Move the tip of the mouse pointer over any part of the selected area.

4. If you want to copy the selection, hold down the Ctrl key while performing the next step. If you want to move it, don't hold down the Ctrl key.

5. Drag the selection to where you want it, and then release the mouse button.

Cut = Ctrl + X

Copy = Ctrl + C

Paste = Ctrl + V

Saving and Printing Your Work

To save your work, use the File Save command. To print, select File Print. To open a file you created and saved, use the File Open command. These operations are the same in most Windows applications. Refer to Chapter 3 for details.

Zooming In (for Detail Work)

As you draw and color your screen, you may not notice that what you are really doing is turning pixels (tiny screen dots) on and off and changing their color. If you are creating a complex illustration, it is sometimes useful to zoom in on a specific area of the screen to control individual pixels. The process can be tedious, but it does give you total control of your drawing. To zoom in and edit individual pixels, here's what you do:

1. Open the View menu and select Zoom In. The mouse pointer turns into a rectangle that you can use to select the area you want to zoom in on.

2. Move the rectangle over the desired area and click the mouse button.

Zoom in to edit individual pixels.   Pixel

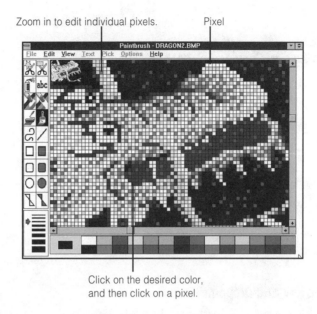

Click on the desired color,
and then click on a pixel.

3. Click on the color you want to use for the pixels. (If you want to use two colors, click on one color and then right-click on the other one. You can then left-click to use the first color and right-click to use the second.)

Use scroll bars To bring areas inTo view

4. Click on the pixel whose color you want to change. The pixel is changed to the color you selected in step 3.

5. When you are done, open the View menu and select Zoom Out.

Cheat Sheet

Moving and Copying Selections

1. Mark the selection you want to copy or move.
2. Open the Edit menu and select Cut or Copy.
3. Move the insertion point to where you want the selection inserted.
4. Open the Edit menu and select Paste.

Viewing the Clipboard Contents

1. Go to the Main group window.

2. Double-click on the Clipboard Viewer icon Clipboard · Viewer

Dragging and Dropping

1. Mark the selection you want to copy or move.
2. Move the mouse pointer over any part of the selection.
3. Hold down the mouse button (and the Ctrl key to copy), while dragging the selection to where you want it.

15

Moving, Copying, and Sharing Information

Windows owes much of its popularity to the fact that it allows you to work with several applications at the same time, and transfer information between applications. In this chapter, you learn how to copy and move information within (and between) documents, and how to use some of Windows' more advanced tools for sharing information between applications.

Basic Survival

Moving and Copying with the Clipboard

The Windows *Clipboard* is a temporary holding area that allows you to copy or move a selection within a document or from one document to another. Whenever you cut or copy a selection, it is placed on the Clipboard, replacing anything that was previously on the Clipboard. You can then paste the selection from the Clipboard into a document.

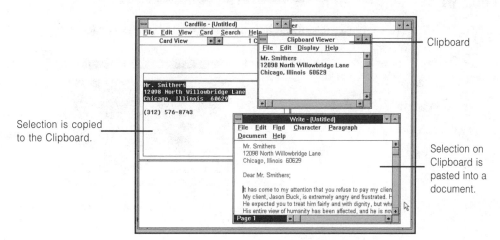

Clipboard

Selection is copied to the Clipboard.

Selection on Clipboard is pasted into a document.

To transfer selections with the Clipboard, here's what you do:

1. Mark the selection you want to copy or move. To select text, drag over it. To select a picture, you can click on it or use the program's selection tool to drag a box around the picture.

Ctrl + C = Copy

2. Open the Edit menu and select Cut (for moving an object) or Copy (for creating a copy of an object). The selection is placed on the Clipboard.

Ctrl + X = Cut

3. Move the insertion point to where you want the selection inserted. (This can be in the same document, in a different document in the same application, or in a different document in a different application.)

Ctrl + V = Paste

4. Open the Edit menu and select Paste. A copy of the selection that's on the Clipboard is pasted into the selected location.

If you attempt to paste a selection into a document created in another application, and the Paste command is dimmed (not available), the application cannot handle the format of the selection that's on the Clipboard. In that case, you cannot paste the Clipboard contents into this document.

Viewing the Clipboard Contents

The Clipboard works in the background, so you rarely see it. However, if you want to see what's on the Clipboard, here's what you do:

1. Go to the Main group window.

2. Double-click on the Clipboard Viewer icon Clipboard Viewer .

Press PrinT Screen key To place a picture of The screen on The Clipboard.

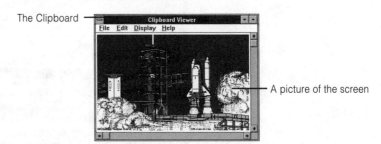

The Clipboard

A picture of the screen

Alt + Print
Screen for only
the current
window.

If you copy a graphic to the Clipboard and then notice that Windows is slowing down (or that you get "Out of Memory" messages), display the Clipboard window, open the Edit menu, and select Delete. A graphic image on the Clipboard can consume a lot of memory. Refer to Chapter 56 for information about freeing up memory in Windows.

Beyond Survival

Dragging and Dropping Selections

Some Windows applications allow you to bypass the Copy, Cut, and Paste commands by using a feature called *Drag and Drop*. If you have an application that offers drag and drop copying and moving, do the following to move or copy selections:

Open two
document
windows and
drag-and-drop

1. Mark the selection you want to copy or move. To select text, drag over it. To select a picture, you can click on it or use the program's selection tool to drag a box around the picture.

2. Move the mouse pointer over any part of the selection.

3. To copy the selection, hold down the Ctrl key while performing the following step. Otherwise the selection is moved instead of copied.

4. Hold down the mouse button, and drag the selection to where you want it.

5. Release the mouse button.

Dynamic Data Sharing

The Windows Clipboard allows you to share information only statically. That is, if you paste information and then later change the source information, the pasted information is not updated to reflect the changes. Windows, and many Windows applications (including Write) offer *dynamic data sharing*, through OLE (Object Linking and Embedding).

With OLE (pronounced "oh-lay"), you can insert objects created in other applications into a document in your current application. When you enter the command to insert an object, Windows runs the application you need to use to create the object. When you exit that application, the object you created is inserted into the current document. Whenever you want to edit the object, simply double-click on it to run the application you used to create it.

OLE gives you two options: *linking* and *embedding*. With linking, the object you insert is linked to its original file. If you modify the file, the object in your document is updated to reflect any changes. With embedding, you place a copy of the object in your document, breaking any link between the object and its file. If you modify the object's file, the changes do not appear in the object.

To insert an object in most applications, perform the following steps:

1. Open the Edit menu and select Insert Object. A dialog box appears, showing the applications you can run to create an object.

Select an application to run it.

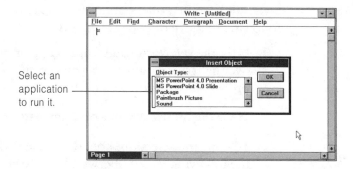

2. Click on the desired application, and then click OK. Windows runs the selected application.

3. Use the application to create the file you want to insert.

ALT + F4 To exit

4. Open the File menu and select Exit and Return To. A dialog box appears asking if you want to update the open embedded object.

5. Click on the Yes button. Windows inserts the object you just created into your document.

Whenever you want to edit the object, simply double-click on it, or click on it, and then choose the appropriate command from the Edit menu.

If you want to embed an object using an application that is not on the list of applications you see when you select Insert Object, use the Object Packager.

Cheat Sheet

Starting Cardfile

1. Go to the Accessories group window.

2. Double-click on the Cardfile icon .

Adding a Card

1. Open the Card menu and select Add.
2. Type a name for the card, and click on OK.
3. Type the information you want to appear on the card.

Deleting a Card

1. Click on the card you want to delete.
2. Open the Card menu and select Delete.
3. Click on the OK button.

Switching to List View

1. Open the View menu and select List.
2. To switch back to Card view, open the View menu and select Card.

16

Making an Address Book with the Cardfile

Windows comes with a simple *database* application (called Cardfile) that acts as an electronic Rolodex. You type names, addresses, phone numbers, and other information onto on-screen cards, that you can later flip through to find the information you need. If you have a modem, you can even use Cardfile to dial phone numbers for you. In this chapter, you learn how to use Cardfile.

Basic Survival

Starting Cardfile

To start Cardfile, follow these steps:

1. Go to the Accessories group window.

2. Double-click on the Cardfile icon. The Cardfile application window appears, displaying a blank card.

3. To create your first card, simply type whatever information you want the card to hold: name, address, phone number, birthday, and so on.

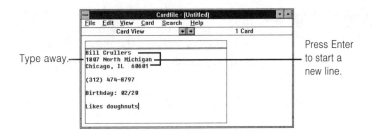

Type away.

Press Enter to start a new line.

Adding and Deleting Cards

Add Card = F7

In Cardfile, you use one card for information about each person or item. To add a card, here's what you do:

1. Open the Card menu and select Add. The Add dialog box appears.

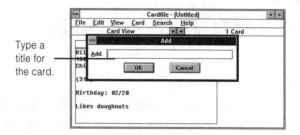

Type a title for the card.

2. Type a name (index line) for the card, and click OK. Cardfile creates a blank card, and inserts the index line you typed at the top of the card. You will learn how to edit a card's index line later. The index line is displayed at the top of the card, and is used to help sort the cards. If you are creating an address book, you may want to type a person's name, last name first.

3. Type the name, address, phone number, and other information you want to appear on the card.

Saving and Opening a Card File

File Print = Print addresses

After you create a few cards, you should save your work to protect it. Use the File Save command, as explained in Chapter 3. Chapter 3 also explains how to use the File Open command to open a file you created and saved.

Beyond Survival

Flipping Through the Cards

As you add cards, the cards are cascaded in alphabetical order, showing all the information typed on the frontmost card, but only the index lines of the other cards. When the stack is too tall to fit inside the window, some cards are completely hidden.

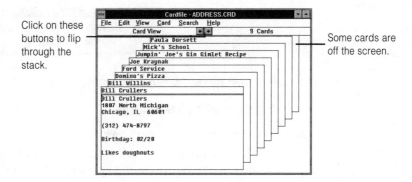

Click on these buttons to flip through the stack.

Some cards are off the screen.

To flip through the cards, perform one of the following steps:

- Click on the left arrow or right arrow ← → in the status bar. The right arrow brings the previous card to the front. The left arrow moves the current card one back and brings the card at the bottom of the stack to the front. You can use the Page Up and Page Down keys to do the same thing.

- Press Ctrl+Home to move the first card (in alphabetical order) to the front of the stack. Press Ctrl+End to move the last card to the front.

- Press Ctrl+Shift+*character* to move the first card whose index line starts with that character to the front of the stack.

- Open the View menu, and select List. Click on the desired card, and then open the View menu and select Card.

Changing a Card's Index Line

At the top of every card is an index line that displays the name of the card. In List view, the index lines appear in alphabetical order. The first card that Cardfile displays when you start the application has no index line. To add an index line to this card (or to edit any card's index line), do the following:

Index = F6

1. Move the card whose index line you want to edit to the front of the stack.

2. Open the Edit menu and select Index. The Index dialog box appears.

Type a new index line here.

3. Type the index line you want to use.

4. Click on the OK button.

Earlier in this chapter, you learned how to flip through a stack of cards. Cardfile offers a couple quicker ways to find a specific card. You can search by index line or search for text that appears on the card. To search by index line, do the following:

Go To = F4

1. Open the Search menu and select Go To. The Go To dialog box appears.

2. Type a few letters or any word in the index line you want to search for. For example, if you want to find your favorite Hobo Stew recipe, type **Hobo** or **Stew** or **Hob**.

3. Click on the OK button. The card you searched for jumps to the front of the stack.

Instead of searching for a card by index line, you may want to search for a card that has a certain entry on it. To search for text on a card, here's what you do:

1. Open the Search menu and select Find. The Find dialog box appears.

2. Type the text you want to search for in the Find What text box.

3. Click on the Find Next button. Cardfile finds the first occurrence of the text, and moves the card that has it to the front of the stack.

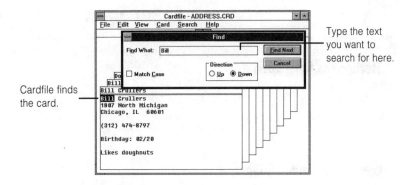

Type the text you want to search for here.

Cardfile finds the card.

Drag Title bar To move Dialog box

4. Repeat step 3 until the desired card is up front.

5. Click on the Cancel button.

Cheat Sheet

Starting the Calendar

1. Open the Accessories group window.

2. Double-click on the Calendar icon .

Entering an Appointment

1. In Day view, click on the time for which you want to set the appointment.

2. Type a description of the appointment.

3. To have an alarm ring at the appointment time, open the Alarm menu and select Set.

4. To have the alarm ring before the appointment time, open the Alarm menu, select Controls, type the number of minutes in advance you want the alarm to ring, and click on OK.

Changing Month/Day View

1. To view a calendar of the current month, open the View menu and select Month.

2. To view the hours of a day, click on the day, open the View menu, and select Day.

Changing the Day Settings

1. Open the Options menu and select Day Settings.

2. Select the desired Interval: 15, 30, or 60 minutes.

3. Select the desired Hour Format: 12 or 24 (military time).

4. In the Starting Time text box, type the hour with which you want your day to start.

5. Click OK.

17

Keeping Appointments with the Calendar

The Windows Calendar allows you to keep track of your daily appointments. You simply enter a description of the appointment at the desired time, and turn on an optional alarm. When the appointment time rolls around, the Calendar interrupts your work and notifies you. In this chapter, you learn how to use the Calendar to keep track of your appointments.

Basic Survival

Starting the Calendar

To start the Calendar, open the Accessories group window, and then double-click on the Calendar icon 🔢 . The Calendar appears, displaying the hours of the current day. You can change the view to display the days of this month by performing the following steps:

Day = F8

1. Open the View menu and select Month.

2. To switch back to Day view, open the View menu and select Day.

MonTh = F9

Click here for the previous day.

Click here to see the next day.

Calendar in Day view.

Show Date
= F 4

Ctrl + Pg Dn
= NexT

Ctrl + Pg Up
= Previous

As you can see in the picture, Calendar provides two buttons that let you move from one day to the next or previous. In Month view, the buttons let you move to the next or previous month. In addition, you can use the following options on the Show menu to move to a day or month:

Today displays the current day according to your computer's internal clock.

Previous displays the previous day.

Next displays the next day.

Date opens a dialog box that prompts you to enter a specific date. Type the desired date, and then click OK.

Entering an Appointment

In Month view, double-click on The desired day To display iT in Day view.

You can enter appointments at any of the listed intervals or at a time between the intervals. To enter an appointment at a time between intervals, skip ahead to the section called "Entering and Removing Special Times." To enter an appointment at one of the times listed, do the following:

1. In Day view, click on the time for which you want to set the appointment. The insertion point appears at the selected time.

2. Type a description of the appointment.

3. To have an alarm ring at the appointment time, open the Alarm menu and select Set. A tiny bell appears to the left of the appointment time. (To turn off an alarm, select Alarm Set again.)

4. To have the alarm ring before the appointment time, open the Alarm menu, select Controls, type the number of minutes in advance you want the alarm to ring, and click on OK.

You can have the alarm ring 1 to 10 minutes in advance.

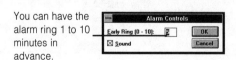

In order for the alarm to notify you of an upcoming appointment, the Calendar must be running. Instead of exiting the calendar when you are done, click on the minimize button, so the Calendar will remain active as you perform other tasks.

Beyond Survival

Changing the Day Settings

Initially, Calendar is set up to start the day at 7:00 a.m., and display times in one-hour intervals. To start the day at another time, or display times in 15- or 30-minute intervals, here's what you do:

1. Open the Options menu and select Day Settings. The Day Settings dialog box appears.

Enter the time you start your day.

Intervals are measured in minutes.

2. Select the desired Interval: 15, 30, or 60 minutes. You can set appointments at times between intervals by using special times, as explained later.

3. Select the desired Hour Format: 12 or 24 (military time).

4. In the Starting Time text box, type the hour with which you want your day to start.

5. Click on the OK button.

Entering and Removing Special Times

Even if you enter Day settings that set up your day in 15-minute intervals, you may need to enter an appointment that does not fall on one of the listed times. To enter an appointment at an off time, here's what you do:

1. Open the Options menu and select Special Time. The Special Time dialog box appears.

Type your special time.

Click on Insert.

Select AM or PM.

*Use File Save
To save your
calendar file.*

2. Type the desired appointment time.

3. Select AM or PM.

4. Click on the Insert button. The special time is inserted, and the insertion point appears at that time, allowing you to type a description of the appointment.

To remove a special time, click on it, and then open the Options menu and select Special Time. Click on the Delete button.

Jotting Down Notes

At the bottom of the Calendar is a scratch pad that can hold up to three lines of text. You can use this area to jot down a reminder about one of your appointments or keep a list of things to do . To write a note, here's what you do:

1. Press the Tab key or click inside the note area.

2. Type your note (up to three lines).

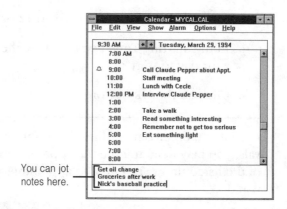

You can jot notes here.

Starting Calendar When You Start Windows

Because Calendar must be running in order to notify you of upcoming appointments, it's a good idea to run Calendar whenever you run Windows. First, save your Calendar file, as explained in Chapter 3. Then, perform the following steps:

1. Hold down the Ctrl key while dragging the Calendar icon from the Accessories group to the Startup group. This copies the Calendar icon into the Startup group, so that Windows will start the Calendar automatically.

2. Open the File menu and select Properties. The Program Item Properties dialog box appears for the Calendar.

3. In the Command Line text box, click at the end of the CALENDAR.EXE command, press the Spacebar, and type the name you gave your calendar file when you saved it. (This tells Calendar to open that file automatically on startup.) If you saved the file in a directory other than \WINDOWS, type the location of the file before the filename. For example, type **c:\data\myfiles\mycal**.

4. Click on the Run Minimized option to put an X in the check box. This runs the Calendar as an application icon to keep it out of your way as you work.

5. Click on the OK button.

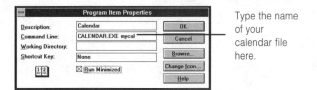

Type the name of your calendar file here.

Now, whenever you start Windows, Windows will start the Calendar and open your calendar file. If you have any appointments on this day, the Calendar is now prepared to notify you.

Cheat Sheet

Starting the Calculator

1. Go to the Accessories group window.

2. Double-click on the Calculator icon 📇 .
   Calculator

Entering Calculations with the Standard Calculator

1. Click on the number buttons to enter the first number.

2. Click on the operator you want to use:

   [+] to add the next number

   [-] to subtract the next number

   [*] to multiply by the next number

   [/] to divide by the next number

3. Click on the number buttons to enter the next number.

4. Repeat steps 2 and 3 until you have performed all the desired calculations.

5. Click on the equal button [=].

Switching Calculators

1. Open the View menu.
2. Click on the calculator you want to use: Scientific or Standard.

18

Go Figure with the Calculator

Windows offers an on-screen calculator you can use just like a hand-held calculator. You key in the numbers and mathematical operators you want to use, and the Calculator performs the calculations for you. In this chapter, you learn how to use the two Windows calculators: Standard and Scientific.

Basic Survival

Starting the Calculator

You start the Calculator as you start any Windows accessory:

1. Open the Accessories group window.

2. Double-click on the Calculator icon 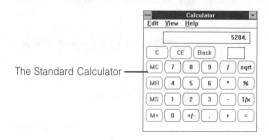 . The Standard calculator appears.

3. To switch to the Scientific calculator, open the View menu and select Scientific. To switch back to the Standard calculator, open the View menu and select Standard.

The Standard Calculator ─

Entering Calculations with the Standard Calculator

The Standard calculator works like a hand-held calculator. You simply click on the buttons to enter numbers and mathematical operators.

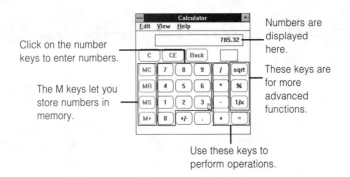

Click on the number keys to enter numbers.

Numbers are displayed here.

The M keys let you store numbers in memory.

These keys are for more advanced functions.

Use these keys to perform operations.

Can also use The number Keys on The Keyboard.

To enter a calculation, perform the following steps:

1. **Click on the number buttons to enter the first number in the calculation.** The number appears in the display area.

2. **Click on the operator you want to use:**

   [+] to add the next number

   [-] to subtract the next number

   [*] to multiply by the next number

   [/] to divide by the next number

3. **Click on the number buttons to enter the next number in the calculation.**

4. **Repeat steps 2 and 3 until you have performed all the desired calculations.**

5. **Click on the equal button [=].**

If you make a mistake while keying in a number, click on any of the following buttons:

[C] Clears all your work up to this point, so you can start over.

[CE] Clears only the current entry. No other entries are affected.

[Back] Deletes the digit you just typed. Keep clicking to remove additional digits.

Backspace = Back button

Beyond Survival

Using the Memory Functions

Sometimes, you may want to store a value in memory while you perform other calculations. For example, say you want to total your last two paychecks, total the taxes, and then divide taxes by gross income to determine what percent is being taken for taxes, you'll want to store the gross pay total in memory until you need it at the end. To use the computer's memory in this way, use the following M buttons:

[MS] Click on this button to store the displayed value in memory.

An **M** appears below the area where values are displayed, to show that a value is stored in memory.

[MR] Click on this button to display the value that's stored in memory.

[MC] Click on this button to clear any value that is stored in memory. The **M** below the value display disappears.

[M+] Click on this button to add the value currently displayed on-screen to the value that's stored in memory.

Calculating a Percentage

The Calculator's % key allows you to calculate sales percentages and perform similar calculations. However, using the key may not be the most intuitive operation. Here's what you do to determine a percentage:

1. Key in the number for which you want to calculate a percent. For example, if you want to determine 7% sales tax on $450, key in **450**.

2. Click on the division button [/].

3. Key in the percentage (for example, 7 for 7%).

4. Click on the percentage button ⬚ % .

Copying and Pasting the Results

Ctrl + C To Copy

Ctrl + V To Paste

If you performed the calculations to plug a number into a letter or other document, you can copy the result and then paste it into the document in the other application. Here's what you do:

1. Open the Edit menu and select Copy.

2. Switch to the document into which you want the result pasted.

3. Move the insertion point to where you want the result.

4. Open the Edit menu and select Paste.

Figuring Averages with the Scientific Calculator

The Scientific calculator contains functions that can determine the sine, cosine, logarithms, and perform other advanced mathematical equations. Although I can't cover them all here, there are two very useful functions: sum and average. The Sum button can total a column of numbers, and Average can determine the average. To use either function, perform the following steps:

1. Open the View menu and select Scientific to display the scientific calculator.

2. Click on the Sta button. The Statistics Box appears, allowing you to enter a column of numbers. You can drag the title bar to move this box to a convenient location.

3. Key in or click on the number buttons to create the first value you want to add to the column.

4. Click on the Dat button. The value is added to the Statistics Box.

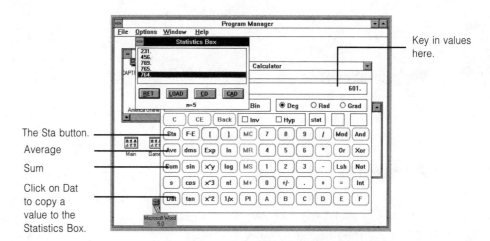

Key in values
here.

The Sta button.

Average

Sum

Click on Dat
to copy a
value to the
Statistics Box.

Click inside
Calculator
Window To
reTurn To iT

5. Repeat steps 3 and 4 for each value you want to add.

6. To determine the total of the numbers, click on the Sum button.

7. To determine the average of the numbers, click on the Ave button.

You may have noticed some buttons at the bottom of the Statistics Box. Here's a list of the buttons and a description of what each button does:

RET returns you to the Calculator. It's easier just to click inside the Calculator window to return to it.

LOAD copies the currently highlighted value to the calculator's data display area.

CD stands for Clear Data. Click on this button to remove the currently-highlighted entry from the list.

CAD stands for Clear All Data. Click on this button to remove all entries from the list.

Cheat Sheet

Displaying the Clock

1. Open the Accessories group window.

2. Double-click on the Clock icon 🕐.

Moving and Resizing the Clock

- The Clock is in its own application window, so you can move and resize it like any window.
- Drag the title bar to move the clock.
- Drag a border to resize the clock.

Making the Clock Stay on Top

Click on the Control-menu box.

Click on Always on Top.

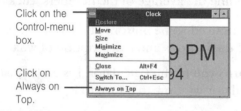

Changing the Clock Type

1. Open the Settings menu.

2. Select Analog for a clock with hands or Digital for a clock with numbers.

19

Tracking Time with the Clock

As you probably know, your computer has a built-in clock that keeps track of the date and time. Windows comes with a clock that can display the system date and time on-screen. In this chapter, you learn how to display the clock and change its settings.

Basic Survival

Displaying the Clock

To display the clock, follow these steps:

1. Open the Accessories group window.

2. Double-click on the Clock icon 🕐 .

To close the Clock, double-click on its Control-menu box.

Double-click here to close the Clock.

Moving and Resizing the Clock

The Clock appears in its own window, so you can move and resize it just as you would move or resize any window. Drag the title bar to move it. Drag any of the window's borders to change its size.

Drag Title bar To move or border To size.

Drag the title bar to move it.

Drag a border to resize.

Beyond Survival

Changing the Clock Type

You can display the Clock as an *analog* clock (with hands) or a *digital* clock (with numbers). To change the Clock type, here's what you do:

1. Open the Settings menu.

2. Select Analog for a clock with hands or Digital for a clock with numbers.

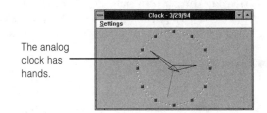

The analog clock has hands.

Changing the Clock Settings

The Clock window has only one menu, the Settings menu. Open the menu for access to the following options:

Set Font lets you select the type style you want to use for the numbers in the digital clock. This option is unavailable for the analog clock. The type size is adjusted automatically, according to the size of the window.

No Title turns the window's title bar and menu bar off, giving the clock more window room. To turn the title and menu bar back on, double-click anywhere inside the Clock window.

Seconds allows you to turn the seconds display off or on.

Date lets you turn the date display on or off.

Double-click inside Title bar To maximize The Clock.

Double-click on clock area (noT Title bar or menu bar) To Turn off Title bar.

Putting the Clock on Top

Most windows retreat automatically to the back whenever you are working in another window. However, you may want the Clock to stay on top as you work. **To keep the Clock window on top, click on the Control-menu box, and select Always on Top.** To turn this option off, select it again.

Minimize clock—Still displays daTe and Time

Click on the Control-menu box.

Click on Always on Top.

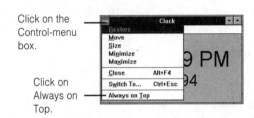

Cheat Sheet

Starting Notepad

1. Open the Accessories group window.

2. Double-click on the Notepad icon .

Inserting the Date and Time

1. Open the Edit menu.
2. Select Time/Date.

Turning Word Wrap On or Off

1. Open the Edit menu.
2. Select Word Wrap.

Undoing an Action

1. Open the Edit menu.
2. Select Undo.

Creating a Time Log

- *Time logs* are useful for keeping track of changes, time spent on a project, or a history of phone calls and contacts.
- Type **.LOG** at the top of the document.
- Whenever you open the document, Notepad inserts the current time and date.

20

Editing Text with the Notepad

Notepad makes plain Text files.

The Windows Help system suggests that Notepad is useful for editing short text files, such as CONFIG.SYS and AUTOEXEC.BAT. Although this is true, Sysedit (described in Chapter 49, "Reading and Editing System Files") works much better. For letters and other documents, Write is better (see Chapters 12 and 13). Write can handle longer documents, and offers more tools for formatting your text.

So what is Notepad good for? A couple of things. First, it is useful for creating text files that you might e-mail to someone on your network (or on an online service). Notepad creates pure text files, so the recipient can open the file in just about any word processing application. Second, Notepad is good for creating date-stamped documents. To have Notepad insert the current date and time whenever you open a file, you can enter the .LOG command in the document. Finally, Notepad is useful for editing .INI and .BAT files that you can't open in Sysedit (see Chapter 49 for details about .INI and .BAT files). In this chapter, you learn how to use Notepad to create and edit text files.

Basic Survival

Starting Notepad: What You'll See

To start Notepad, follow these steps:

1. Open the Accessories group window.

2. Double-click on the Notepad icon .

The Notepad window

Typing in Notepad

Edit Undo (Alt + Backspace) To cancel an action

Once you've started Notepad, you can start typing or use the File Open command to open a text file. You type just as you type in Write (see Chapter 12). The only difference between Write and Notepad is that Notepad does not wrap the text automatically from one line to the next. You have to press Enter at the end of each line. However, you can turn word wrap on by performing the following steps:

1. Open the Edit menu.

2. Select Word Wrap.

Beyond Survival

Inserting the Date and Time

Time/Date = F5

Sometimes it's useful to insert the date and time in a file to keep track of notes and revisions. You could type the date as normal text, or have Notepad insert the date and time from your computer's internal clock:

1. Open the Edit menu.

2. Select Time/Date.

Creating a Time Log

If you need to keep track of phone calls and contacts (for legal or billing purposes), or if you need to keep track of the dates on which you entered changes to a file, you can use Notepad to create a time log. With a time log, Notepad inserts the current date and time at the bottom of the file whenever you open it, and positions the insertion point below the date and time. To create a time log, type **.LOG** at the top of the document.

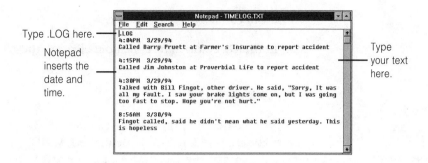

Type .LOG here.

Notepad inserts the date and time.

Type your text here.

Creating a Batch File

Batch files contain a series of commands that run automatically when you run the batch file. The most famous batch file is AUTOEXEC.BAT, which runs whenever you boot your computer. You can use Notepad to create your own batch files. For example, say you often enter the command **win c:\word5\word.exe letter.doc** to start Windows. The command starts Windows, runs Word, and opens the document LETTER.DOC. You can create a batch file that enters the command for you. Here's how you do it:

1. Start Notepad.

2. Type the command or commands that you want the batch file to carry out. If you are entering two or more commands, press Enter at the end of each command line.

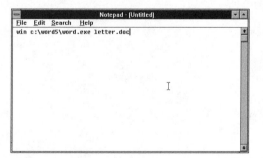

3. Open the File menu and select Save. The Save dialog box appears.

4. Type a name for the file (up to eight characters), type a period, and type **bat**. For example, type **windows.bat**.

5. From the Drives list, select c:.

6. In the Directories tree, double-click on the c:\ at the top of the tree.

7. Click on OK.

Make W.BAT
ThaT conTains
command Win :

To run the batch file, type the file's name at the DOS prompt and press Enter. For example, to run a file named WINDOWS.BAT, you would type **windows** at the DOS prompt and press Enter.

Cheat Sheet

Playing Solitaire

1. Open the Games group window.

2. Double-click on the Solitaire icon .

To start over, select Deal from the Games menu.

Click to flip through the deck.

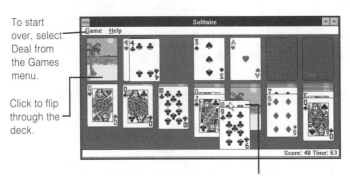

Drag cards from one pile to another.

Playing Minesweeper

1. Open the Games group window.

2. Double-click on the Minesweeper icon .

Left-click to clear blocks

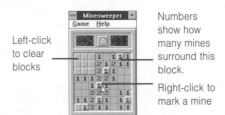

Numbers show how many mines surround this block.

Right-click to mark a mine

21

Playing the Windows Games

Windows comes with two very addictive games that can help you become less productive and have more fun at work: Solitaire (the old standard) and Minesweeper. With Minesweeper, you attempt to discover the location of hidden mines without getting blown up. In this chapter, you learn the basics of how to play these games and how to set options to make the games more interesting.

Basic Survival

Playing Solitaire

Solitaire is a good game if you need to practice using your mouse. It gives you lots of practice with clicking and dragging. To run Solitaire, follow these steps:

1. Open the Games group window.

Tell boss you need mouse practice

2. Double-click on the Solitaire icon 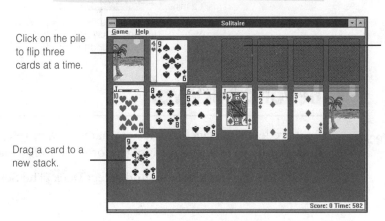. Solitaire deals the cards.

3. All you have to do to play is click and drag.

Click on the pile to flip three cards at a time.

When you get an Ace, drag it up here.

Drag a card to a new stack.

137

Playing Minesweeper

Think—don't click on a block unless you're sure

Minesweeper is slightly more risky than Solitaire. To run Minesweeper, follow these steps:

1. Open the Games group window.

2. Double-click on the Minesweeper icon ⚫ Minesweeper . You get a mine field with 10 hidden mines. The object of the game is to figure out where the mines are without getting blown up. Take the following actions to clear the mine field:

   • Left-click on a block to clear it. Under each block is a mine or a number. If you click on a mine, you're history. If you get a number, the number represents how many mines surround this block. So, if you get a 1, only 1 of the 8 blocks that surround this square has a mine.

   • Right-click on a block to flag it as a mine. If you're not sure, right-click on the block again to flag it with a question mark. If you decide later that the block does not have a mine, you can left-click on it.

   • To start the game over, click on the smiley face (if you won) or sad face (if you lost).

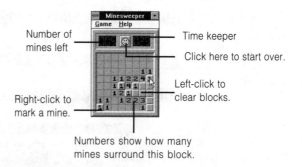

Number of mines left

Time keeper

Click here to start over.

Right-click to mark a mine.

Left-click to clear blocks.

Numbers show how many mines surround this block.

Beyond Survival

Changing Decks in Solitaire

Solitaire lets you select the design that you want to appear on the backs of the cards. To select a design, perform the following steps:

1. Open the Games menu and select Deck. The Select Card Back dialog box appears.

2. Click on the desired design.

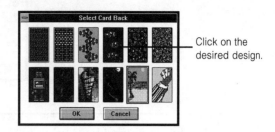

Click on the
desired design.

3. Click on the OK button.

Setting the Solitaire Options

Solitaire offers several options for controlling the game. To enter your settings, follow these steps:

1. Open the Games menu and select Options.

2. Select the desired options, as follows:

Draw One is easier

Draw tells Solitaire how many cards to flip when you click on the deck. Draw One is easier, but you lose 100 points for each pass through the deck. Draw Three is more difficult.

Scoring tells Solitaire how to keep score. With Standard, you get 5 points when you move a card from the deck down to a stack, 10 points for moving a card from a lower stack to an upper (Ace) stack (you lose 15 points if you have to move a card back). You lose 20 points for each pass through the deck after three passes (100 points if you are set to Draw One). With Vegas scoring, you pay 52 bucks for each deal, and you get 5 bucks each time you move a card from a lower stack to an upper (Ace) stack. If you choose Vegas, you can choose Keep Score to keep a running total from game to game.

Timed game keeps track of how many seconds you've been playing... just in case your boss is curious.

Status bar turns the status bar on or off.

Outline dragging keeps the card you are dragging in its original position. An outline of the card appears as you drag. When you release the mouse button, the card is moved to the outline's location.

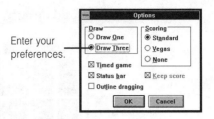

Enter your
preferences.

Making a Bigger Mine Field in Minesweeper

The Beginning level mine field is an 8-by-8 grid (64 blocks) that contains 10 mines. If you want a real challenge, you can create a bigger mine field with more mines. Simply open the Games menu and choose the desired option:

- **Intermediate** provides a 16-by-16 grid that contains 40 mines.

- **Expert** provides a 16-by-30 grid with 99 mines.

- **Custom** allows you to specify the grid size and number of mines you want to use.

Setting the Game Options in Minesweeper

In addition to letting you select the level at which you want to play, the Games menu contains two options that let you control the behavior of the game:

Marks (?) turns the right-click question mark feature on or off. Initially, this is on. If you turn it off, right-clicking on a block turns the flag mark on or off without displaying a question mark.

Color turns the screen color for the game on or off.

The Challenge

To check your best times in Minesweeper, open the **Games** menu and select **Best Times**. Mine are 22 seconds for Beginner and 136 for Intermediate. Beat that! Also, with Solitaire set to Vegas scoring, I once had the score up to $3000! Notice, however, I haven't quit my day job. This is *only* a game.

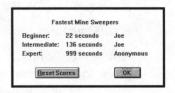

Cheat Sheet

Starting Terminal

1. Open the Accessories program group.
2. Double-click on the Terminal icon .

Selecting Modem Commands for Your Modem

1. Open the Settings menu and select Modem Commands.
2. In the Modem Defaults group, select the type of modem you have.
3. In the Dial text box, type **ATDT** for tone or **ATDP** for rotary.
4. Click on the OK button.

Entering Communications Settings

- Communications settings must match the settings of the remote computer or service you are calling, and the COM port must indicate the proper location of your modem.

- To enter settings, open the Settings menu and select Communications. Enter your settings and click on OK.

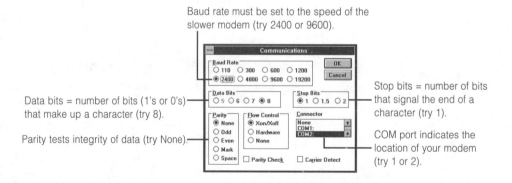

Baud rate must be set to the speed of the slower modem (try 2400 or 9600).

Data bits = number of bits (1's or 0's) that make up a character (try 8).

Parity tests integrity of data (try None).

Stop bits = number of bits that signal the end of a character (try 1).

COM port indicates the location of your modem (try 1 or 2).

Calling a Remote Computer

1. Open the Settings menu and select Phone Number.
2. Type the phone number needed to connect to the remote modem.
3. Click on OK.
4. Open the Phone menu, and select Dial.

22

Dialing Out with the Terminal

If you have a modem connected to your computer and to the phone line, you can use the Windows Terminal to transfer files to and from another computer and to connect to an electronic bulletin board, your city library's computerized card catalogue, or any other system that allows computers to call in and connect. In this chapter, you learn how to dial out with your modem and transfer files.

Basic Survival

Starting the Terminal

To start the Terminal, follow these steps:

1. Open the Accessories program group.

2. Double-click on the Terminal icon .
Terminal

The Terminal application window

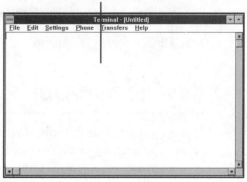

Selecting Modem Commands for Your Modem

In order for Terminal to be able to dial a number using your modem and terminate a call, it must know the commands required to tell the modem what to do. Most modems use *Hayes commands*, and require a specific startup command sequence to do anything. Before you try calling out with your modem, you should perform the following steps to check the modem commands:

1. **Open the Settings menu and select Modem Commands.** The Modem Commands dialog box appears.

Select the modem type that matches yours, or try Hayes.

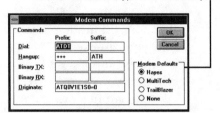

2. **In the Modem Defaults group, select the type of modem you have.** If you're unsure, select Hayes or None. Terminal enters the default commands for the selected modem type.

3. **In the Dial text box, type ATDT if you have tone phone service or ATDP if you have rotary service.** If you're not sure, pick up your phone and dial a couple numbers. If you hear tones, you have tone service. If you hear clicks, you have rotary service.

To reset The commands, select The modem Type again.

4. Check your modem documentation to determine if you need to change any other modem settings, then enter your changes. **If you are unsure, don't touch the settings.**

5. **Click on the OK button.**

Beyond Survival

Entering Communications Settings

If you connect your computer to another computer (or to an on-line service), you must make sure both computers are using the same *communications settings.* Otherwise, errors may result during data transfer. For example, if one modem is talking at 9600 baud and the other is listening at 2400 baud, it's likely that some information will get lost. To change your communications settings, follow these steps:

1. **Open the Settings menu and select Communications.** The Communications dialog box appears.

The Communications dialog box—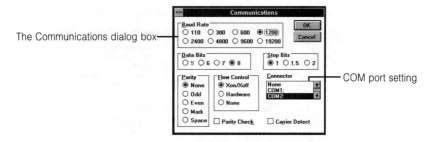

COM port setting

2. Check the following settings:

COM port   Most computers have two COM ports—one for the mouse and one for the modem. Usually, the mouse is on COM1, and the modem is on COM2. Try COM2 first. If you try to dial out with the modem, and you get a message that Terminal could not find the modem, try a different COM port.

Baud Rate   The speed at which the two modems transfer data. The transfer can only be as fast as the slower of the two modems allows. Baud rate is commonly measured in bits per second (bps). Try 2400 or 9600.

Parity   Tests the integrity of the data sent and received. A common setting is None or No Parity.

Data Bits   Indicates the number of bits in each transmitted character. A common setting is Eight.

Stop Bits   Indicates the number of bits used to signal the end of a character. A common setting is One bit.

Try a fast baud rate at first, like 9600.

Selecting a Terminal Emulation

Large mainframe computers (used for online services, libraries, and other institutions) sometimes require the computer that's calling in to act like (emulate) a specific type of computer. Check with the service to determine which type of emulation is required. To change the emulation, follow these steps:

1. Open the Settings and select Terminal Emulation. The Terminal Emulation dialog box appears.

Select an emulation.

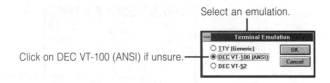

Click on DEC VT-100 (ANSI) if unsure.

2. Select the required emulation.

3. Click on OK.

If you selected DEC VT-100 (ANSI), press the Scroll Lock key to turn it on. This allows you to use the function keys to pass commands along to the mainframe computer. If Scroll Lock is off, the function keys enter Windows commands. For example, if you press F1, you'll get the Terminal Help screen.

DEC VT-100 (ANSI)? Turn Scroll Lock on.

Connecting to Another Computer

To connect to a remote computer, the remote computer must be on and must be waiting for a call. If you're connecting with your friend's computer across the street, you may have to make a phone call to let her know you'll be making a modem call. When you are ready, perform the following steps to place the call:

1. Make sure your modem is turned on.

2. Open the Settings menu and select Phone Number. The Phone Number dialog box appears.

Type the number you want to dial here.

Comma Tells modem To pause before dialing remaining numbers

3. Type the phone number needed to connect to the remote modem. If you need to dial 9 (or some other number) to get an outside line, type the number—followed by a comma—before the phone number. Don't put any spaces in the phone number.

4. Click on OK.

5. Open the Phone menu, and select Dial. Terminal dials the number and connects to the remote computer.

Once you are connected, you can type messages to have them appear on the other user's screen. Whatever the other user types will appear on your screen. To hang up the phone (and disconnect), open the Phone menu and select Hang Up.

Saving Your Settings

Before you quit Terminal, you should save your terminal settings so you won't have to enter the same settings the next time you want to place a call. Perform the following steps:

1. Open the File menu and select Save. The Save dialog box appears.

Save your settings so you won't
have to re-enter them next time.

2. Type a name for the file (up to eight characters). Terminal will add the extension **.TRM** to the end of the filename.

3. Click on OK. Terminal saves the communications settings, modem commands, terminal emulation, and phone number you entered.

The next time you want to call the same number, open the File menu, select Open, select the terminal file you created, and then click on OK. To place the call, open the Phone menu and select Dial.

Sending a Text File

To send a text file, you must be connected to the remote computer, and that computer must be set up to receive the file. You can type a message telling the other user that you are about to send a file, and instructing the user to set up to receive it. Make sure the other user sets up to receive a text file, not a binary file. Perform the following steps to send the file:

TexT files Typically end in .TXT

1. Open the Transfers menu and select Send Text File. The Send Text File dialog box appears.

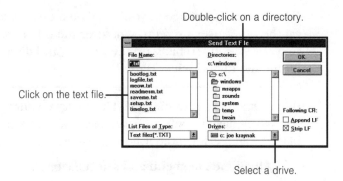

Double-click on a directory.

Click on the text file.

Select a drive.

2. Select the drive, directory, and file name of the text file you want to send.

3. If the remote computer adds carriage returns and line feeds to the file (to advance text on the screen), select Strip LF. If the remote computer does not add them, select Append LF.

4. Click on the OK button. Terminal sends the file.

Sending a Binary File

Protocol = communica- Tions rules

A *binary file* is any file that's not a text file. If you want to transfer a program file, graphic file, or a document file that has formatting, you must use the binary file transfer method. Here's what you do.

1. Open the Settings menu and select Binary Transfers. The Binary Transfers dialog box appears, prompting you to select a protocol. You must select a protocol that matches the one used by the receiving computer.

2. Select XModem/CRC or Kermit, then click on OK.

3. Open the Transfers menu and select Send Binary File. The Send Binary File dialog box appears.

4. Select the drive, directory, and file name of the text file you want to send.

5. Click on the OK button. Terminal sends the file.

Preparing to Receive a File

To receive a file, you must first make sure that you are using the proper settings for the desired file transfer. If you plan on receiving a text file, open the Settings menu and select Text Transfers. If you plan on receiving a binary file, open the Settings menu and select Binary

Transfers. Select the transfer protocol and settings so that they match those of the calling computer.

When the other user is ready to send the file, perform the following steps to receive it:

1. Open the Transfers menu.

2. Select Receive Text File (to receive a text-only file) or Receive Binary File (to receive any other type of file). A dialog box appears, prompting you to type a name for the file.

3. Type a name for the file (up to eight characters), type a period, and type an extension for the file. If you are receiving a text file, use the extension **.TXT**.

4. Select the drive and directory in which you want the file saved.

5. Click on the OK button. A message appears at the bottom of the window indicating that the file is being received. When the remote computer starts sending the file, the message will change to show the progress of the operation.

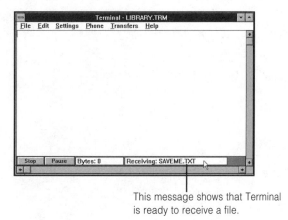

This message shows that Terminal is ready to receive a file.

Cheat Sheet

Recording a Sound

1. Open the Accessories window.
2. Double-click on the Sound Recorder icon .
3. Click on the Record button and start talking into the microphone.
4. Click on the Stop button.
5. Open the File menu and select Save.
6. Type a name for the file (no extension) in the File Name text box.
7. Click OK.

23

Recording Sounds with the Sound Recorder

If you have a sound board (such as SoundBlaster) and a microphone, you can use the Windows Sound Recorder to record music, your voice, or any other sounds—and store them in a file on disk. Then you can attach the sounds to certain events in Windows, to play the sounds whenever the event occurs. For example, you can have a short piece of music play whenever you start Windows.

If you don't have a sound board, you can still do some nifty things with sounds, such as play back prerecorded sounds. In order to do this, you need a PC speaker driver, a program that makes your computer's puny speaker act sort of like a sound board. For details, see Chapter 45.

Basic Survival

Recording a Sound

The Sound Recorder lets you record a sound and save it in a .WAV file. To start the Sound Recorder and record a sound, here's what you do:

1. Open the Accessories window.

2. Double-click on the Sound Recorder icon 🎤 . The Sound Recorder application window appears.

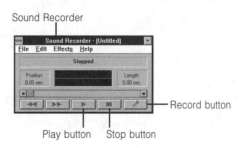

Sound Recorder

Play button   Stop button

Record button

Position mouse pointer over Stop button so you can stop quickly

3. When you are ready to record, click on the Record button and start talking, playing music, or making other sounds into the microphone.

4. When you're done talking, click on the Stop button.

5. Open the File menu and select Save. The Save File dialog box appears.

6. Type a name for the file (up to eight characters, no extension) in the File Name text box.

7. Use the Drives and Directories lists to change to the drive and directory where you want the file saved.

8. Click on the OK button.

Playing Back Sound Files

Once you've recorded a sound, you'll want to listen to it. Simply click on the Play button. If nothing happens, try clicking on the Rewind button, and then clicking on the Play button.

You can also open a sound file at any time and play it. Here's what you do:

1. Run Sound Recorder.

2. Open the File menu and select Open.

3. Select the drive, directory, and name of the sound file you want to play. Sound files end in the .WAV extension.

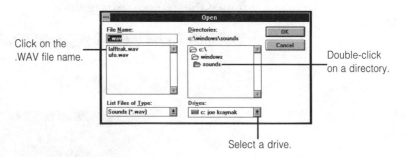

Click on the .WAV file name.

Double-click on a directory.

Select a drive.

4. Click on the OK button. Sound Recorder opens the file.

5. Click on the Play button. Sound Recorder plays the sound.

Beyond Survival

Adding Special Effects

Sound Recorder comes with a couple of tools you can use to increase or decrease the volume of a sound, add an echo, or play the sound in reverse (useful for analyzing Led Zeppelin songs). To add any of these effects, open the Effects menu and select the desired effect:

Increase Volume   Increases the volume by 25%.

Decrease Volume   Decreases the volume by 25%.

Increase Speed   Plays the sound faster.

Decrease Speed   Plays the sound slower.

Add Echo   Adds an echo that reverbs your sound.

Reverse   Plays the sound backward.

To change volume for all sounds, use Speaker Driver—explained in Chapter 45

Open the Effects menu.

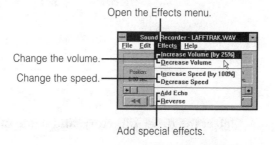

Change the volume.

Change the speed.

Add special effects.

Combining and Mixing Sounds

The Edit menu contains a couple commands for inserting and mixing sounds. *Inserting* a sound sticks the sound from one file inside another. *Mixing* lays one sound over the other. To insert a sound, here's what you do:

1. Open the sound file into which you want the other sound inserted.

2. Use the Play and Stop buttons to go to the point at which you want the other sound inserted. (Use Fast Forward to go to the end of the sound, or Rewind to go to the beginning.)

Use The scroll bar for more precise positioning

This area shows the sound.

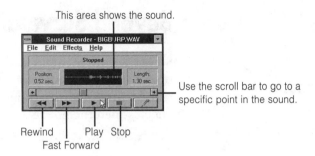

Rewind | Play | Stop
Fast Forward

Use the scroll bar to go to a specific point in the sound.

3. **Open the Edit menu and select Insert File.** The Insert File dialog box appears.

Double-click on a directory.

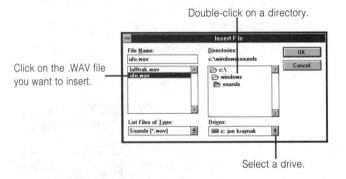

Click on the .WAV file you want to insert.

Select a drive.

4. **Select the drive, directory, and name of the file you want to insert.**

5. **Click on the OK button.** The selected file is inserted into the open sound file.

Cheat Sheet

Working with Macros

- A *macro* is a recording of keystrokes and mouse actions that you can play back to automate tasks in Windows.
- When recording a macro, use the mouse sparingly. Mouse actions may have unexpected results if a window or menu is in a different location when you play back the macro.
- You can stop a macro that you're playing by pressing Ctrl+Break.

Running the Recorder

1. Open the Accessories group window.
2. Double-click on the Recorder icon .

Recording a Simple Macro

1. Display the screen where you want to start recording the macro.
2. Run the Recorder, or switch to it if it is already running.
3. Open the Macro menu and select Record.
4. Type a name for the macro (up to 40 characters).
5. Click on the Start button.
6. Press the keys and use the mouse (sparingly) as you normally would to perform the task.
7. Click on the Recorder icon or press Ctrl+Break.
8. Click on Save Macro.
9. Click OK.

Playing a Recorded Macro

1. Display the screen where you want the macro to start playing.
2. Run the Recorder, or switch to it if it is already running.
3. Open the Macro file that contains the macro you want to run.
4. Double-click on the macro you want to play.

24

Automating Windows with the Recorder

Windows comes with a tool called the Recorder, which allows you to record and play back keystrokes and mouse actions. You use the Recorder to record the steps, and then you can play back the steps simply by selecting the macro from a list, or by pressing a shortcut key combination (if you assigned a key combination to the macro). For example, you could use the Recorder to enter the File Open command in Write, change to a drive and directory, select a file, and open the file. In this chapter, you learn how to record and play back macros.

Basic Survival

Running the Recorder

Before you can record or run a macro, the Recorder must be active. To run the Recorder, open the Accessories group window and double-click on the Recorder icon. Leave the Recorder on as you work through the rest of this chapter. To get the Recorder out of the way and leave it running, click on its Minimize button.

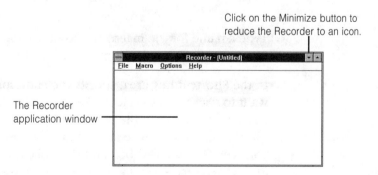

Click on the Minimize button to reduce the Recorder to an icon.

The Recorder application window

Recording a Macro

Ctrl + Esc = Switch To

To record a macro, you turn on the Recorder and then perform the steps required to do a task. The Recorder keeps track of all your mouse clicks and keystrokes and then saves them when you stop recording. To record a series of steps, here's what you do:

1. Display the screen where you want to start recording the macro. For example, if you want to create a macro that opens a file in Write, you should have the Write screen displayed, and any files that you have been working on should be saved.

2. Run the Recorder, or switch to it if it is already running. (Refer to the previous section, "Running the Recorder.")

3. Open the Macro menu and select Record. The Record Macro dialog box appears.

Type a name for the macro.

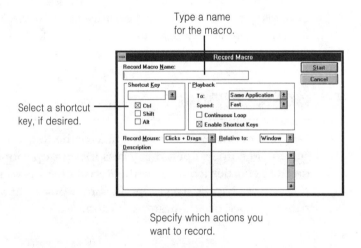

Select a shortcut key, if desired.

Specify which actions you want to record.

4. Type a name for the macro (up to 40 characters). This name will appear in the Recorder application window.

5. In the Shortcut Key area, specify the shortcut key combination you want to use. You can select a key from the drop-down list, or type a letter or number in the text box. Click on the Ctrl, Shift, and/or Alt options to add those keys to the combination. For example, if you type **O** in the text box and then place an X in the Ctrl and Shift check boxes, the key combination would be Ctrl+Shift+O.

6. In the Playback area, select any of the following options:

To   Select Same Application to have this macro work only in the current application. Select Any Application to run the macro in other applications as well.

Speed   Click on Fast to have the macro run as quickly as possible. Otherwise, click on Recorded Speed.

Continuous Loop   If you want to use a macro as a demo that keeps playing over and over, click on this option to turn it on.

To set defaults, use Options Preferences.

Enable Shortcut Keys   Turn this option off if you are using an application that uses shortcut keys that match the shortcut keys you assigned to your macros. You will still be able to run macros by selecting them in the Recorder, but you will not be able to run them using shortcut keys.

7. From the Record Mouse drop-down list, select one of the following options:

Clicks + Drags records all keystrokes and mouse clicking and dragging actions. This is the default setting, and is usually best for most tasks.

Ignore Mouse records only keystrokes. Select this option if you plan to run the macro on another computer that may have a display that differs from yours.

Everything records every action, including mouse moves across the screen. Selecting this option can cause problems during playback.

8. From the Relative to drop-down list, select Window if you are running the application in a window, or Screen if you are running the application in a maximized window.

9. (Optional) To add a description for the macro, tab to the Description area and type the desired description.

10. Click on the Start button. The Recorder is reduced to a blinking Recorder icon at the bottom of the screen (you may not see it).

11. Press the keys and use the mouse as you normally would to perform the task.

Use mouse sparingly— rely more on keyboard

12. When you're finished, click on the Recorder icon or press Ctrl+Break. The Recorder dialog box appears, showing you that the macro recording operation has been suspended.

Select Save Macro.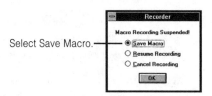

13. Click on Save Macro, and click on the OK button. The name of the new macro is added to the Recorder's macro list.

Playing a Macro

When you record a macro, it is added to the macro list in the Recorder application window. You can run a macro by selecting it from the list or by pressing the shortcut key combination you assigned to the macro (assuming you assigned a shortcut key combination). Here's what you do:

1. Display the screen where you want the macro to start playing. For example, if you created a macro to insert a string of text, run the required application, open the desired document, and move the insertion point where you want the text inserted.

2. Make sure the Recorder is running. (If you want to run the macro by selecting it from the list, switch to the Recorder application window.)

The macros you created are listed.

3. Perform one of the following steps:

• Press the shortcut key combination you assigned to the macro.

- Double-click on the name of the macro you want to run.

- Click on the name of the macro you want to run, open the Macro menu, and select Run.

Saving and Opening a Macro File

As you create macros, they are added to the Recorder's macro list, but they are not automatically saved in a file. In other words, if you quit the Macro Recorder, your macros will be lost. To save the macros you created, perform the following steps:

1. Open the Recorder's File menu and select Save.

2. Type a name for the file (up to eight characters) in the File Name text box.

Recorder adds the .REC extension
for you even if you don't see it here.

Type a name for the file.

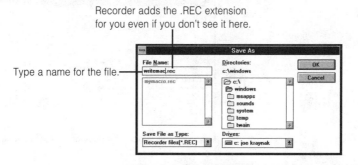

3. (Optional) Select a drive from the Drives list and a directory from the Directories list to specify where you want the file saved.

Save macro files in The Windows directory.

4. Click on the OK button. The Recorder saves all the macros in the macro list to the file you just named. In order to run any of these macros, the Recorder must be running, and the macro file must be opened.

Whenever you run Recorder, it does not automatically open the macro file you created and saved. In order to use the macros in a file, you must open the file. Use the File Open command to open the desired macro file. For more details about opening files, refer to Chapter 3, "Running and Using Applications."

Beyond Survival

Changing a Macro's Properties

When you record a macro, you are prompted to name the macro, assign it a shortcut key, provide a description, and enter other settings. To change these settings for a particular macro, perform the following steps:

1. Click on the macro whose properties you want to change.

2. Open the Macro menu and choose Properties. The Macro Properties dialog box appears.

You can change the macro's name.   You can change the playback settings.

You can add or change the shortcut key.

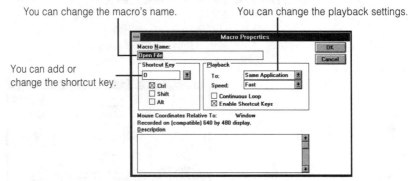

View macro conTenTs = Hold down ShifT and selecT Macro ProperTies

3. Enter the desired changes.

4. Click on the OK button.

Setting Up the Recorder to Open a Macro File Automatically

You can configure the Recorder to open a specific macro file automatically whenever you run the Recorder. First, click on the Recorder icon (in the Accessories group window), open the File menu, and select Properties. Then, in the Command Line text box, after the RECORDER.EXE command, type a space and then the name of the macro file you want to open (for example, MYMACRO.REC). Click on OK to save your changes.

Run
Recorder
auTomaTically:
drag iTs icon
inTo STarTup
group

Type the macro file name after RECORDER.EXE.

Cheat Sheet

Running Character Map

1. Open the Accessories group window.
2. Double-click on the Character Map icon .

Inserting a Character or Symbol

1. Run Character Map.
2. Open the Font list and click on a font.
3. Double-click on each character you want to insert.
4. Click on the Copy button.
5. Switch to the application and document you want to paste the characters in.
6. Move the insertion point where you want the characters.
7. Select the same font you selected in step 2.
8. Open the Edit menu and select Paste.

25

Inserting Characters and Symbols with Character Map

Character Map allows you to insert special characters and symbols into your documents—characters and symbols that may or may not appear on your keyboard. With Character Map, you select the characters and/or symbols you want to insert, copy them to the Clipboard, and then paste them into your document. Keep in mind, however, that Character Map works only in Windows applications.

Basic Survival

Running Character Map

To run Character Map, perform the following steps:

1. Open the Accessories group window.

2. Double-click on the Character Map icon ⬦ . The Character Map application window appears.

Character Map contains several sets of special characters and symbols.

If you use Character Map often, keep it running. You may even want to assign it a shortcut key combination so you can quickly call it up while you're working in another application. If you want to assign a shortcut key to it, refer to the section called "Editing a Program-Item Icon" in Chapter 9, "Setting Up Applications."

Inserting a Character or Symbol

You can use Character Map to insert symbols and characters that do not appear on your keyboard. Here's what you do:

1. Run Character Map.

2. Open the Font list and click on a font. A grid full of characters and symbols for the selected font appears.

3. Move the mouse pointer over a character or symbol and hold down the mouse button to see it more clearly.

Use arrow Keys To move from one characTer To The nexT

Select a font for access to symbols and characters in that font.

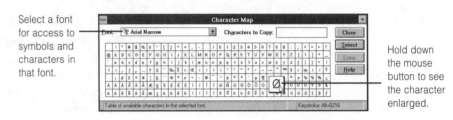

Hold down the mouse button to see the character enlarged.

Double-click on a characTer

4. Click on a character, and then click on the Select button to add the character to the Characters to Copy text box. The characters in this text box will be copied to the Clipboard.

5. Repeat steps 3 and 4 to add more characters and symbols to the Characters to Copy text box. To remove a character, click to the right of it inside the text box, and then backspace over it.

6. Click on the Copy button. The characters in the Characters to Copy text box are placed on the Windows Clipboard.

7. Switch to the application and document into which you want to paste the characters. (Press Ctrl+Esc and use the Task List, or press Alt+Tab to switch to an application. See Chapter 3 for details.)

8. Move the insertion point to where you want the characters.

9. Select the same font you selected in step 2.

10. Open the Edit menu and select Paste. The characters from the Clipboard are pasted at the insertion point.

Registered trademark symbol

Copyright symbol

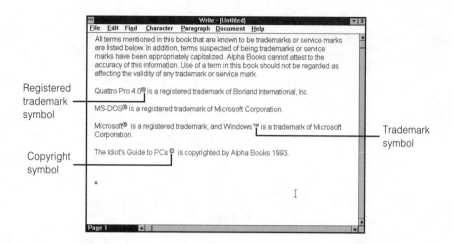

Trademark symbol

PART 4

Managing Disks, Files, and Directories

If you normally perform your file, disk, and directory management at the DOS prompt—using commands like MD (make directory), CD (change directory), COPY, DISKCOPY, FORMAT, and so on—you know how clumsy the DOS prompt can be. In this section, you learn how to use the Windows File Manager to perform those same tasks, faster and more easily. You learn how to copy files by clicking and dragging, how to format a disk by selecting the Format command from a menu, and how to change to a directory simply by clicking on its icon. Here's what you learn:

- Starting and Exiting File Manager
- Changing Drives and Directories
- Sorting and Filtering Files
- Searching for Files
- Selecting Files and Directories
- Copying and Moving Files and Directories
- Renaming Files and Directories
- Deleting and Undeleting Files
- Formatting Floppy Disks
- Copying Disks
- Making and Deleting Directories
- Running Applications from File Manager
- Customizing File Manager

Cheat Sheet

Starting File Manager

1. Open the Main program group window.

2. Double-click on the File Manager icon 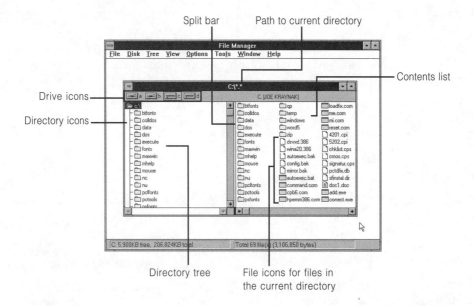.

Parts of the File Manager Window

Changing Views in File Manager

1. Open the View menu.

2. Select one of the following options:

Tree and Directory to view the directory tree on the left and the current directory's contents on the right.

Tree Only to view only the directory tree, not the file list.

Directory Only to view only the current directory's contents, not the directory tree.

26

Starting and Exiting File Manager

Windows File Manager allows you to keep track of—and manage—your files, directories, and disks. You can use File Manager to copy, move, and delete files; you can also format and copy disks, and create and delete directories on a disk. But before you can perform these tasks, you must run the File Manager. In this chapter, you learn how to run the File Manager, change the directory and file views, and exit when you're done.

Basic Survival

Starting File Manager

To start File Manager, perform the following steps:

1. Open the Main group window.

2. Double-click on the File Manager icon ![File Manager icon]. The File Manager application window appears.

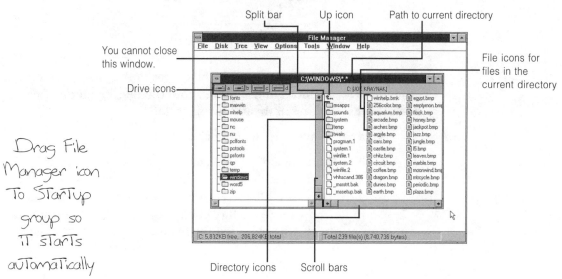

Split bar Up icon Path to current directory

You cannot close this window.

Drive icons

File icons for files in the current directory

C:\WINDOWS*.*

C: [JOE KRAYNAK]

Drag File Manager icon To StarTup group so IT sTarTs auTomaTically

Directory icons Scroll bars

You can exit the File Manager at any time by opening the File menu and selecting Exit. Or, double-click on the Control-menu box in the upper left corner of the window.

Beyond Survival

Changing Views

Initially, File Manager is set up to display the current drive's directory tree on the left and the files in the current directory on the right. To change views, open the View menu, and select one of the following options:

WindowNew Window opens another Window.

Tree and Directory to view the directory tree on the left and the current directory's contents on the right.

Tree Only to view only the directory tree, not the file list.

Directory Only to view only the current directory's contents, not the directory tree.

With Tree Only view, you can manage your directories more efficiently.

Showing File Details

Initially, File Manager shows only the names of the files in the current directory. To see more information about the files, open the View menu and select one of the following options:

Name displays only the file names and directory names.

All File Details displays the names of all files and directories, and the dates and times they were created. Also displays the size and file attributes for all files. (File attributes are settings that tell the computer how to treat a file. For example, if a file has the read-only attribute, you can open the file but you cannot change it.)

Partial Details opens a dialog box that allows you to specify which details you want displayed. Click on all the details you want to turn on, and then click on the OK button. (An X inside an option's check box indicates the option is on. To turn an option off, click on it again.)

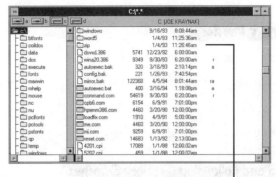

With All File Details on, File Manager shows the date, time, and attributes of your files.

Moving the Window Split

View Split moves window split

In Tree and Directory view, there's a directory tree on the left and a file list on the right. To move the split between the sides, and give one side more screen space, here's what you do:

1. Move the mouse pointer over the split until the pointer turns into a two-headed arrow.

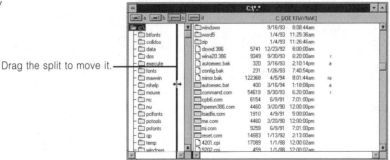

Drag the split to move it.

2. Hold down the mouse button and drag the split left or right.

3. Release the mouse button.

Cheat Sheet

Changing to a Drive

1. Make sure there is a formatted disk in the drive.
2. Click on the drive's icon.

Changing to a Directory

1. Click on the directory's icon in the tree.
2. Double-click on the subdirectory's icon in the contents list.

   or

   Double-click on the Up icon 🔼 .

Expanding and Collapsing Directory Branches

- To expand a branch, double-click on the directory icon in the tree.
- To collapse a branch, double-click on the directory icon again.
- To expand all branches, select Tree Expand All.

Opening Another Directory Window

- Select Window New Window.
- Double-click on a drive icon.
- Hold down Shift while double-clicking on a directory icon in the tree.

Changing Drives and Directories

In order to work with the files on a disk or in a directory, you must first activate the drive and directory in which the files are stored. In this chapter, you learn how to change to a drive and directory, and how to work with the directory tree.

Basic Survival

Changing to a Drive

At the top of the directory window are *drive icons* that represent the drives installed on your system. These drives may include floppy disk drives, hard disk drives, network and CD-ROM drives, and RAM drives. (If you've set up part of your computer's memory to act as a disk drive, refer to Chapter 52, "Speeding Up Windows.") To change to a drive, perform the following steps:

1. Make sure there is a formatted disk in the drive.

2. Click on the drive's icon. The directory tree and contents list will change to display the directories and files on the current drive.

CTrl + Drive leTTer = Change drives

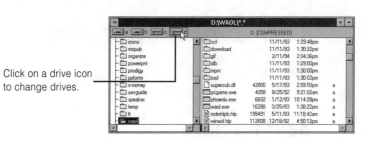

Click on a drive icon to change drives.

Changing to a Directory

Down arrow = Next directory

Up arrow = Previous directory

Home = Root directory

End = Last directory

All disks have at least one directory, the *root directory*. Hard disks usually have additional directories and *subdirectories* to group related files. To change to a directory, do one of the following:

- **Click on a directory icon in the directory tree.** The folder icon for the directory appears opened, and the contents list displays the directories and files in that directory.

- **Double-click on a directory icon in the contents list.** The contents list changes to display the subdirectories and files in that directory.

- **Double-click on the Up icon at the top of the contents list.** This moves you up one directory in the directory tree.

Double-click on the Up icon to move up one level in the tree.

Double-click on a directory icon here.

Click on a directory icon here.

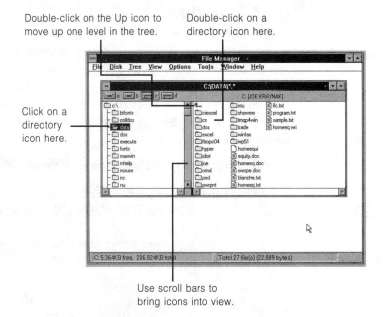

Use scroll bars to bring icons into view.

Beyond Survival

Expanding and Collapsing Directory Branches

Directories may have subdirectories, which may also contain subdirectories. Initially, File Manager shows only the root directory of the current drive, and any directories under the root directory. Subdirectories are hidden. To display the subdirectories, perform the following steps:

1. Click on the directory icon (in the tree, not in the contents list) whose subdirectories you want to view. To view the directories under the root directory, click on the drive letter at the top of the tree.

Double-click on direcTory icon To expand

2. Open the Tree menu.

3. Select one of the following options:

    Expand One Level displays one level of directories under the current directory.

    Expand Branch displays all directory levels under the current directory.

    Expand All expands all directory levels under the root directory, so you can see all directories and subdirectories on the current drive.

[+] = Expand One Level

[*] = Expand Branch

[−] = Collapse Branch

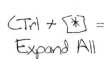
CTrl + [*] = Expand All

Expand Branch shows all directory levels.

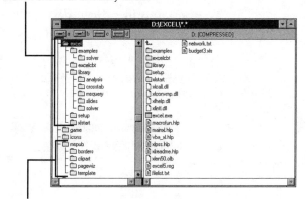

Expand One Level shows the next level of directories.

To collapse a branch, select the directory icon again, open the Tree menu, and select Collapse Branch.

File Manager can help you determine whether a directory is expandable or collapsible. Open the Tree menu and select Indicate Expandable Branches. The icons for expandable directories contain a plus sign. Icons for collapsible directories contain a minus sign.

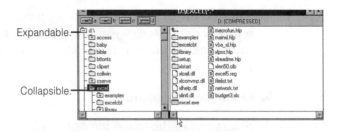

Expandable
Collapsible

Opening Another Directory Window

Expand all =
Shift + Click
on drive icon

File Manager initially displays only one directory window, and you cannot close it. You can, however, open additional directory windows to display the contents of another drive or directory. This can be useful if you are copying or moving files from one drive or directory to another. To open another directory window, do one of the following:

To open another drive: Make sure there is a formatted disk in the drive. Double-click on the drive icon in the currently opened window.

To open another directory: Hold down the Shift key while double-clicking on the directory's icon in the tree.

To open the same drive and directory: Open the Window menu and select New Window. You can then change to the desired drive and directory, as explained earlier in this chapter.

Having two windows opened helps when you copy or move files.

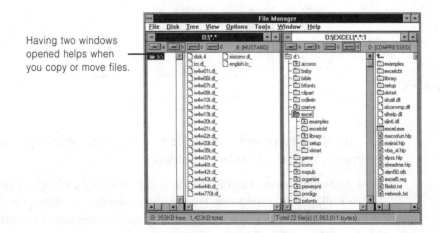

Side-by-side
windows =
Hold down
ShiET while
selecTing
Window Tile

Whenever you open another window, the new window covers part or all of the original window. You can resize and move the windows to rearrange them, as explained in Chapter 5, "Working with Windows." You can also use Window Tile or Window Cascade to have File Manager rearrange the windows for you.

Cheat Sheet

Sorting Files in the List

1. Open the View menu.
2. Select one of the following options:

   Sort by Name sorts files alphabetically by name.

   Sort by Type sorts files alphabetically by extension. For example, all .BAT files will be listed, and then .COM files, and then .EXE files.

   Sort by Size sorts files by file size, largest files first.

   Sort by Date sorts files by date and time, most currently changed files first.

Filtering the List

1. Open the View menu and select By File Type.
2. Select any of the following options (removing the X from the check box) to prevent a specific item from appearing in the list:

   Directories prevents directories from appearing in the contents list. Directories still appear in the tree.

   Programs prevents files with the extension .BAT, .COM, .EXE, and .PIF from appearing in the list.

   Documents prevents files that are associated to specific applications from appearing in the list.

   Other Files prevents all other files from appearing in the list.
3. To display hidden and system files in the list, click on the Show Hidden/System Files option.
4. Click OK.

28

Sorting and Filtering Files

The File Manager's contents list is initially set up to display all directory and file names in alphabetical order. You can filter the files, however, so that the list displays only files of a specific type. You can also sort the files by name, extension, date, or size if you are looking for specific files. In this chapter, you learn how to take control of your file lists.

Basic Survival

Sorting Files in the List

Initially, the contents area of the directory window displays the directory and file names in alphabetical order. You can sort the files and directories in a different order by selecting a sort order from the View menu. These sorting commands affect only the contents area; they do not affect the directory tree. To change the sorting order, here's what you do:

1. Change to the directory window whose contents you want to sort.

2. Open the View menu.

3. Select one of the following options:

Sort by date for recently modified files

   Sort by Name lists directories first and sorts files alphabetically by name. This is the default setting.

   Sort by Type lists directories first and sorts files alphabetically by extension. For example, all .BAT files will be listed, and then .COM files, and then .EXE files.

   Sort by Size lists directories first and sorts files by file size, listing the largest files first.

   Sort by Date sorts directories and files by date and time, listing the most currently changed files first.

The sorting option you select affects only the current window (and any new windows you create from it). You can select a different sorting order for two different windows.

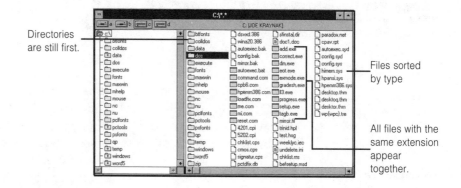

Directories are still first.

Files sorted by type

All files with the same extension appear together.

Filtering the List

The contents area normally contains the names of all the files in the current directory, except for hidden files and system files (files you probably shouldn't mess with). To display a specific group of files, you can filter the contents list. Here's what you do:

1. Open the View menu and select By File Type. The By File Type dialog box appears.

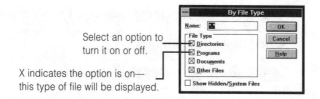

Select an option to turn it on or off.

X indicates the option is on— this type of file will be displayed.

2. (Usually, you will perform step 2 or 3 but not both.) To display a group of files that have similar names, type a wild-card entry using an asterisk (*) to stand in for a group of characters or a question mark (?) to stand in for individual characters. Here are some examples:

*.doc displays only those files that have the .DOC extension.

sales??.xls displays files named SALES01.XLS, SALES02.XLS, and so on.

. displays all files. This is the default.

3. Select any of the following options (removing the X from the check box) to prevent a specific item from appearing in the list:

Directories prevents directories from appearing in the contents list. Directories still appear in the tree.

Programs prevents files with the extension .BAT, .COM, .EXE, and .PIF from appearing in the list.

Documents prevents files that are associated to specific applications from appearing in the list.

Other Files prevents all other files from appearing in the list.

Keep Show Hidden/ System Files off.

4. To display hidden and system files in the list, click on the Show Hidden/System Files option. System files are files that you shouldn't copy, move, delete, or edit. These include IO.SYS and MSDOS.SYS. If you turn this on, File Manager displays the names of hidden and system files but includes a red exclamation point (!) in the icons that mark those files.

5. Click on the OK button. The contents list changes to reflect your selections.

To view all files, repeat these steps. In the Name text box, type *.* and make sure there is an X in each of the File Type check boxes.

Beyond Survival

Refreshing a Directory Window

Usually, File Manager updates the directory tree and contents list automatically whenever you enter a command, copy or move a file, or change disks or directories. If the list is not updated, perform the following steps:

Refresh = F5

1. Open the Window menu.

2. Select Refresh.

Cheat Sheet

Searching for a File

1. Select File Search.
2. Type the name of the file or a wild-card entry in the Search For text box.
3. Tab to the Start From text box.
4. Type a path to the drive and directory you want to search.
5. Click on the Search All Subdirectories option.
6. Click OK.

Understanding Wild-Card Entries

- Wild-card entries let you search for and select files that have similar names.
- Two wild-card characters are available, the asterisk (*) and the question mark (?). The asterisk stands in for two or more characters. The question mark stands in for a single character.
- **Example:** To find a group of files that have the extension .TXT, type *.txt.
- **Example:** To find a group of files that start with CHPT, have a two digit number, and end in .TXT, type **chpt??.txt**. This would find CHPT01.TXT, CHPT02.TXT, and so on.

Searching for Files

29

Sometimes you'll save a file and not know which drive or directory you saved it to. You could sift through all the files in your directories to look for it, but that could take awhile. An easier way is to have File Manager sniff out the file for you. In this chapter, you learn how to send the File Manager on a search.

Basic Survival

Searching for a File

To search for a file, you have to tell File Manager where to search, and what to search for. Here's how you do it:

1. **Open the File menu and select Search.** The Search dialog box appears.

Type a file name or wild-card entry here.

Type a path to the drive and directory you want to search.

Make sure this option is selected to search subdirectories of the search directory.

2. **Type the name of the file, or type a wild-card entry in the Search For text box.** For more details on wild-card entries, skip to the next section.

3. **Tab to the Start From text box.**

4. **Type a path to the drive and directory you want to search.** Follow these examples:

185

C:\ searches the root directory of drive C. If the Search All Subdirectories option is on (see next step), File Manager searches all the directories on drive C.

C:\DATA searches only the \DATA directory on drive C.

C:\DATA\LETTERS searches only the \DATA\LETTERS directory on drive C.

5. Click on the Search All Subdirectories option to place an **X** in its check box. This tells File Manager to search the directory (*and* any of its subdirectories) as you specified in step 4.

6. Click on the OK button. File Manager performs the search, and displays a window that contains all files that matched your search instructions. You can now select these files as explained in Chapter 30, "Selecting Files and Directories."

Search one directory = Turn off Search All Subdirectories

These are the files that match the search instructions.

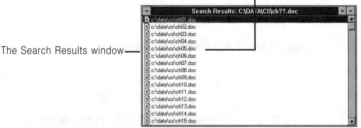

The Search Results window

To further narrow the list of files, perform another, more specific search on the files in the Search Results window.

Beyond Survival

Understanding Wild-Card Entries

A *wild-card character* is any character that takes the place of another character or a group of characters. Think of a wild-card character as a "wild card" in a game of poker. If the Joker is wild, you can use it in place of any card in the entire deck. To search for (or select) a group of files, you can use two "wild" characters: a question mark (**?**) and an asterisk (*). The question mark stands in for any single character. The asterisk stands in for any group of characters. Here are some examples:

. = all files

*.txt finds all files that have the .TXT extension—for example, CHAPTER.TXT, LETTER.TXT, SALES12.TXT.

chapter.* finds all files named CHAPTER with any extension—for example, CHAPTER.TXT, CHAPTER.DOC, CHAPTER.BAK, CHAPTER.BK.

sales??.xls finds all files that start with SALES and one or two additional characters, and have the extension .XLS—for example, SALES12.XLS, SALES01.XLS, SALES1.XLS.

s???.* finds every file whose file name starts with S and has four letters or fewer—for example, SORT.DOC, SAVE.TXT, SYS.INI.

Cheat Sheet

Selecting a Single File or Directory

1. Change to the drive and directory that contains the directory or file you want to select.
2. Click on the desired directory or file in the contents list.

Selecting a Group of Neighboring Items

1. Click on the first directory or file in the group.
2. Hold down Shift while clicking on the last directory or file in the group.

Selecting Non-Neighboring Items

1. Click on the first directory or file in the group.
2. Hold down Ctrl while clicking on additional items.

Selecting Files Using a Wild-Card Entry

1. Change to the drive and directory that contains the files you want to select.
2. Choose File Select Files.
3. Type the name of the file, or type a wild-card entry.
4. Click the Select button.
5. Repeat steps 3 and 4 to select additional files.
6. Click on the Close button.

30

Selecting Files and Directories

In order to copy, move, rename, or delete files or directories, you must first select them. In this chapter, you learn how to select individual files and directories and groups. In later chapters, you'll learn how to copy, move, rename, and delete selected items.

Basic Survival

Selecting Individual Files and Directories

If you want to perform some action on a single file or directory, perform the following steps to select it.

1. Change to the drive and directory that contains the directory or file you want to select.

2. Click on the desired directory or file in the contents list.

Tab To contents list, and use arrow keys

Click on a directory or file to select it.

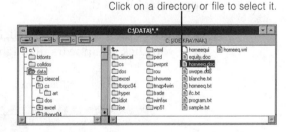

Beyond Survival

Selecting a Group of Neighboring Items

If you want to copy or move several files or directories, you don't want to have to do it one-by-one. If the files or directories are listed next to each other in the contents area, perform the following steps to select them:

1. Click on the first directory or file in the group. A group can include all files, all directories, or a mix of files and directories. You must, however, select the directories and files in the contents area; you cannot select directories in the tree *and* files in the contents area.

*Shift +
Arrow Keys
= ExTend
currenT
selecTion*

2. Hold down the Shift key while clicking on the last directory or file in the group. The first and last items you clicked on and all items in between are selected and appear highlighted.

Click on the first item.   Shift+Click on the last item.

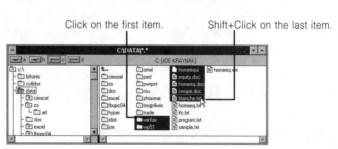

Selecting Non-Neighboring Items

If you want to work with a group of files or directories that are not next to each other in the list, perform the following steps to select them:

1. Click on the first directory or file in the group. This item will appear highlighted.

2. Hold down the Ctrl key while clicking on additional items. Each item you click on appears highlighted.

Use Ctrl+Click to select non-neighboring items.

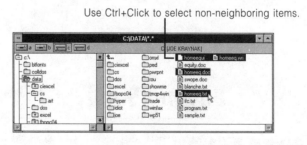

190

Selecting Separate Groups of Files

You can use a combination of techniques to select multiple files. For example, you can select two separate groups of neighboring files by performing the following steps:

1. Click on the first directory or file in the group.

2. Hold down the Shift key while clicking on the last directory or file in the group.

3. Hold down the Ctrl key while clicking on the first file or directory in the next group.

4. Hold down the Ctrl+Shift keys while clicking on the last file or directory in the group.

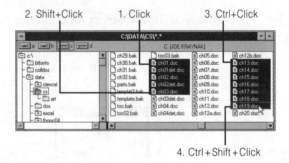

$Deselect = Ctrl + Click$

Deselecting Individual Files

To deselect a selected file, hold down the Ctrl key and click on the file again. To deselect all the selected files, click on any file in the contents area.

Selecting Files Using a Wild-Card Entry

Chapter 29 explains how to search for files using wild-card entries. You can use a similar technique to select groups of files. Here's what you do:

1. Change to the drive and directory that contains the files you want to select.

2. Open the File menu and choose Select Files. The Select Files dialog box appears.

Type a file name or wild-card entry here.

Click here to select files.

Click here to deselect.

Click here to return to
the directory window.

3. Type the name of the file you want to select, or type a wild-card
entry. For example, type ***.txt** to select all files that have the .TXT
extension. (Refer to Chapter 29, "Searching for Files," for details
about wild-card entries.)

. selects
all files

4. Click on the Select button. The contents list shows selected files
with boxes around them.

Boxes indicate these files are selected.

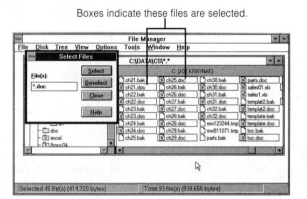

5. Repeat steps 3 and 4 to select additional files.

6. Click on the Close button. The Select Files dialog box disappears,
and all selected files appear highlighted.

If you want to select most of the files in the contents list, type *.* in the
Files text box, and click on Select. This selects all the files in the directory. Then, type another entry in the Files text box, and click on Deselect to deselect the group of files you do not want to include (or
Ctrl+Click on any files you want to omit).

Cheat Sheet

Dragging to Copy or Move

1. Select the files or directory you want to copy or move.
2. Make sure the destination (drive icon, directory icon, or directory window) is visible.
3. Move the mouse pointer over any of the selected files or directory.
4. While performing the next step, hold down Shift to move files or Ctrl to copy files.
5. Drag the mouse pointer over the destination icon or window.
6. Release the mouse button, and then release the key you were holding down.
7. Click on the Yes button.

Copying Files or Directories with File Copy

1. Select the files or directories you want to copy.
2. Select File Copy.
3. Type a path to the drive and directory to which you want the files or directories copied.
4. Click OK.

Moving Files and Directories with File Move

1. Select the files or directories you want to move.
2. Select File Move.
3. Type a path to the drive and directory to which you want the files or directories moved.
4. Click OK.

31

Copying and Moving Files and Directories

You may want to move files from one drive or directory to another to reorganize your files. You may also want to copy files from your hard drive to a floppy drive or vice versa to exchange files with other users. Or, you may want to create a copy of a file on the same drive so you can edit the file without changing the original. Whatever the reason, this chapter teaches you how to copy and move files with File Manager.

Basic Survival

Copying Files with the Mouse

The easiest way to copy or move files and directories is to use the mouse to drag the selected files or directories from one drive or directory to another. To copy files or directories, here's what you do:

1. Select the files or directories you want to copy. (Refer to Chapter 30, "Selecting Files and Directories," for details.)

2. Make sure the source and destination are visible. The *source* is the directory window that contains the selected files or directories. The *destination* can be any of the following:

    Drive icon You can drag the files up to a drive icon at the top of the source directory window. The files will be copied to the current directory of that drive. (Using a drive icon is good if you are copying files to a floppy disk. If you are copying them to a hard disk, make sure the desired directory icon is visible, as explained next.)

Directory icon   To copy files to a specific directory, make sure the directory's icon is visible. You may have to open another window to see the directory icon. (See "Opening Another Directory Window" at the end of Chapter 27.)

Directory window   You can drag files into the contents area of another directory window. Just make sure the desired directory is selected in the directory tree.

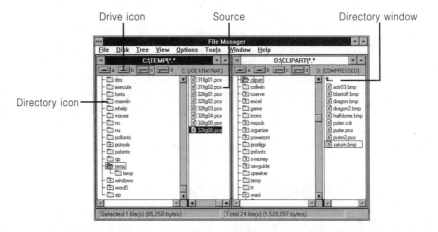

3. Move the mouse pointer over any of the selected files.

No CTrl if copying To different drive

4. Hold down the Ctrl key and the mouse button while dragging the pointer over the destination icon or window. As you drag, an icon appears with a plus sign (+) in it. This means the files will be copied. If the plus sign does not appear, the files will be moved; hold down the Ctrl key.

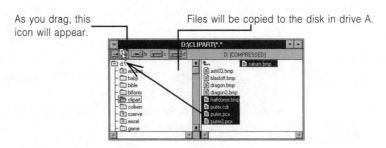

196

*Cancel
operation =
Drag files
back To source*

5. Release the mouse button, and then release the Ctrl key. A confirmation dialog box appears. To prevent the Confirmation dialog box from appearing, see Chapter 38, "Customizing File Manager."

6. Click on the Yes button. File Manager copies the selected files to the destination.

If the destination contains a file that has the same name and extension as one of the files you are copying, you'll get a warning box that asks if you want to overwrite the existing file. Click on No to skip this file and proceed copying the other files, or click on Yes to overwrite the existing file with the copy.

If you try to copy
one file over another
of the same name,
File Manager warns
you.

Moving Files with the Mouse

You can move files or directories by dragging them from one drive or directory to another. Here's what you do:

1. Select the files or directories you want to move. (Refer to Chapter 30, "Selecting Files and Directories," for details.)

2. Make sure the source and destination are visible. The source is the directory window that contains the selected files or directories. The destination can be a drive icon, directory icon, or directory window.

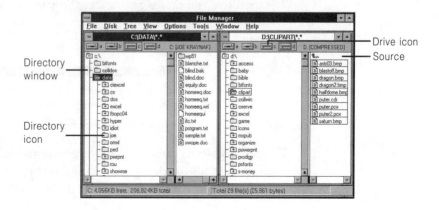

Directory
window

Directory
icon

Drive icon
Source

197

No Shift if moving on The same drive

3. Move the mouse pointer over any of the selected files.

4. Hold down the Shift key and the mouse button while dragging the pointer over the destination icon or window. As you drag, a file icon appears. If the icon has a plus sign, the files will be copied (not moved); hold down the Shift key.

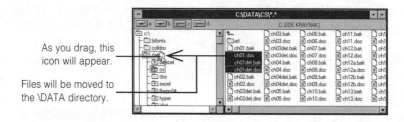

As you drag, this icon will appear.

Files will be moved to the \DATA directory.

5. Release the mouse button, and then release the Shift key. A confirmation dialog box appears. To prevent the Confirmation dialog box from appearing, see Chapter 38, "Customizing File Manager."

6. Click on the Yes button. File Manager moves the files.

Beyond Survival

Using File Copy and File Move

Move = F7

Copy = F8

With copying and moving, dragging is definitely the way to go. If you prefer using menus, however, perform the following steps to copy or move files:

1. Select the files or directories you want to copy or move.

2. Open the File menu and select Copy or Move. The Copy or Move dialog box appears (they look about the same), prompting you to specify a destination.

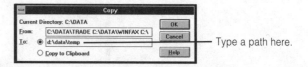

Type a path here.

3. Type a path to the drive and directory to which you want the selected files or directories copied or moved. For example, type **c:\data** to move the files or directories to the C:\DATA directory.

4. Click on the OK button. If you try to copy a file that has the same name as a file already on the destination drive, a confirmation dialog box appears.

5. Click on the Yes button. The selected files or directories are copied or moved to the specified destination.

Creating a Copy of a File with a Different Name

Sometimes it is useful to create a copy of a document so you can edit it without changing the original. For example, you may have a resumé cover letter that you want to change and send to another company. You have two options: you can copy the file to a different drive or directory using the same file name (as explained earlier), or you can copy the file to the same directory using a different file name. Here's how you copy a file to the same directory:

1. Select the file you want to copy.

Copy = F8

2. Open the File menu and select Copy. The Copy dialog box appears.

3. Type a new name for the copy.

To copy a file to the same directory, give the copy a unique name.

4. Click on the OK button. File Manager creates a copy of the selected file and assigns it the specified name.

Copying a File to Insert It in Another Document

Drag file icon from FM inTo application/ document window

You may have noticed that the Copy dialog box has a Copy to Clipboard option. This option allows you to copy the selected file to the Windows Clipboard and then paste it into another document as a linked or embedded file. Here's what you do:

1. Select the file (only one) that you want to embed in another document.

2. Open the File menu and select Copy. The Copy dialog box appears.

3. Click on Copy to Clipboard.

4. Click on the OK button. The selected file is placed as a packaged object on the Windows Clipboard.

5. Switch to the application and document in which you want the file embedded.

6. Move the insertion point where you want the file inserted.

7. Open the Edit menu and select Paste. An icon representing the file appears in the document.

Cheat Sheet

Renaming a Single File

1. Click on the file you want to rename.
2. Select File Rename.
3. Type a new name for the file.
4. Click OK.

Renaming a Directory

1. Click on the directory you want to rename.
2. Select File Rename.
3. Type a new name for the directory.
4. Click OK.

Renaming a Group of Files

1. Select the files you want to rename.
2. Select File Rename.
3. Type a wild-card entry.
4. Click OK.

32

Renaming Files and Directories

As you accumulate more and more files on your hard disk, you may have to rename files to make the names more descriptive (or to assign previously used names to other files). In this chapter, you learn how to rename files and directories.

When renaming files, remember to rename only the files you create, or the data files that someone gives you. Do not rename system files or program files. If you rename program files, the program may not run.

Basic Survival

Renaming a Single File

Use arrow keys To select file

You can rename a file at any time, just as long as you don't use a name that is already being used by a file in the same directory. To rename a file, here's what you do:

1. Click on the file you want to rename. The selected file appears highlighted.

2. Open the File menu and select Rename. The Rename dialog box appears, displaying the file's current name, and prompting you to enter a new name.

Type the new name here.

3. Type a new name for the file. Names can be up to eight characters, followed by a period, followed by an extension of up to three characters.

4. Click on the OK button. File Manager renames the file.

If you try to use a name that is already in use by a file in this directory, File Manager displays a dialog box that warns you that the name is already being used. Select OK, and then repeat the steps trying a different name.

You cannot use a name that is already in use by another file in this directory.

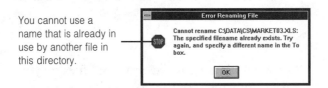

Renaming a Directory

You rename a directory the same way you rename a file:

1. Click on the directory you want to rename. The directory appears highlighted.

2. Open the File menu and select Rename. The Rename dialog box appears.

Leave extensions off directory names.

3. Type a new name for the directory. Names can be up to eight characters, followed by a period, followed by an extension of up to three characters. With directories, it is best to leave off the extension so you won't have so much to remember and type later.

4. Click on the OK button. File Manager renames the directory.

Beyond Survival

Renaming a Group of Files

Sometimes you may want to rename an entire group of files. For example, you might have a directory full of old documents that you want to mark as old. You can rename them, giving them all the extension **.OLD**. To rename a group of files, here's what you do:

1. Select the files you want to rename.

2. Open the File menu and select Rename. The Rename dialog box appears, prompting you to type a new name for the files.

3. Type a wild-card entry that will produce the desired results. This is tricky. Here are a couple of examples to give you some ideas:

Extension rename   This is easy. Type *. followed by the extension you want to use. For example, to change the extension of all files to .MY, type ***.my**.

Rename multiple files by changing their extensions.

File names   This can be complicated. If all the files start with or end with the same group of characters, you can type those characters and use question marks in place of the characters that differ. For example, say you have files named MARKET01.TXT, MARKET02.XLS, and MARKET03.DOC, and you want to name them QSALES01.TXT, QSALES02.XLS, and QSALES03.DOC. You would type **qsales??.***.

Files to be renamed. ——

File extensions will all be changed to .OLD.

4. Click on the OK button. The files are renamed.

Cheat Sheet

Deleting Files

1. Select the files you want to delete.
2. Select File Delete.
3. Click OK.
4. Select one of the following options:

    Yes to delete this file and go on to the next one.

    Yes to All to delete all selected files without asking you again.

    No to skip this file and go on to the next one.

    Cancel to abort the operation.

Can You Undelete Files from Windows?

- If you have DOS 6 or later, and you selected to install Undelete for Windows, you can undelete files.
- Open the File Manager's File menu, and look for the Undelete command.

Undeleting Files with DOS 6 Undelete for Windows

1. Change to the drive and directory that contains the accidentally deleted files.
2. Select File Undelete.
3. Click on each file you want to undelete.
4. Click on the Undelete button.
5. Type the first character of the file's name, and click OK.
6. Repeat step 5 for all selected files.
7. Select File Exit.

Deleting and Undeleting Files

To keep disks from getting cluttered with obsolete programs and with data files that you no longer need, you should back up these old files (or copy them), and then delete them from your hard disk. In this chapter, you learn how to delete files from disks and directories. If you have DOS 6 or later, and you installed Undelete for Windows, you also learn how to restore accidentally deleted files.

Basic Survival

Deleting Files

Before you delete files, make sure you will never *ever* need the files again, or at least make sure you have a copy of the files on floppy disks in a safe storage area. Once you've done that, take the following steps to delete one or more files:

1. Select the file(s) you want to delete.

Del Key = DeleTe file

2. Open the File menu, and select Delete. The Delete dialog box appears, displaying the names of the files that are going to be deleted.

3. Click on the OK button. A dialog box appears, prompting you to confirm the deletion. (To turn off these confirmation messages, refer to Chapter 38, "Customizing File Manager.")

File Manager asks you to confirm.

4. Select one of the following options:

   Yes to delete this file and go on to the next one. You will be prompted again to confirm the deletion of the next file.

Yes to All to delete all selected files without asking you again.

No to skip this file and go on to the next one.

Cancel to abort the operation.

5. Follow any on-screen messages that appear to complete the operation.

Beyond Survival

Undeleting Files with DOS 6 Undelete for Windows

Accidentally deleted files can be restored.

Whenever you delete a file, the computer does not erase all the data in the file; it erases only the first character of the file's name. This tells the system that the file name may be used by another file, and that the disk space is no longer reserved. If you delete a file accidentally, stop what you're doing, and take the following precautions:

- **Don't copy or move any files to the disk from which you deleted the files.** If you copy files to the disk, you risk overwriting the data contained in the file.

- **Don't quit Windows or turn off your computer.** Whenever you start your computer or Windows, you take a risk that the system may write something to disk, overwriting the data contained in the file.

If you have DOS 6, and you installed Microsoft Undelete for Windows, you may have just what you need to get your accidentally deleted files back. Open the File Manager's File menu and look for an Undelete command. If you see it, you're in luck. You can perform the following steps to undelete your files:

1. Change to the drive and directory that contains the accidentally deleted files. You won't see the deleted files in the contents list.

2. Open the File menu and select Undelete. The Microsoft Undelete window appears, showing the names of the recently deleted files. Note that the names have a question mark in place of their first characters.

Microsoft Undelete can help restore accidentally deleted files.

The condition of the file

Partial file names

Recently deleted files

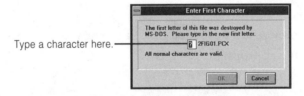

3. Click on each file you want to undelete. Each file you click on appears highlighted. To deselect a file, click on it again.

Undelete To a different drive = use "File Undelete To"

4. Click on the Undelete button. The Enter First Character dialog box appears, prompting you to type the first character of the file's name.

Type a character here.

5. Type the first character of the file's name. If you can't remember, type any character for now. You can rename the files later, as explained in Chapter 32, "Renaming Files and Directories."

6. Click on OK. Undelete restores the file to its original drive and directory.

7. Repeat steps 5 and 6 for all selected files. The Enter First Character dialog box goes away after you enter the character for the last file you selected.

8. Open the File menu and select Exit. You return to the File Manager window.

If the restored files do not appear in the contents area, open the Window menu and select Refresh. Sometimes File Manager cannot provide an immediate update of information that has changed on a disk.

Cheat Sheet

Formatting a Floppy Disk

1. Insert a blank disk in drive A or B.
2. Select Disk Format Disk.
3. In the Disk In drop-down list, select the appropriate drive.
4. In the Capacity drop-down list, select the capacity.
5. Click OK.
6. Click on Yes.

Making a Bootable Disk

1. Insert a blank, formatted disk in drive A.
2. Select Disk Make System Disk.
3. If a dialog box appears, click OK.

Labeling a Disk

1. Make sure there is a formatted disk in the drive.
2. Click on the appropriate drive icon.
3. Select Disk Label Disk.
4. Type a label.
5. Click OK.

34

Formatting Floppy Disks

Before you can use a floppy disk to store files, the disk must be formatted. *Formatting* divides a disk into small storage areas, and creates a *file-allocation table* (FAT) on the disk that acts as a map, telling your computer the location of all its storage areas. Whenever you save a file to disk, it is saved in one or more of these storage areas. In this chapter, you learn how to format a floppy disk, label the disk, and make a disk that you can use to start your computer.

Basic Survival

Disk and Drive Capacities

High-density = High-capacity

Although the procedure for formatting floppy disks is fairly simple, understanding the drive and disk capacities can be confusing. The problem is that the disk's manufacturers, the drive's manufacturers, and File Manager itself may all use different terms to describe capacities. For example, the disk label may describe the disk as "3.5-inch high-density," and File Manager will ask whether the disk is "1.44M or 720K." Use the following table to translate:

Disk Size	Density	Capacity
3.5-inch	High-Density (HD)	1.44M (High)
3.5-inch	Double-Density (DD)	720K (Low)
5.25-inch	High-Density (HD)	1.2M (High)
5.25-inch	Double-Density (DD)	360K (Low)

No high-capacity disks in low-capacity drives

You should also know that floppy disk drives come in high-capacity and low-capacity models, as well. If you have a high-capacity disk drive (1.44M or 1.2M), you don't have to worry—you can format both high-density and double-density disks. If you have a low-capacity drive, you will be able to format only double-density disks (360K or 720K).

Formatting a Floppy Disk

FormaTTing desTroys any daTa on The disk.

In general, you format a disk only once—when it is brand new. If you format a disk that has already been formatted, you risk destroying any files that may already be on the disk. It's better to just delete the files (see Chapter 33, "Deleting and Undeleting Files"). If you have a new disk, or one that is old and needs to be reformatted, perform the following steps to format the disk:

1. Insert a blank disk in drive A or B, and close the drive door, if necessary.

2. Open the Disk menu and select Format Disk. The Format Disk dialog box appears, asking you to specify a drive letter and disk capacity.

Specify the letter of the drive.

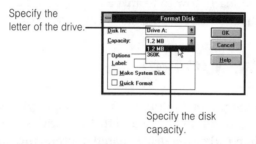

Specify the disk capacity.

3. Click on the arrow to the right of the Disk In option, and select the drive that contains the blank disk.

4. Click on the arrow to the right of the Capacity option, and select the capacity of the disk. If you are formatting a double-density disk (360K or 720K) in a high-density drive (1.2M or 1.44M), make sure you select the capacity of the *disk*, not the drive.

5. (Optional) Select any of the following options:

   Label   Click inside the Label text box, and type a label for the disk (up to 11 characters). If you add a disk label, the label will appear to the right of the disk icons in the directory window for this disk.

   Make System Disk   Select this option to make the disk *bootable* (this means you can use it to boot up your computer). File Manager copies the files IO.SYS, MSDOS.SYS, and COMMAND.COM from the hard disk to the floppy.

Reformat
disk = Quick
Format on

Quick Format   If the disk was previously formatted, and the disk has no bad sectors (areas), you can select this option to refresh the disk.

6. Click on the OK button. A dialog box appears, warning you that formatting will erase any data on the disk, and asking if you want to proceed.

7. Click on the Yes button. File Manager formats the disk. When done, File Manager displays a message asking if you want to format another disk.

8. Click on No to quit, or Yes to format another disk.

Beyond Survival

Making a Formatted Disk Bootable

Make bootable
disk To
recover from
crashes

You should always have at least one bootable floppy disk on hand in case your system crashes and you can't boot from your hard disk. You can stick the bootable floppy disk in drive A, reboot, and at least call up your files and programs. In the previous section, you learned how to make a floppy disk bootable when formatting it. If you already formatted the disk, perform the following steps to make it bootable:

1. Insert a blank, formatted disk in drive A. You can boot a computer only from a disk in drive A.

2. Open the Disk menu and select Make System Disk. If your computer has two floppy disk drives, the Make System Disk dialog box appears, prompting you to select a drive.

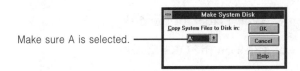

Make sure A is selected. ——

3. If a dialog box appears, make sure drive A is selected.

4. Click on the OK button. File Manager copies the files IO.SYS, MSDOS.SYS, and COMMAND.COM from the hard disk to the floppy. (IO.SYS and MSDOS.SYS are hidden files that do not usually appear in a file list. To display hidden files in File Manager, see Chapter 28.)

You may also want to copy the files AUTOEXEC.BAT and CONFIG.SYS from the root directory of drive C to the floppy disk, and the files WIN.INI and SYSTEM.INI from the WINDOWS directory. Then *write-protect* the disk (place a write-protect sticker over the write-protect notch in a 5.25-inch disk, or slide the write-protect tab so you can see through the window of a 3.5-inch disk). This ensures that nothing will happen to the files on the disk.

Adding or Editing a Disk Label

Label appears in directory window

The best way to label a disk is to write a description of the disk's contents on a stick-on label, and put it on the disk. However, you can also label a disk electronically. The label will then appear in the directory window for that disk. You can add a label when you format a disk—or you can add or edit it later, by performing the following steps:

1. Make sure there is a formatted disk in the drive. You can label floppy disks or your hard disks. (Although most computers have only one hard disk, C, some computers have the hard disk partitioned into two or more drives: C, D, E, and so on. You can give each partition a different label.)

2. Click on the drive icon for the drive that contains the disk you want to label.

3. Open the Disk menu and select Label Disk. The Label Disk dialog box appears.

Type a label here. —————

4. Type a label for the disk.

5. Click on the OK button.

214

Cheat Sheet

Copying Disks Using One Disk Drive

1. Select Disk Copy Disk.
2. Open the Source In list; click on the letter of the drive to use for copying disks.
3. Open the Destination In list; click on the same drive letter you selected in step 2.
4. Click OK.
5. Click Yes.
6. Insert the disk you want to copy.
7. Click OK, then wait until a message appears telling you to insert the destination disk.
8. Remove the source disk and insert the destination disk.
9. Click on OK.

Copying Disks Using Two Drives of the Same Capacity

1. Select Disk Copy Disk.
2. Open the Source In list; click on the letter of the drive to use for the original disk.
3. Open the Destination In list; click on the letter of the drive you want to use for the blank disk.
4. Click OK.
5. Click Yes.
6. Insert the original disk in the source drive, and the blank disk in the destination drive.
7. Click OK.

35

Copying Disks

Whenever you get a new computer program, you should write-protect the original floppy disks, and then copy the disks. You should use the copies, rather than the originals, to install and use the program. Doing this is a good precaution against damaging the original disks accidentally. In this chapter, you learn how to copy floppy disks with File Manager.

Basic Survival

Disk Copying Rules and Regulations

Source = Original disk

Destination = Blank disk

If you have copied disks before, you know the rules you need to follow. If you're new to all this, here are the rules:

- You can copy a disk only to a disk of the same size and capacity. You can't copy a 5.25-inch disk to a 3.5-inch disk, or a 360K disk to a 1.2M disk. You can copy a 3.5-inch 1.44M disk only to a 3.5-inch 1.44M disk.

- If you have two disk drives of the same size and capacity, you can copy the disk in one drive (the source) to the disk in the other drive (the destination).

- If you do not have two disk drives of the same size and capacity, you must use the same drive for both the source and the destination. You'll have to swap disks into and out of the drive during the process.

- The destination disk (the blank one) does not have to be formatted. The copy operation will format the disk for you.

Copying Disks Using One Disk Drive

If you have only one floppy drive that is the size and type you need to copy your disks, perform the following steps:

1. Write-protect the original disk (not the blank disk). This prevents the disk from being ruined if you accidentally try to copy the destination disk over the source disk.

Down
arrow =
change drive

2. Open the Disk menu and select Copy Disk. The Copy Disk dialog box appears.

3. Open the Source In drop-down list, and click on the letter of the drive to use for copying disks.

4. Open the Destination In drop-down list, and click on the same drive letter you selected in step 3. Because you are using the same drive for both the source and destination disks, the Source In and Destination In settings must be the same.

Make sure you select the same drives.

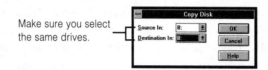

5. Click on the OK button. A warning message appears, telling you that any information on the destination disk will be erased.

See Chapter
38 To Turn
off warning
messages.

6. Click on Yes. A dialog box appears, telling you to insert the source disk in the drive.

7. Insert the disk you want to copy in the floppy drive you selected, and close the drive door, if necessary. (On 5.25-inch drives, *drive doors* are levers that lock the disk in place; 3.5-inch drives don't have them.)

8. Click on OK. File Manager copies the disk to memory and then displays a message telling you to insert the destination disk.

File Manager lets you know when you need to insert the destination disk.

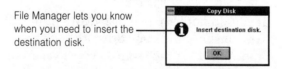

9. Remove the source disk and insert the destination disk.

10. Click on the OK button. File Manager writes the data from memory to the disk.

Beyond Survival

Copying Disks Using Two Drives of the Same Capacity

Drive A—
  Source

Drive B—
  Destination

If you have two drives of the same size and capacity, say two 3.5-inch 1.44M drives, you can copy a disk without having to swap the source and destination disks in the drive. Here's what you do:

1. Write-protect the original disk (not the blank disk). This prevents the disk from being ruined if you accidentally try to copy the destination disk over the source disk.

2. Open the Disk menu and select Copy Disk. The Copy Disk dialog box appears, prompting you to specify the drives you want to use.

3. Open the Source In drop-down list, and click on the letter of the drive to use for the original disk (usually drive A).

4. Open the Destination In drop-down list, and click on the letter of the drive you want to use for the blank disk (usually drive B).

Make sure the source and destination drives are different.

5. Click on the OK button. A warning message appears, telling you that any information on the destination disk will be erased.

6. Click on Yes. A dialog box appears, telling you to insert the source and destination disks in the drives.

7. Insert the original disk in the source drive, and the blank disk in the destination drive, and close the drive doors, if necessary.

8. Click on OK. File Manager copies the source disk to the destination disk.

Cheat Sheet

Making a Directory

1. Select the directory under which you want the new directory to appear.
2. Select File Create Directory.
3. Type a name for the directory.
4. Click OK.

Deleting an Empty Directory

1. Click on the directory.
2. Select File Delete.
3. Click OK.
4. Click on Yes.

Deleting a Directory and Its Files

1. Click on the directory.
2. Select File Delete.
3. Click OK.
4. Click on Yes to All.
5. Click on Yes to All.

36

Making and Deleting Directories

Keep directory
Trees
shallow—no
more Than 4
layers deep.

Hard disks can store thousands of files. In order to keep those files from getting lost, you should organize them using directories. *Directories* are logical divisions that keep related files together. For example, you might create a \DATA directory to store all the files you create, and create a subdirectory called \PERSONAL for all your personal letters and diaries. In this chapter, you learn how to create directories, and delete directories that you no longer use.

Basic Survival

Making a Directory

Root
directory of
C is C:\

All disks have at least one directory, the *root directory*, which you cannot name or change. You can, however, add directories under the root directory and under any existing directories. Here's how you do it:

1. Select the directory under which you want the new directory to appear.

Select the root directory to have the new directory appear one level below it.

Select a directory to make a subdirectory under it.

2. Open the File menu and select Create Directory. The Create Directory dialog box appears, prompting you to type a name for the new directory.

Type a name for the directory.

221

3. Type a name for the directory (up to eight characters). You can type a period and an extension, but you probably shouldn't use an extension. This makes the directory name cumbersome to work with.

4. Click on the OK button. The new directory is created and appears in the directory tree.

Refresh = F5

If the new directory does not appear immediately in the directory tree, open the Window menu and select Refresh. File Manager rereads the disk, updating the tree and contents area.

Beyond Survival

Deleting an Empty Directory

File Manager allows you to delete directories whether they contain files or not. Because of this, the safest way to delete a directory is to first move or delete any files in the directory and then delete the empty directory. That way, you know what you're deleting. After you have moved (Chapter 31) or deleted the files (Chapter 33), perform the following steps to delete the directory:

Click on directory, press Del

1. Click on the directory you want to delete.

2. Open the File menu and select Delete. The Delete dialog box appears, showing the name of the directory that will be deleted.

This directory will be deleted.

3. Click on the OK button. A warning box appears, asking you to confirm the deletion.

4. Click on the Yes button. File Manager deletes the empty directory.

If you click on the Yes button, and File Manager displays another dialog box asking you to confirm the deletion of a subdirectory, the directory you tried to delete was not empty. It still contains a subdirectory or files. To be on the safe side, click on the Cancel button, and then look back through those directories to see if you want to save anything.

Deleting a Directory and Its Files

If you have a directory that's packed with obsolete or old files that you know you will never ever need again, you can delete the directory (including all its subdirectories and files) by simply deleting the directory. Here's what you do:

1. Click on the directory you want to delete.

2. Open the File menu and select Delete. A dialog box appears, showing the name of the directory that will be deleted.

3. Click on the OK button. The Confirm Directory Delete prompt appears, asking you to approve the deletion.

4. Click on the Yes to All button. This tells File Manager to delete this directory and any of its subdirectories. If the directory or subdirectories contain files, a Confirm File Delete dialog box appears, asking you to approve the file deletions.

Yes = Safest

Yes To All = Fastest

This dialog box appears if the directory you want to delete or any of its subdirectories contain files.

5. Click on one of the following buttons:

Yes tells File Manager to delete this file and go on to the next one. Choose this if you want to see the name of each file before it is deleted.

Yes to All tells File Manager to delete all the files without asking you to confirm.

Cheat Sheet

Running an Application

1. Change to the drive and directory that contains the program's files.
2. Double-click on the application's executable file.

Opening a Document in an Application

1. Open two directory windows.
2. In one window, display the name of the document file.
3. In the other window, display the name of the file that runs the application.
4. Drag the document file icon over the application file icon.
5. Release the mouse button.
6. Click on Yes.

Associating a Document with an Application

1. Select the document file you want to associate with an application.
2. Select File Associate.
3. In the Associate With list, click on the application you want the document file associated with.
4. Click OK.

Opening an Associated Document File

1. Change to the drive and directory that contains the document file.
2. Double-click on the file you want to open.

37

Running Applications from File Manager

Usually you run applications from the Program Manager by double-clicking on a program-item icon. The File Manager provides another, sometimes faster, method. With File Manager, you can double-click on a program file to run the program, or double-click on a document file—which runs the application you used to create the document, *and* opens the document in the application. In this chapter, you learn how to do all this.

Basic Survival

Running an Application from File Manager

Bypass
menu =
Double-click
on file

Every program has an executable program file that starts the program. In almost all cases, the file ends in .BAT, .EXE, .COM, or .PIF. In Chapter 3, you learned how to run a DOS application by using the Program Manager's File Run command. You can use a similar technique to run DOS or Windows applications from File Manager. Here's what you do:

1. Change to the drive and directory that contains the program's files.

2. Click on the file that runs the application. Executable program files have a unique icon ▭.

3. Open the File menu and select Run. The Run dialog box appears, displaying the name of the selected file.

The name of the executable file

4. Click on the OK button. File Manager runs the application.

If you have a hard time sifting through the file lists to find executable program files, open the View menu and select By File Type. In the File Type group, turn off all options except Program, and then click on the OK button.

With only Program selected, all you see are executable program files.

Opening a Document in an Application

Drag & Drop To open document

If you want to run an application and open a document file automatically, you can drag the document's icon over the program icon. Here's how you do it:

1. Open two directory windows. You need two directory windows so you can see both the document and program icons.

2. In one window, display the name of the document file you want to open. Document file icons look like this: 📄.

3. In the other window, display the name of the program file that runs the application. Program icons look like this: 🔲.

4. Drag the document file icon over the program file icon.

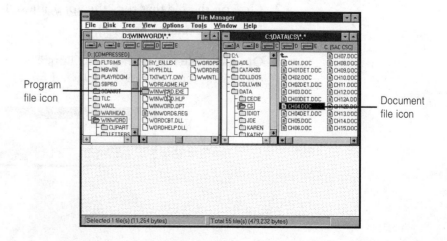

Program file icon

Document file icon

Ionize File Manager when running an application

5. Release the mouse button. A confirmation dialog box appears, asking if you are sure you want to do this.

6. Click on the Yes button. File Manager runs the application and automatically opens the selected document file.

Running applications in full-screen consumes memory and processing power. To free up system resources, it's a good idea to minimize any application windows you are not using. To have File Manager minimize itself whenever you run an application from it, open the Options menu and select Minimize on Use.

Beyond Survival

Associating a Document with an Application

In the previous section, you learned how to open a document file in an application by dragging the document icon over the program icon. There's an easier way to open a document and an application together. You can *associate* a type of document file with a particular application. For example, you can associate all files that have the extension .DOC with Word for Windows. Once the file association is set up, just double-click on a document file icon to run the associated application and open the document. To create an association, here's what you do:

1. Select a document file that has the extension you want to associate with an application. For example, to associate all .PCX files with an application (say Paintbrush), click on any file that has the .PCX extension.

2. Open the File menu and select Associate. The Associate dialog box appears. The extension of the file you selected is inserted in the Files with Extension text box.

The extension of the selected file appears here.

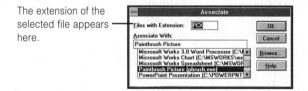

3. In the Associate With list, click on the application you want the document file associated with. If the application is not listed, click on the Browse button, and use the Browse dialog box to select the drive, directory, and file name of the application you want to run with this document. Then click on the OK button to go back to the Associate dialog box.

Select an application, or click on the Browse button.

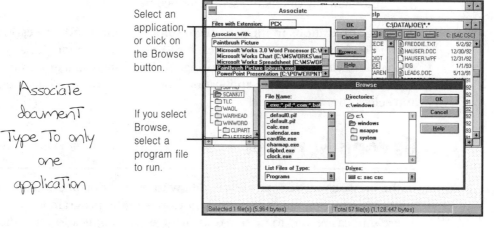

Associate document Type To only one application

If you select Browse, select a program file to run.

4. Click on the OK button. The association is set up.

Opening an Associated Document File

Once a document file is associated with an application, you can open the document in the application simply by double-clicking on the document file you want to open.

To open a document file, double-click on it.

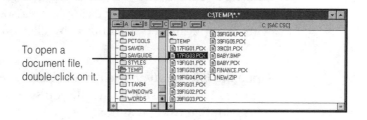

Cheat Sheet

Turning Off Confirmation Messages

1. Select Options Confirmation.
2. Select the confirmation message(s) you don't want to appear.
3. Click OK.

Saving Your Settings

1. Open the Options menu.
2. Select Save Settings on Exit to place a check mark next to it.

Changing the On-Screen Font

1. Select Options Font.
2. Select the type style, enhancement, and size of the text you want to use in the directory windows.
3. Select Lowercase, if you want.
4. Click OK.

Turning the Status Bar On or Off

1. Open the Options menu.
2. Select Status Bar.

38

Customizing the File Manager

In earlier chapters, you learned how to customize the File Manager by opening additional directory windows, sorting and filtering the file lists, and arranging directory windows on-screen. In this chapter, you learn how to further customize File Manager by selecting the type style and font used in displays and by turning confirmation messages on or off.

Basic Survival

Turning Confirmation Messages On or Off

As you copy and move files, format or copy disks, or drag-and-drop document icons onto program items, you may notice that File Manager questions you every step of the way. Although File Manager's "safety net" can help you avoid catastrophes, it can get annoying. If you want to turn off some or all of the confirmation messages, here's what you do:

1. Open the Options menu and select Confirmation. The Confirmation dialog box appears, showing a list of actions that call up confirmation messages.

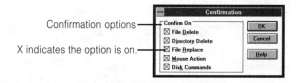

Confirmation options ──
X indicates the option is on. ──

2. Select one or more of the following options to turn them off:

   File Delete   With this off, File Manager does not ask for your final approval before deleting a file.

Directory Delete   Turn this off, and File Manager will not display a warning message when you are about to delete a directory.

File Replace   With this option off, File Manager allows you to copy or move files over existing files of the same name without warning you.

Mouse Action   Normally, File Manager warns you whenever you try to drag and drop a file with the mouse (to copy or move the file or open a document file in an application). Select this option to turn off mouse confirmation.

Disk Commands   Turn this option off if you want to prevent confirmation message appearing for disk commands such as Copy Disk and Format Disk.

3. Click on the OK button.

To turn any confirmation message back on, select Option Confirmation, and click on the option again. This places an **X** in the option's check box, turning it on.

Saving Your Settings

The File Manager Options menu has a Save Settings on Exit command that saves your current File Manager setup when you exit. If you turn this on, the next time you start File Manager, it starts with the same directory windows and arrangement, the same confirmation settings, and any other settings you may have entered. To see if Save Settings on Exit is on, open the Options menu, and make sure there is a check mark next to the option. If there is no check mark, click on Save Settings on Exit.

Make sure there is a check mark here.

Turn Save Settings off To use these settings only for current session

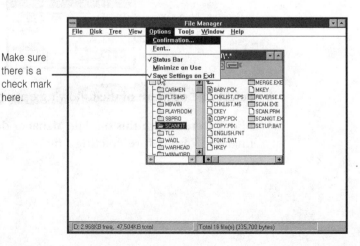

When you have File Manager set up the way you want to use it, turn Save Settings on, and then exit File Manager. Restart File Manager, and then turn Save Settings off. This ensures that your setup will not get changed later.

Beyond Survival

Changing the On-Screen Font

File Manager lets you change the type style and size it uses to display file names and directory names in the directory windows. If you want more file names to fit in the window, you may want to select a smaller font. If you are having trouble reading the file names in the current font, you may want to select a larger (or bold) font. To change the font, here's what you do:

1. Open the Options menu and select Font. The Font dialog box appears, prompting you to select a type style, type size, and enhancement for the font.

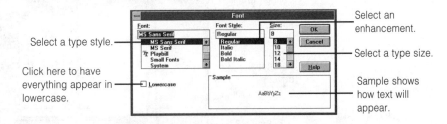

Select a type style.

Click here to have everything appear in lowercase.

Select an enhancement.

Select a type size.

Sample shows how text will appear.

Fonts marked TT give more control over Type size

2. From the Font list, select the type style you want to use. Keep an eye on the Sample area to see what the selected font will look like. Some fonts can be almost impossible to read.

3. From the Font Style list, select an enhancement for the font, if desired. Enhancements include italic and bold.

4. From the Size list, select the desired type size in points. (There are 72 *points* in an inch.) For TrueType fonts (fonts marked with **TT**), you can type a setting in the Size text box that does not appear in the list.

5. Select Lowercase if you want all text to appear in small letters. For example, with Lowercase on, a file name such as LETTER.DOC will appear as letter.doc in the file list.

6. Click on the OK button. File Manager changes the display according to the new settings.

Turning the Status Bar On or Off

At the bottom of the File Manager window is a *Status Bar* that displays some useful information about the selected drive, directory, and files. For example, if you are copying files from one drive to another, the status bar displays the amount of space required by the selected files and the amount of space available on the disk. That way, you'll know whether there is enough space to copy the files to the destination. You can turn the status bar off or on by performing the following steps:

1. Open the Options menu.

2. Select Status Bar. A check mark next to the option indicates that it is on.

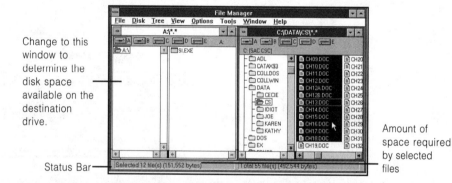

Change to this window to determine the disk space available on the destination drive.

Status Bar

Amount of space required by selected files

Drag File Manager icon To StartUp group Window

One more way to customize File Manager is to have it start whenever you start Windows. Simply hold down the Ctrl key while dragging the File Manager icon from the Main group window to the StartUp group. This places a copy of the icon in the StartUp group window.

Using the Windows Control Panel

The Windows Control Panel allows you to change the appearance and function of several Windows features. You can use the Control Panel to change the screen colors, to control how fast the mouse pointer moves across the screen, to set up your printer, to set the date and time on your computer, and much more. In this section, you learn what you can do with the Control Panel, and how to customize Windows to suit your needs. Specifically, you learn how to perform the following tasks:

- Seeing What's in the Control Panel
- Changing the Screen Colors
- Working with Fonts
- Controlling Your Mouse and Keyboard
- Controlling Your Desktop
- Setting the System Date and Time
- Working with System Sounds
- Changing the 386 Enhanced Settings
- Setting Up and Selecting a Printer
- Using the Windows Print Manager

Cheat Sheet

Starting the Control Panel

1. Open the Main group window.

2. Double-click on the Control Panel icon .

The Control Panel Icons

 Pick Windows color scheme.

 Add and remove fonts.

 Control serial ports.

 Control mouse speed.

 Choose a background color, and turn on screen saver.

 Change key repeat speed.

 Add, remove, and select printers.

 Set date, time, and currency format for various countries.

 Set the system date and time.

 Set sound driver priorities.

 Assign system resources to applications.

 Install and set up drivers for optional devices.

 Link sounds to system events.

39

Seeing What's in the Control Panel

The Control Panel allows you to enter settings for many Windows features. In this chapter, you learn how to start the Control Panel, and you learn about the various Control Panel icons that let you enter settings.

Basic Survival

Starting the Control Panel

Learn abouT icon—Click on iT, Then press F1

Before you can use the Control Panel, you have to start it. Here's how:

1. Open the Main group window.

2. Double-click on the Control Panel icon ![icon] . The Control Panel appears.

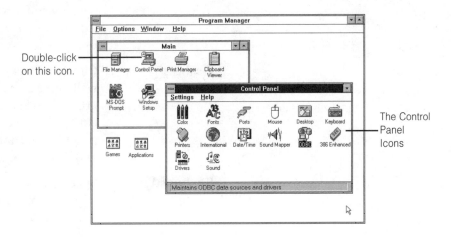

Double-click on this icon.

The Control Panel Icons

Beyond Survival

The Control Panel Icons

To change a system setting using the Control Panel, you can choose an option from the Settings menu, or you can double-click on an icon. Following is a list of the icons and a description of each:

FonT = Type
sTyle and size

Icon	Name	Description
Color	**Colors**	Pick a Windows color scheme or create your own color scheme.
Fonts	**Fonts**	Add and remove fonts.
Ports	**Ports**	Enter communications settings for your serial ports. Communications settings tell a serial device, such as a modem or serial printer, how to send and receive data.
Mouse	**Mouse**	Change the speed that your mouse pointer travels across the screen, and control how fast you have to click twice for a double-click. Configure mouse for left-handed use.
Desktop	**Desktop**	Choose a background color or wallpaper that acts as a background, turn on a screen saver, control how fast the insertion point blinks, and change the look and spacing of icons.
Keyboard	**Keyboard**	Specify how long you have to hold down a key before it starts repeating a character, and change how fast the key repeats the character.
Printers	**Printers**	Add and remove printers, select a default printer, and change the quality of print.

Try The
Windows
screen saver

238

International   Set the date, time, currency, and other format settings for various countries. These settings will control any Windows applications that support international settings for sorting or managing information. This does not change the language used for Windows commands and options.

Date/Time   Set the date and time on your computer's internal clock. This is much easier than using the DOS DATE and TIME commands.

Sound Mapper   Set the sound driver priorities if you have two or more sound drivers installed on your system; for example, a sound board driver and a PC speaker driver.

386 Enhanced   Assign system resources to applications running in the foreground and background, specify how much disk space you want to use as memory, tell Windows how to handle simultaneous requests from two applications wanting to use the same device.

Drivers   Install and set up drivers for optional devices, such as sound cards.

Sound   Link sounds to system events, such as Windows start and exit.

386 Enhanced To use disk space as memory

When you use the Control Panel to make a change, changes are saved in a file called WIN.INI that is run whenever you run Windows. You can open this file and edit commands (as explained in Chapter 49), but it is usually easier and safer to make the changes with the Control Panel.

Cheat Sheet

Picking a Color Scheme

1. Open the Main group window.
2. Double-click on the Control Panel icon .
3. Double-click on the Color icon .
4. Open the Color Schemes list; click on the desired color scheme.
5. Click OK.

Selecting a Custom Color

1. Open the Main group window.
2. Double-click on the Control Panel icon .
3. Double-click on the Color icon .
4. Open the Color Schemes list, and click on the desired color scheme.
5. Click on the Color Palette button.
6. Open the Screen Element list, and click on the item whose color you want to change.
7. Click on the desired color in the Basic Colors area.
8. Repeat steps 6 and 7 for each item.
9. Click on the Save Scheme button.
10. Type a name for the color scheme, and click on OK.
11. Click OK.

40

Changing the Screen Colors

Windows uses a default color scheme that is easy on your eyes. If you want a color scheme that's a little more wild or interesting, you can select one of Windows other color schemes or design your own. This chapter shows you how.

Basic Survival

Picking a Windows Color Scheme

Windows comes with several color schemes, including Black Leather Jacket (tough black and purple) and Hotdog Stand (festive red and yellow). You can select one of these prefabricated color schemes by performing the following steps:

1. Open the Main group window.

2. Double-click on the Control Panel icon ![Control Panel] . The Control Panel window appears.

3. Double-click on the Color icon ![Color] . The Color window appears, prompting you to select a color scheme.

Windows Default = original setting

4. Click on the arrow to the right of the Color Schemes drop-down list, and click on the desired color scheme.

Select a color scheme from the drop-down list.

5. Click on the OK button. The selected color scheme is activated.

Beyond Survival

Designing Your Own Color Scheme

Each color scheme defines colors for various screen elements, such as title bars, borders, and backgrounds. You can change the color used for any of these elements to create your own custom design. You can then save the color scheme you created to add it to the Color Schemes drop-down list. Here's how you do it:

1. Open the Main group window.

2. Double-click on the Control Panel icon ⬛. The Control Panel window appears.

3. Double-click on the Color icon 𝐈𝐈𝐈. The Color window appears, prompting you to pick a color scheme.

SelecT existing scheme and ediT iT

4. Open the Color Schemes drop-down list, and click on a color scheme that looks most like the one you have in mind. You can then change colors for individual screen elements.

5. Click on the Color Palette button. The Color Palette appears. The Palette contains a list of the screen elements and a list of basic colors. If you want to create your own colors, skip ahead to the next section.

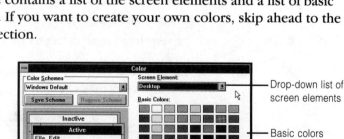

Drop-down list of screen elements

Basic colors

6. Open the Screen Element drop-down list, and click on the item whose color you want to change. For example, you can select Active Title Bar to change the color of the active window's title bar.

Arrow keys, space bar To change color

7. Click on the desired color in the Basic Colors area. A selection box appears around the color, and the selected color is applied to the preview area.

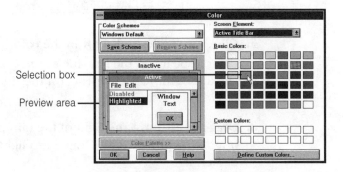

Selection box ——

Preview area ——

8. Repeat steps 6 and 7 for each item whose color you want to change.

9. Click on the Save Scheme button. The Save Scheme dialog box appears, prompting you to type a name for the new color scheme.

10. Type a name for the color scheme (up to 32 characters), and click on OK.

11. Click on the OK button. The new color scheme is activated.

Creating Custom Colors

At the bottom of the Color Palette is a button labeled Define Custom Colors. If you click on this button, and you get the Custom Color Selector that lets you mix colors to create your own color and add it to the Color Palette. Here's what you do:

1. Click on the Define Custom Colors button. The Custom Color Selector appears.

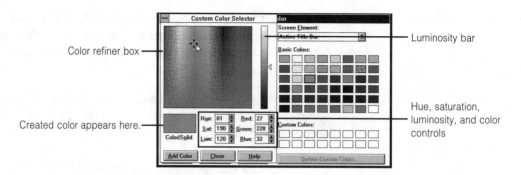

Color refiner box

Created color appears here.

Luminosity bar

Hue, saturation, luminosity, and color controls

Hue = Color
Saturation = Purity
Luminosity = Brightness

2. Click on the desired color in the color refiner box. The selected color appears on the left side of the Color/Solid box. The solid version of this color appears on the right side of the Color/Solid box.

3. Drag the arrow to the right of the luminosity bar to change the brightness of the color. Drag up to lighten the color or down to darken it.

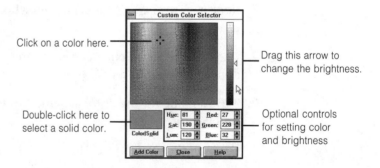

Click on a color here.

Double-click here to select a solid color.

Drag this arrow to change the brightness.

Optional controls for setting color and brightness

Solid colors = Faster display

4. To use the solid version of the color, double-click on the right side of the Color/Solid box.

5. Click on the Custom Colors box in which you want the new color added.

6. Click on the Add Color button.

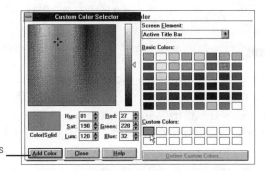

Add Color button adds created color here.

7. Repeat steps 2–6 to add more colors.

8. **Click on the Close button.** The Color window now contains the colors you created. You can select an item from the screen element drop-down list, and then select one of your custom colors to apply it to the selected element.

These steps describe the easiest way to create a color. However, you could also use the Hue, Sat, Lum, Red, Blue, Green settings to create a color. You can type settings directly in the text boxes (or click on the arrows to the right of the text boxes) to increase or decrease the settings. The settings range from 0 to 255.

Cheat Sheet

Types of Fonts

- *Printer fonts* are built into the printer. They are made available when you select a printer.
- *Screen fonts* are fonts Windows uses to display options, messages, and text on-screen. They control the way text is displayed, not printed.
- *Soft fonts* come on disk, and include both printer and screen fonts. Most come with their own installation program.
- *TrueType fonts* are soft fonts designed especially for Windows. They act as both printer and screen fonts.

Adding Soft Fonts

1. Open the Main group window.
2. Double-click on the Control Panel icon .
3. Double-click on the Fonts icon ![Fonts].
4. Click on the Add button.
5. Insert the disk that contains the fonts you want to install.
6. Change to the drive and directory that contains the fonts.
7. Press Ctrl while clicking on each font you want to install.
8. Click OK.

Removing Fonts

1. Open the Main group window.
2. Double-click on the Control Panel icon ![Control Panel] .
3. Double-click on the Fonts icon ![Fonts].
4. Press Ctrl while clicking on each font you want to remove.
5. Click on the Remove button.
6. Click on Yes to All.

Working with Fonts

Windows comes with several fonts (type styles and sizes) that are installed automatically when you set up Windows for the first time. You can remove some of these fonts to free up computer memory, and you can reinstall them to make them available on font lists in your Windows applications. In addition, you can purchase and install more fonts. In this chapter, you learn how to add and remove fonts in Windows.

Basic Survival

Understanding Fonts

Printer fonts are installed when you select a printer

A *font* is any text that has the same typeface and size. For example, Courier 12-point is a font. Courier is the typeface, and 12-point is the size. Fonts come from different sources, depending on the type of font. Here's a list of the most common font types:

- *Printer fonts* are built into the printer. When you select a printer (see Chapter 47), the printer setup installs the screen fonts (used to display the selected fonts on-screen) and the printer fonts (used to create the fonts on paper). You don't need the information in this chapter to install printer fonts.

- *Cartridge fonts* are additional fonts that you can plug into some printers (usually laser or dot-matrix printers). They act as additional printer fonts. To view such fonts as they will appear in print, you must install corresponding screen fonts.

- *Screen fonts* are fonts Windows uses to display options and messages on-screen. Screen fonts may also be included with printers, cartridges, and soft fonts to make the type appear on-screen as it will in print. If Windows does not have a screen font that matches the selected printer or cartridge font, Windows uses a screen font that most closely matches the selected font. Most cartridges and soft fonts come with an installation program that installs the screen fonts for you. If no setup program exists, you can follow the instructions in this chapter to install the fonts.

• *Soft fonts*, such as Adobe fonts, come on disk. Most of these fonts come with their own installation program and include both the screen and printer fonts. If no installation program exists, you can follow the instructions in this chapter to install the fonts.

• *TrueType fonts* are soft fonts designed especially for Windows. TrueType fonts act as both printer and screen fonts. Unlike other fonts that come in a fixed number of sizes, TrueType fonts allow you to select any size and rotate the text. Follow the instructions in the next section to install TrueType fonts.

*TrueType
fonts = TT
in font lists*

Installing Screen Fonts and TrueType Fonts

*Install only
fonts you
intend to
use*

You'll need to use the Windows Font Installation program if the fonts you want to install did not come with an installation program, or if you want to add previously installed fonts back into your fonts lists (if you removed them, as explained later in this chapter). To install fonts using the Installation program, here's what you do:

1. Open the Main group window.

2. Double-click on the Control Panel icon ![Control Panel icon]. The Control Panel window appears.

3. Double-click on the Fonts icon ![Fonts icon]. The Fonts dialog box appears.

4. Click on the Add button. The Add Fonts dialog box appears, prompting you to specify the disk and directory that contains the font files.

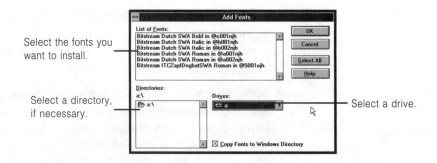

Select the fonts you want to install.

Select a directory, if necessary.

Select a drive.

5. Insert the disk that contains the fonts you want to install. (If you are reinstalling fonts that you uninstalled earlier, but did not remove from disk, skip this step.)

248

6. Change to the drive and directory that contain the fonts. A list of fonts in the selected drive and directory appears in the List of Fonts list.

7. Select each font you want to install:

   Single font   Click on it.

   Group of neighboring fonts   Click on the first one in the group, and then hold down the Shift key while clicking on the last font in the group.

   Group of non-neighboring fonts   Hold down the Ctrl key while clicking on each font you want to install.

8. To copy the selected fonts to the Windows directory, make sure there is an **X** in the Copy Fonts to Windows Directory check box. This option is useful if you are installing fonts from a floppy disk. If you are installing from a directory on your hard disk or from a CD, you may want to turn this option off.

9. Click on the OK button. The selected fonts are installed, and you are returned to the Fonts dialog box.

10. Click on the Close button.

The fonts you installed will now appear in the Fonts lists of your Windows applications.

Beyond Survival

Removing Screen Fonts and True-Type Fonts

More fonts slow down system

Whenever you install fonts, the font names are added to a file called WIN.INI that Windows reads into memory at startup. This slows down your computer in two ways. First, Windows takes longer to start. Second, these additional fonts take up computer memory that your applications can use to run. If you never use a font, it's a good idea to remove it.

There's one exception. Do *not* remove the font called MS Sans Serif. Windows uses this font (which is easy to read) to display text in its windows, menus, and dialog boxes. If you remove this font, you may not be able to read all the on-screen text.

To remove a font, here's what you do:

1. Open the Main group window.

2. Double-click on the Control Panel icon 🖳 .
   Control Panel

3. Double-click on the Fonts icon 𝕬𝕭ℂ. The Fonts dialog box appears,
   Fonts
   showing a list of installed fonts.

4. Select each font you want to remove:

   Single font   Click on it.

   Group of neighboring fonts   Click on the first one in the
   group, and then hold down the Shift key while clicking on the last
   font in the group.

   Group of non-neighboring fonts   Hold down the Ctrl key while
   clicking on each font you want to remove.

Select the fonts you
want to remove.

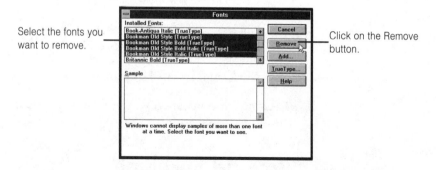

Click on the Remove
button.

5. Click on the Remove button. The Remove Font dialog box appears.

6. (Optional) If you want the font files removed from disk, click on
   the Delete Font File From Disk option. If you leave this option off,
   the font is removed from the font lists, and does not consume
   memory, but the file is left on disk. You can then reinstall the font
   easily.

Remove
fonts from
disk To free
up disk
space

Select this option if you
want the font files
removed from disk.

7. Click on Yes to remove this font and go on to the next one, or click on Yes to All to remove all selected fonts without asking for your okay. You are returned to the Fonts dialog box.

8. Click on the Close button.

Setting TrueType Options

Windows allows you to disable TrueType fonts as a group or make it so that only TrueType fonts appear on your font lists. To set these options, here's what you do:

1. Open the Main group window.

2. Double-click on the Control Panel icon .

3. Double-click on the Fonts icon . The Fonts dialog box appears, showing a list of installed fonts.

4. Click on the TrueType button. The TrueType dialog box appears.

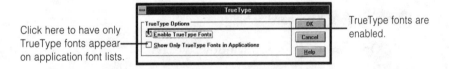

Click here to have only TrueType fonts appear on application font lists.

TrueType fonts are enabled.

5. To disable TrueType fonts, click on the Enable TrueType Fonts option to remove the **X** from its check box.

You can use TrueType fonts exclusively

6. To have only TrueType fonts appear on the font lists in your applications, click on the Show Only TrueType Fonts in Applications option to place an **X** in its check box. (Some applications do not support this option. If you select this option and all your TrueType fonts disappear from the fonts lists, turn this option off.)

7. Click on the OK button. If you turned Enable TrueType Fonts on or off, a dialog box appears, asking if you want to restart Windows now. (The change will not take effect until you restart Windows.) Click on the desired choice.

Cheat Sheet

Changing Your Mouse Settings

1. Open the Main group window.

2. Double-click on the Control Panel icon 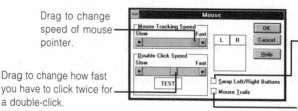 .

3. Double-click on the Mouse icon .

4. Change the mouse settings, as shown.

Drag to change speed of mouse pointer.

Select this option if you are left-handed.

Drag to change how fast you have to click twice for a double-click.

Select this if you want the mouse pointer to leave a shadow as it moves across the screen.

5. Click on OK.

Changing Your Keyboard Settings

1. Open the Main group window.

2. Double-click on the Control Panel icon .

3. Double-click on the Keyboard icon .

4. Change the keyboard settings, as shown.

Drag to control how long you have to hold down a key to start repeating the character.

Drag to control how fast the character repeats.

5. Click OK.

42

Controlling Your Mouse and Keyboard

Have you ever wished your mouse pointer would travel faster or slower across the screen, or that you could click twice more slowly to enter a double-click? With the Control Panel, you can change the mouse settings to make your mouse behave the way you want it to. In addition, you can change the keyboard settings so you don't have to hold down a key so long to have it repeat a character. In this chapter, you learn how to change your mouse and keyboard settings.

Basic Survival

Changing Your Mouse Settings

A mouse that operates too fast or too slow can be frustrating. Fortunately, you can change the way your mouse behaves. Here's what you do:

1. Open the Main group window.

2. Double-click on the Control Panel icon .

3. Double-click on the Mouse icon. The Mouse dialog box appears.

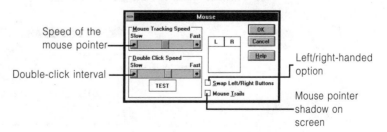

Speed of the mouse pointer

Double-click interval

Left/right-handed option

Mouse pointer shadow on screen

Double-click on Test button To check double-click speed.

System security— Swap mouse buttons before going home

4. To change the speed at which the mouse pointer travels across the screen, drag the Mouse Tracking Speed button left (to slow the pointer) or right (to quicken it).

5. To change the speed at which you have to click twice for a double-click, drag the Double Click Speed button left (so you don't have to be so fast) or right (if you have a quick finger).

6. To use the mouse as a left-handed mouse, click on the Swap Left/Right Buttons option. (To change back, you have to right-click on this option, because the right button now acts as the left button.)

7. To have the mouse pointer leave steps across the screen as you move it, click on the Mouse Trails options.

8. Click on the OK button. Your changes are saved, and the mouse acts the way you instructed it to.

Beyond Survival

Changing Your Keyboard Settings

Whenever you hold down a key on your keyboard, it starts to repeat its character. The Keyboard option lets you control how long you have to hold a key down before it starts repeating, and how fast the character repeats once it starts. To change these settings, perform the following steps:

1. Open the Main group window.

2. Double-click on the Control Panel icon ⌨. The Control Panel window appears.

3. Double-click on the Keyboard icon ⌨.

Key repeat interval ———

Key repeat speed

4. To change how long you have to hold down a key before it starts repeating, drag the Delay Before First Repeat button left (so you have to hold down the key longer) or right (so the character will start repeating right away).

5. To change how fast the character repeats when it starts repeating, drag the Repeat Rate button left (to repeat slowly) or right (for a more frenetic pace).

6. Click on the OK button. Your changes are saved, and your keyboard will start acting as instructed.

Click inside
TesT box,
hold down
Key

255

Cheat Sheet

Accessing the Desktop Settings

1. Open the Main group window.
2. Double-click on the Control Panel icon .
3. Double-click on the Desktop icon .

Select a background color.

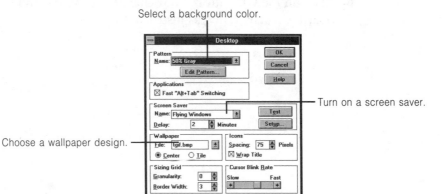

Turn on a screen saver.

Choose a wallpaper design.

Changing the Background Pattern

1. Open the Pattern Name drop-down list.
2. Click on the desired pattern.
3. Click OK.

Turning On a Screen Saver

1. Open the Screen Saver Name drop-down list.
2. Click on a screen saver.
3. Tab to the Delay text box, and type the number of minutes you want your computer to be inactive before the screen saver kicks in.
4. Click OK.

Selecting a Wallpaper Design

1. Open the Wallpaper File drop-down list.
2. Click on the graphics file you want to use.
3. Click OK.

43

Controlling Your Desktop

You may think that you're stuck with the standard Windows look—the plain gray background that sits behind Program Manager. Not true. You can use the Desktop option in the Control Panel to select an interesting Windows background, and to turn on a screen saver that just might keep your monitor from going south. In this chapter, you learn what you can do with the Desktop.

Basic Survival

Choosing a Background Pattern

If Program Manager or an application window is in full-screen view, you won't see the Windows background. However, if you minimize all the windows on your screen, you'll see a plain gray background (or another color if you changed the screen colors in Chapter 40). You can select a different background by performing the following steps, or you can skip ahead to the section called "Using a Graphics File as Wallpaper" for more interesting backgrounds. To change the background design, here's what you do:

Skip This and go To The Wallpaper section.

1. Open the Main group window.

2. Double-click on the Control Panel icon . The Control Panel window appears.

3. Double-click on the Desktop icon . The Desktop dialog box appears, allowing you to change the Desktop settings.

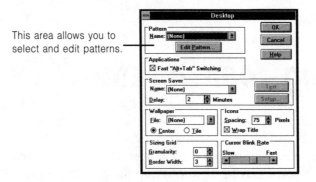

This area allows you to select and edit patterns.

4. Open the Pattern Name drop-down list. A list of available patterns appears. Patterns are made up of black squares arranged gray or color background.

5. Click on the desired pattern.

6. To change the pattern, click on the Edit Pattern button. The Desktop - Edit Pattern dialog box appears.

Click on a square to make it black if it is gray, or gray if it is black.

Sample shows how your design will look.

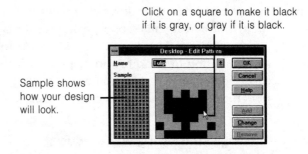

7. Click on a square to toggle it between black and the background color. For example, if you click on a gray square, it turns black. Click on a black square, and it turns gray.

8. Click on the OK button. You are returned to the Desktop dialog box.

9. Click on the OK button again. Your changes are made, and the new design appears on the Windows background.

Beyond Survival

Using a Graphics File as Wallpaper

Background patterns are fairly boring. If you want something more graphic, you should select a wallpaper. Windows 3.1 comes with several eye-catching wallpapers you can use as backgrounds. To select one, here's what you do:

1. Open the Main group window.

2. Double-click on the Control Panel icon . The Control Panel window appears.

3. Double-click on the Desktop icon . The Desktop dialog box appears, allowing you to change the Desktop settings.

Try DRAGON.BMP.

4. Open the Wallpaper File drop-down list. A list of graphics files, all having the extension .BMP, appears.

5. Click on the graphics file you want to use as your Windows background.

Make original wallpaper with Paintbrush (see Chapter 57).

6. Click on Center or Tile. If the image you select is not big enough to fill the screen, Windows centers the image, or tiles several copies of the image to fill the screen.

7. Click on the OK button. The selected graphic appears on-screen, if you have your windows minimized.

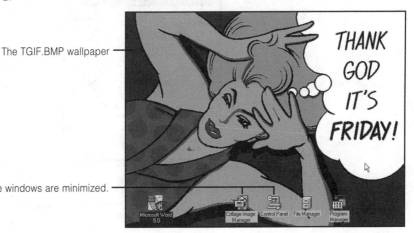

The TGIF.BMP wallpaper —

These windows are minimized. —

Now that you've had your fun, I have to tell you that these interesting backgrounds consume memory. If your applications seem slow, or you're getting **Out Of Memory** messages, try turning off the wallpaper (select None) or use a solid background.

Turning On the Screen Saver

If you leave one image on your screen for an extended period, the image can get burnt into the screen, permanently damaging it. To prevent this from happening, you should use a *screen saver*. Screen savers typically blank the screen, or display images that move across the screen. The screen saver starts when the computer is inactive for a certain amount of time. Windows contains several screen savers that you can turn on by performing the following steps:

1. Open the Main group window.

2. Double-click on the Control Panel icon . The Control Panel window appears.

3. Double-click on the Desktop icon. The Desktop dialog box appears, allowing you to pick a screen saver.

4. Open the Screen Saver Name drop-down list. A list of available screen savers appears.

5. Click on the name of the screen saver you want to use. You can preview it later.

Flying Windows is cool!

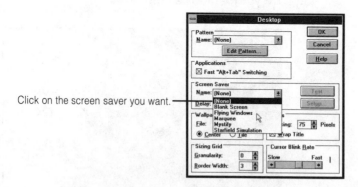

Click on the screen saver you want.

6. Tab to the Delay text box, and type the number of minutes you want your computer to be inactive before the screen saver kicks in. You can also click on the up or down arrow to the right of the text box to change the setting.

7. To see what the screen saver will look like, click on the Test button. When you're done previewing, move the mouse or press a key to stop it.

8. To change the screen saver settings, click on the Setup button, enter the desired settings, and click on OK.

9. Click on the OK button. You are returned to Windows, and your screen saver will kick in when you leave your computer inactive for the specified amount of time.

Enter a password To secure your system.

You may have noticed that the Screen Saver setup lets you enter a password. If you enter a password, the screen saver won't allow you to return to Windows until you type the required password. As a cheap way to secure your system, consider cranking the screen saver delay time down to one minute, adding a password, and setting up Windows to run automatically when you start your computer (by adding **WIN** to the end of your AUTOEXEC.BAT file, as explained in Chapter 49). If anyone tries to mess with your computer, they'll be locked out as soon as the screen saver kicks in.

Other Desktop Options

The Desktop dialog box contains other options that are not quite as exciting as backgrounds, screen savers, and wallpaper. Here is a list of the options and a description of each (or a reference telling you where to look for more information):

Fast Alt+Tab Switching 'enables you to jump among active application windows by pressing Alt+Tab. If you need to use the Alt+Tab key combination for one of your applications, you can turn this option off.

Cursor Blink Rate controls the speed at which the insertion point blinks on and off.

Sizing Grid lets you control window placement and border width. See Chapter 5 for details.

Icon Spacing lets you change the spacing between program-item icons. See Chapter 6 for details.

Cheat Sheet

Changing the Date and Time

1. Open the Main group window.
2. Double-click on the Control Panel icon 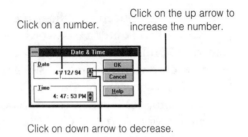 .
3. Double-click on the Date/Time icon .
4. Click on the number you want to change.

5. Click on the up or down arrow to change the number.
6. Repeat steps 4 and 5 for each number you want to change.
7. Click on OK.

Changing the Date and Time (Keyboard Steps)

1. Open the Main group window.
2. Arrow key over to the Control Panel icon, and press Enter.
3. Arrow key to the Date/Time icon, and press Enter.
4. Tab to the number you want to change.
5. Type the desired number.
6. Repeat steps 4 and 5 for each number you want to change.
7. Press Enter.

44

Setting the System Date and Time

Most PCs have a battery-operated internal clock. Like most clocks, the computer clock may run a little fast or slow, and you may have to reset the date or time. In this chapter, you learn how.

Basic Survival

Changing the Date and Time

The Control panel has a Date/Time option that lets you set the date and time on your computer's clock. To set the date and time, here's what you do:

1. Open the Main group window.

2. Double-click on the Control Panel icon . The Control Panel window appears.

3. Double-click on the Date/Time icon [Date/Time]. The Date & Time dialog box appears.

Tab To a number and Type.

4. Click on the number you want to change. For example, to change the hour, click on the number that represents the hour.

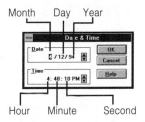

5. Click on the up or down arrow to the right of the number to change it. The Up arrow increases the number, the down arrow decreases it.

6. Repeat steps 4 and 5 for each number you want to change.

7. Click on the OK button. Your computer's clock is changed. The changes you entered now appear on the Clock in Accessories (see Chapter 19). The change will also affect the date and time you insert in your documents.

Cheat Sheet

Can Windows Play Sounds?

- Your computer must have a sound board or a PC speaker driver.
- A speaker driver is a program that enables the computer's built-in speaker to play more complex sounds.
- You can get a PC speaker driver from a user group, a friend, or an online service.

Attaching a Sound to an Event

1. Open the Main group window.

2. Double-click on the Control Panel icon Control Panel .

3. Double-click on the Sound icon Sound .

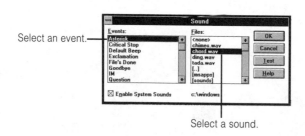

Select an event.

Select a sound.

4. Click on the Windows event to which you want to assign a sound.

5. Click on the .WAV file you want to use.

6. Click OK.

45

Working with System Sounds

In Chapter 23, you learned how to record sounds if your computer has a sound board and a microphone. In this chapter, you learn how to attach those sounds (and other sounds stored in .WAV files) to system events that occur in applications. For example, you can make Windows play some wild sound whenever it starts up, or have it say "Good-bye" whenever you exit.

Basic Survival

Can You Use System Sounds?

For Windows to make sounds, your computer needs a sound board or a PC speaker driver (a program that enables your computer's tiny speaker to make more interesting sounds). To find out if your computer has what it takes to play sounds, here's what you do:

1. Open the Main group window.

2. Double-click on the Control Panel ▣ Control Panel. The Control Panel window appears.

3. Double-click on the Sound icon ♫ Sound. The Sound dialog box appears. If the list of sounds and events are dimmed, Windows cannot play sounds.

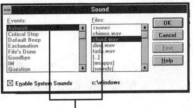

If these items are dimmed, Windows can't make sounds.

4. Click on the Cancel button.

Attaching a Sound to an Event

An inexpensive way to enable your computer to make sounds is to install a PC speaker driver. Skip ahead to the section called "Installing a PC Speaker Driver" for details.

If your computer makes sounds in Windows, you can assign sounds to certain events in Windows, such as Windows startup and Windows exit. The sounds attached to other events vary depending on the Windows application you're using.

What kinds of sounds can you attach to an event? Here's a list:

- Sounds that you recorded in Chapter 23. For example, your voice, bits of music, your dog barking, or other unusual sounds.

- Boring sound files that came with Windows. These include CHIMES.WAV, CHORD.WAV, DING.WAV, and TADA.WAV, all in the \WINDOWS directory.

- Sound files from friends or other users. The files must have the extension .WAV. You can get share sound files at user groups or download (copy) them from online services.

To attach a sound to an event, Here's what you do:

1. Open the Main group window, and double-click on the Control Panel icon ⌨ Control Panel .

2. Double-click on the Sound icon 🔊 Sound . The **Sound** dialog box appears.

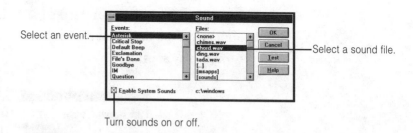

Select an event. / Select a sound file. / Turn sounds on or off.

Click on a file and select Test to hear it

3. In the Events list, click on the Windows event to which you want to assign a sound.

4. In the Files list, change to the drive and directory that contains the sound file you want to attach to the event.

5. Click on the name of the .WAV file you want to use.

6. Click on the OK button.

At the bottom of the Sound dialog box is the Enable System Sounds option. Initially, this is on (has an **X** in the check box). If you get tired of hearing sounds, you can turn off *all* sounds (except Windows Start and Exit) by clicking on this option. Click on it again to turn on the sounds.

Beyond Survival

Installing a PC Speaker Driver

If you don't have a sound board, you can get a program called a *speaker driver* that can make your computer's speaker play .WAV files. Where do you get one? Check with a local computer user group, ask your friends if their computers make sounds in Windows, or (if you have an online service, such as CompuServe or America Online), *download* (copy) the speaker driver from the service. Once you have the file you need, perform the following steps to install it:

1. Open the Main group window, and double-click on the Control Panel icon 🖥️ Control Panel .

Steps similar To installing a sound board

2. Double-click on the Drivers icon 🔊 Drivers . The Drivers dialog box appears, showing a list of installed drivers.

Check the list for a PC Speaker Driver.

3. Check the list for a driver called PC Speaker Driver (or a similar name). If you see the driver, it is already installed. You may not hear the sounds for some other reason; for example, Enable System Sounds in the Sounds dialog box may be turned off.

4. If no speaker driver is listed, click on the Add button. The Add dialog box appears.

These options install a
sound driver for a popular —
sound board.

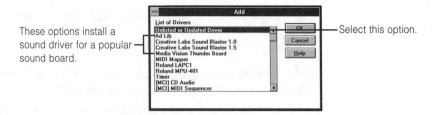

Select this option.

5. Click on Unlisted or Updated Driver, and click on OK. The Install
Driver dialog box appears.

6. If driver is on a floppy disk, insert the disk, and close the drive
door (if necessary).

7. To specify the location of the driver, do one of the following:

- Type a path to the drive and directory that contains the file.

- Click on the Browse button, and use the Browse dialog box
  to select the drive and directory (you won't select a file,
  just select the drive and directory). Click on the OK button
  to return to the Install Driver dialog box.

8. Click on the OK button. The Add Unlisted or Updated Driver
dialog box appears, showing a list of drivers in the selected drive
and directory.

Driver on the specified drive —

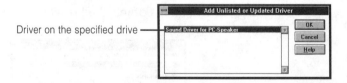

9. Click on the desired driver, and then click on OK. Windows
installs the driver, and instructs you to restart Windows to activate
the driver.

10. Follow the on-screen instructions.

Changing the Speaker Driver Setup

Most PC speaker drivers have a dialog box that lets you control the
speed, volume, and time limit for sounds. If your sounds are too soft,
or if you can play only three seconds of a 60-second recording, check
the speaker driver setup. Here's how you do it:

PC driver controls all sounds

Sound Recorder controls volume for ONE sound

1. Open the Main group window, and double-click on the Control Panel icon ![Control Panel].

2. Double-click on the Drivers icon ![Drivers]. The Drivers dialog box appears, showing a list of installed drivers.

3. Click on the PC Speaker Driver, and then click on the Setup button. A dialog box appears, allowing you to adjust the settings.

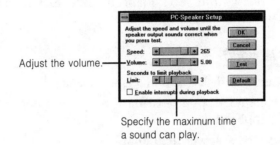

Adjust the volume.

Specify the maximum time a sound can play.

4. Adjust the settings as desired, and then click on the OK button. You are returned to the Drivers dialog box.

5. Click on the Close button.

Cheat Sheet

Is Windows in 386 Enhanced Mode?

- This chapter requires that Windows run in 386 Enhanced mode.
- Enhanced mode needs 2 megabytes of RAM.
- To find out which mode Windows is in: open the Program Manager Help menu, and select About Program Manager.
- To force Windows into 386 Enhanced mode: exit, then start Windows with the **WIN /3** command.

What Is Virtual Memory?

- Virtual memory is disk space that is used as RAM.
- With more memory (RAM + virtual), your computer can run more and bigger applications.
- Virtual memory is slower than RAM.

Changing the Amount of Virtual Memory

1. Open the Main group window.
2. Double-click on the Control Panel icon
3. Double-click on the 386 Enhanced icon
4. Click on the Virtual Memory button.
5. Click on the Change button.
6. Type the desired amount of virtual memory in the New Size text box.
7. Click OK, then click on Yes.
8. Click OK.

46

Changing the 386 Enhanced Settings

In 386 Enhanced mode, Windows can perform some operations that must be managed carefully to ensure that all applications get the system resources they need. In this chapter, you learn how to enter your preferences for the following system resources:

Virtual memory = disk space used as RAM

Virtual memory   You can control how much disk space Windows will use for virtual memory (disk space that is used as memory).

Hardware devices   If a Windows application and a non-Windows application try to use a serial printer or modem at the same time, communications can get garbled. You can tell Windows how to manage these conflicts.

Processor time   When running two or more applications, you can tell Windows how much relative processor time to give to the various applications—those you are using, and those running in the background.

Basic Survival

Is Windows in Enhanced Mode?

No 386 Enhanced icon in Control Panel = Standard mode

Before you enter 386 Enhanced settings, make sure Windows is running in Enhanced mode. Here's how:

1. Switch to the Program Manager.

2. Open the Help menu.

3. Select About Program Manager. The About Program Manager dialog box appears, indicating the current mode.

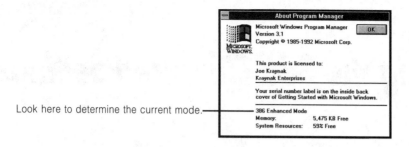

Look here to determine the current mode.

4. Click on the OK button.

WIN /3
runs
Windows in
Enhanced
mode

Windows starts in the optimum mode for your system. If your system has at least two megabytes of RAM, Windows should start in Enhanced mode. If it doesn't, you should buy and install more RAM, or upgrade your version of DOS to 6.0 or 6.2 and use the MEMMAKER command to wring some more RAM out of your system. (See Chapter 56, "Coping with Out of Memory Error Messages" for more ideas.) You might also try exiting Windows and restarting it with the WIN /3 command, which forces Windows to run in Enhanced mode.

Giving Your System More (Virtual) Memory

In 386 Enhanced mode, Windows can use disk space as memory (*virtual memory*). Windows creates a *swap file* on the disk, and then swaps data back and forth between RAM and the swap file as you work. The extra "memory" allows you to run more applications, and more complex applications. The downside is that virtual memory is slower than RAM, because of all the swapping required. However, if you need more memory, slow memory is better than no memory.

Do disk
maintenance
first

Before you try setting up a swap file to use as virtual memory, you may want to clean up your hard disk (as explained in Chapter 51, "Uncluttering Your Disk"), and perform some disk maintenance (as explained in Chapter 52, "Speeding Up Windows"). You'll want to do three things: remove unnecessary files, save or delete misplaced file parts, and cram all your files together so Windows has a clean area on disk to create a swap file. You can proceed without doing all this, but you'll have a faster swap file if you prepare in advance.

When you're ready to increase or decrease the amount of virtual memory, here's what you do:

1. Open the Main group window.

274

2. Double-click on the Control Panel icon  . The Control Panel window appears.

3. Double-click on the 386 Enhanced icon . The 386 Enhanced dialog box appears. (Don't worry about all those options. They're explained later in this chapter.)

Don't worry about these options. ⎯

Click here.

1024 =
1 megabyte

4. Click on the Virtual Memory button. The Virtual Memory dialog box appears, showing the drive used for the swap file and the file's size and type.

5. Click on the Change button. A New Settings area appears in the dialog box, allowing you to specify a new drive, and a swap file size and type.

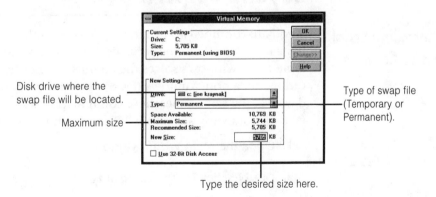

Disk drive where the swap file will be located.

Maximum size

Type of swap file (Temporary or Permanent).

Type the desired size here.

6. (Optional) Open the Drive drop-down list, and select the letter of the drive you want to use for the swap file. For example, if you have a drive that has more free disk space, select that drive.

7. (Optional) Open the Type drop-down list, and select one of the following options:

Temporary is the safest option. Windows uses any free space on the disk for swap files. However, a temporary swap file can be stored in several places on the disk, making it slower than a permanent swap file.

Permanent is better if disk space is no issue.

Permanent creates a swap file using the largest block of free space on the selected drive. Because the swap file is in one location on the disk, Windows can read and write to it more quickly. However, if you don't have a large block of free space on your hard disk, Windows won't let you create a permanent file.

8. In the New Size text box, type the desired size for the swap file. This number must be less than or equal to the Maximum Size listed.

9. Click on the OK button. A confirmation message appears, asking if you're sure you want to make these changes.

10. Click on the Yes button. This returns you to the 386 Enhanced dialog box.

11. Click on the OK button.

Beyond Survival

Controlling Serial Device Conflicts

If you are running two or more Windows applications, and the applications try to use the same serial device (serial printer or modem) at the same time, Windows solves the conflict. However, if a Windows application and a non-Windows (DOS) application try to use the same device at the same time, there could be problems. To avoid problems, take the following steps to tell Windows how to handle such conflicts:

If default settings work—leave them

1. Open the Main group window.

2. Double-click on the Control Panel icon ![Control Panel icon] Control Panel . The Control Panel window appears.

3. Double-click on the 386 Enhanced icon ![386 Enhanced icon] 386 Enhanced . The 386 Enhanced dialog box appears.

4. In the Device Contention area, select the port to which the device is connected. For example, if you want to enter device-contention settings for your modem, and it is connected to COM2, select COM2.

Specify how you want conflicts resolved.

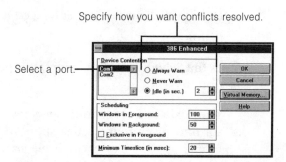

Select a port.

5. Select one of the following options for solving conflicts:

Always Warn tells Windows to display a warning whenever there is a conflict. You then choose which application gets to use the device.

Never Warn tells Windows to ignore any conflicts. Choose this only if you know you will never try to use a device from two or more applications at the same time.

Idle (in sec.) tells Windows that when a conflict occurs, the application currently using the device gets to keep using it. When the application stops using the device for the specified number of seconds, the second application gets control of the device. This is the default setting.

6. Click on the OK button.

Always use
Warn or
Idle, not
Never
Warn.

Managing System Resources

Whenever you're running two or more applications at the same time, Windows allots processor time to all the applications, usually giving more time to the application that you are currently using. For example, if you are printing a document, and then you start typing in another application (while still printing), Windows allots some processor time to the printing (background) application, and more time to the application you are typing in (foreground application). To control the relative amounts of processor time allotted to foreground and background applications, here's what you do:

1. Open the Main group window.

2. Double-click on the Control Panel icon 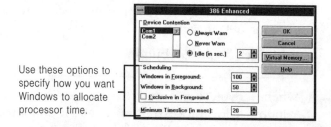. The Control Panel window appears.

3. Double-click on the 386 Enhanced icon . The 386 Enhanced dialog box appears.

4. In the Scheduling area, enter your preferences for the following options:

Windows in Foreground specifies the relative amount of processor time given to the active application. You can type an entry from 1 to 10000, or click on the arrow buttons to increase or decrease the setting. These numbers represent the number of *time slices* allocated to an application.

Windows in Background specifies the relative amount of processor time given to Windows applications running in the background, and to non-Windows applications running in the foreground. You can type an entry from 1 to 10000, or click on the arrow buttons to increase or decrease the setting.

Exclusive in Foreground allows you to prevent any non-Windows applications from running when a Windows application is running in the foreground. The Windows application gets all the processor time.

Use these options to specify how you want Windows to allocate processor time.

5. In the Minimum Timeslice text box, type the number of milliseconds an application can be inactive before Windows lets another application have control of the processor. Here are your options:

Enter a smaller number. Windows switches from one application to another very quickly, allowing all applications to get a little done each time. All applications get their work done in a smooth fashion, but the switching strains the system resources.

Enter a larger number. Windows switches between applications slowly, but each application does more in the time it has. For example, an application that is printing will print more before Windows turns control of the processor over to another application. The switching becomes more apparent, but overall, the work gets done in less time.

For DOS
apps, edit
PIF.

6. Click on the OK button.

The system resource settings you enter using the 386 Enhanced option will affect Windows applications. To change system resource settings for a specific DOS application, edit the application's PIF as explained in Chapter 50, "Editing PIFs for Stubborn DOS Applications."

Cheat Sheet

Adding a Printer

1. Open the Main group window.
2. Double-click on the Control Panel icon Control Panel.
3. Double-click on the Printers icon Printers.
4. Click on the Add button.
5. Click on the name of the printer you want to add in the List of Printers.
6. Click on the Install button.
7. Insert the requested Windows disk in the drive.
8. Click OK.

Selecting a Default Printer

1. Open the Main group window.
2. Double-click on the Control Panel icon Control Panel.
3. Double-click on the Printers icon Printers.
4. Click on the printer in the Installed Printers list.
5. Click on the Set As Default Printer button.
6. Click on Close.

Changing the Printer Settings

1. Select the printer you want to use.
2. Click on the Setup button.
3. Enter the desired settings.
4. Click OK.

47

Setting Up and Selecting a Printer

Printer driver : file That Tells Windows how To Talk To printer

Before Windows, each application came with its own *printer driver*, a file that tells the application how to communicate with the printer. For each application, you had to install a new printer driver and play with it until you got your printer working. With Windows, you install the printer driver only once. All Windows applications then use the Windows printer driver to control the printer. In this chapter, you learn how to install a printer driver in Windows and how to change the settings for your printer.

Basic Survival

Adding a Printer

When you installed Windows, the installation program prompted you to select a printer. If you selected a printer, you can probably skip this section. However, if you did not select a printer (or if you have since obtained a new printer), you can perform the following steps to add a printer to Windows:

1. Open the Main group window.

2. Double-click on the Control Panel icon . The Control Panel window appears.

3. Double-click on the Printers icon . The Printers dialog box appears, indicating the current default printer and any additional printers you installed.

4. Click on the Add button. A list of available printer drivers appears. These are the drivers that came on the disks you used to install Windows. If your driver is not on the list, skip to the section called "Installing an Unlisted Printer."

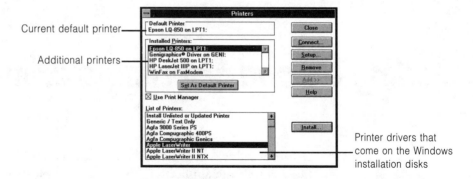

Current default printer —

Additional printers —

Printer drivers that come on the Windows installation disks

Drivers copied To \WINDOWS \SYSTEM

5. In the List of Printers list, click on the name of the printer you want to add.

6. Click on the Install button. A dialog box appears, telling you to insert one of the Windows installation disks in one of the floppy drives.

7. Insert the requested Windows disk in the drive.

8. Click on the OK button. Windows copies the printer driver for the selected printer from the disk to the \WINDOWS\SYSTEM directory. The printer now appears in the Installed Printers list.

9. To use this printer, click on the Set As Default Printer button.

10. Click on the Close button.

Selecting a Default Printer

If you use two or more printers, say a color and a black-and-white printer, you can select which printer you want to use as the default printer by doing the following:

1. Open the Main group window.

2. Double-click on the Control Panel icon

3. Double-click on the Printers icon . The Printers dialog box appears, showing a list of the installed printers.

4. Click on the printer you want to use as the default printer. This printer will be used by most applications unless you specify in that application to use a different installed printer.

5. Click on the Set As Default Printer button. The name of the selected printer appears in the Default Printer box.

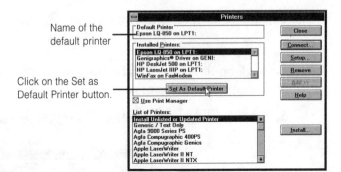

Name of the default printer

Click on the Set as Default Printer button.

In Application, select File Print Setup

6. Click on the Close button.

Most Windows applications contain a Print Setup option, usually on the File menu or as a button in the dialog box that appears when you try to print a document. If you select this option, you usually get a dialog box that lets you select the default printer or a specific printer for this work session. This is an easy way to select a specific printer without changing the default.

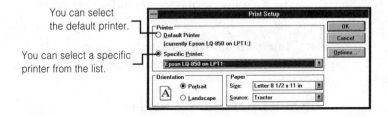

You can select the default printer.

You can select a specific printer from the list.

Beyond Survival

Selecting a Printer Port

Whenever you install a printer, Windows assumes the printer is connected to parallel printer port (LPT1). If your printer is connected to a different parallel port or to a serial port (COM2 for example), you must specify the port, so Windows will know where to send printing data. To select a port, here's what you do:

1. Open the Main group window.

2. Double-click on the Control Panel icon 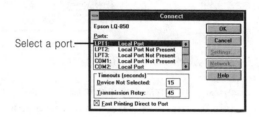. The Control Panel window appears.

3. Double-click on the Printers icon ![Printers]. The Printers dialog box appears.

4. Click on the printer in the Installed Printers list, whose port assignment you want to change.

5. Click on the Connect button. The Connect dialog box appears.

PorT :
OuTleT on
sysTem uniT

Select a port.

```
┌─────────────────────────────────────────────┐
│ ═  │            Connect                       │
├─────────────────────────────────────────────┤
│ Epson LQ-850                    ┌──────────┐ │
│ Ports:                          │    OK    │ │
│ │LPT1:   Local Port         │▲  ├──────────┤ │
│ │LPT2:   Local Port Not Present│ │  Cancel  │ │
│ │LPT3:   Local Port Not Present│ ├──────────┤ │
│ │COM1:   Local Port Not Present│ │ Settings…│ │
│ │COM2:   Local Port         │▼  ├──────────┤ │
│ ┌─ Timeouts (seconds) ──────┐    │ Network  │ │
│ │ Device Not Selected:  │15│    ├──────────┤ │
│ │ Transmission Retry:   │45│    │   Help   │ │
│ └───────────────────────────┘    └──────────┘ │
│ ⊠ Fast Printing Direct to Port                │
└─────────────────────────────────────────────┘
```

MosT
prinTers
connecT To
parallel porT

6. Click on the port that the printer is connected to. If you're not sure, try various ports until you get one that works.

7. Click on the OK button. The Installed Printers list is updated to show the new port assignment for this printer.

Changing the Printer Settings

Most printers are initially set up to print on 8.5-by-11-inch paper, in portrait orientation, at a certain resolution. To change these settings, here's what you do:

1. Open the Main group window.

2. Double-click on the Control Panel icon ![Control Panel].

3. Double-click on the Printers icon ![Printers].

4. Select the printer whose settings you want to change.

5. Click on the Setup button. The setup dialog box for the selected printer appears.

PrinTer
seTTings =
paper size,
prinT
qualiTy,
graphics
resoluTion

In
application,
selecT File
PrinTer
SeTup

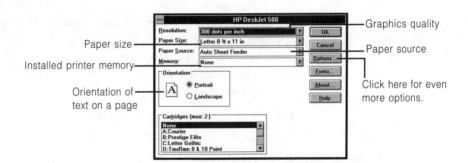

Graphics quality

Paper size

Paper source

Installed printer memory

Click here for even
more options.

Orientation of
text on a page

6. Open the Resolution drop-down list, and select the desired print quality for pictures. Print quality is measured in dots per inch. The more dots, the higher the quality, but it takes longer to print. This does not affect text quality unless you choose to print text as graphics.

7. Open the Paper Size drop-down list, and select the desired paper or envelope size you want to print on.

8. Open the Paper Source drop-down list, and select the device that you intend to use to feed paper into the printer. For example, some printers come with two paper trays that you can use for different size or color papers.

DonT
change
Memory
unless you
insTalled
memory on
your prinTer.

9. If a Memory drop-down list is visible, you can open it and select the amount of memory installed in the printer. Some printers let you plug in a cartridge (or add memory chips) to increase the amount of information the printer can process.

10. In the Orientation area, select one of the following options:

Portrait prints text across the short side of the page, as in a personal or business letter.

Landscape prints text across the longer side of a page so the page is wider than it is tall. This is useful for wide spreadsheets and graphics.

11. If you plugged extra font cartridges into your printer, click on the cartridge in the Cartridges list. You can purchase font cartridges for most printers, and plug them into a socket on the printer.

12. To further adjust the print quality, click on the Options button, and enter the following preferences:

Dithering Select None for black-and-white graphics (no gray shading), Coarse if you selected a resolution of 300 dots per inch or more, Fine if you selected a resolution of 200 dots per inch or less, or Line Art if you want clearly defined lines to appear between shaded areas.

Intensity Drag the button in the Intensity Control bar to control the lightness or darkness of graphic images.

Print Quality Open the drop-down list, and select the desired print quality for text. Letter Quality is high, but somewhat slower, and consumes more ink. Draft Quality is low, but faster, and consumes less ink.

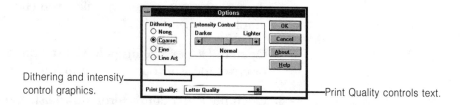

Dithering and intensity control graphics.

Print Quality controls text.

13. Click on the OK button. You are returned to the setup dialog box for your printer.

14. Click on the OK button to save your changes.

Installing an Unlisted Printer

If your printer did not appear on the list of printers, you have several options:

- Select a printer that is like the one you have. For example, if an older model of the brand of your printer is listed, select the older model. You may not be able to use the advanced features of the new model.

- Select Generic/Text Only to print plain text. You won't be able to print fancy fonts or enhancements.

- Call the printer manufacturer or Microsoft Corporation, and ask them to send you a Windows printer driver for your printer.

Once you have the printer driver you need, take the following steps to install it:

1. With the list of available printers displayed, double-click on the Unlisted or Updated Driver option.

Extra drivers might be in WINDOWS \SYSTEM.

2. Insert the disk that contains the driver into the disk drive, and close the door (if necessary). (If the driver file is in a directory on your hard disk, you don't have to insert it on a floppy.)

3. Type a path to the drive and directory where the printer driver files are stored. For example, if the files are on a disk in drive A, type **A:**. If the files are in the WINDOWS\SYSTEM directory on drive C, type **C:\WINDOWS\SYSTEM**.

Type a path to the drive and directory that contain the printer driver files.

4. Click on the OK button. Windows displays a list of drivers that are on the disk.

5. Click on the driver you want to install, and then click on the OK button. Windows copies the printer driver for the selected printer from the disk to the \WINDOWS\SYSTEM directory. The printer now appears in the Installed Printers list.

Removing a Printer Driver

If you no longer use a particular printer driver, you can remove it from disk (and from your list of installed printers) by performing the following steps:

1. Open the Main group window.

2. Double-click on the Control Panel icon .

3. Double-click on the Printers icon .

4. In the Installed Printers list, click on the printer you want to remove.

5. Click on the Remove button. A message appears asking for your confirmation.

6. Click on the Yes button.

7. Click on the Close button.

Cheat Sheet

What Is Print Manager?

- Print Manager allows you to print documents in the background while you work in other Windows applications.
- DOS applications running from Windows do not use Print Manager.

Turning On Print Manager

1. Open the Main group window.
2. Double-click on the Control Panel icon .
3. Double-click on the Printers icon .
4. Place an X in the Use Print Manager check box.
5. Click on Close.

Pausing and Resuming a Print Job

1. Press Ctrl+Esc.
2. Click on Print Manager.
3. Click on the Switch To button.
4. Click on the printer you want to pause.
5. Click on the Pause button.
6. To resume printing, click on the Resume button.

Cancelling a Print Job

1. Press Ctrl+Esc.
2. Click on Print Manager.
3. Click on the Switch To button.
4. Click on the print job you want to cancel.
5. Click on the Delete button.
6. Click OK.

48

Using the Windows Print Manager

The Windows Print Manager allows you to print documents (from Windows applications) in the background while you are working in other applications. Print Manager acts as a "middle man" standing between your application and your printer. When you print a document from a Windows application, Print Manager intercepts it, and then feeds the document to the printer. In this chapter, you learn how to use Print Manager to pause, resume, or cancel your print jobs.

Basic Survival

Turning on Print Manager

Low on memory? Don't use Print Manager!

Chances are, Print Manager is already on. Whenever you select the File Print command in a Windows application, the file is sent to Print Manager and then sent on to your printer. If Print Manager is not on, the application sends the document directly to the printer, and you have to wait until the printing process is done before you can do anything else or use other applications. Take the following steps to see if Print Manager is on and to turn it on or off:

1. Open the Main group window.

2. Double-click on the Control Panel icon .

3. Double-click on the Printers icon . The Printers dialog box appears. If there's an X in the Use Print Manager check box, Print Manager is on.

Print Manager is on. ———

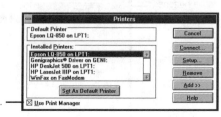

4. If Print Manager is on and you want it off, or vice versa, click on the Use Print Manager option to clear or remove the X in the check box.

5. Click on the Close or Cancel button.

Pausing and Resuming Printing

If you selected to use the Print Manager, it runs whenever you print a document from a Windows application. As you print documents, they are added to a *queue* (a list) in Print Manager. The Print Manager appears as an application icon at the bottom of the screen (it may be hidden by the Program Manager window or an application window). If you want to view the queue—or pause, resume, or cancel print jobs in the queue—you have to maximize the Print Manager or switch to it. The following steps explain how to switch to the Print Manager and pause a print job:

Minimize all windows To see Print Manager icon

1. Press Ctrl+Esc. The Task List appears, displaying the names of the applications you are running.

2. Click on Print Manager; it will then appear highlighted.

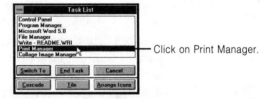

Click on Print Manager.

Double-click on Print Manager icon

3. Click on the Switch To button. The Print Manager window appears, showing a list of installed printers and a list of the documents being printed on each printer.

4. Click on the printer you want to pause. The printer appears highlighted.

Click on the Pause buttons.
Select the printer you want to pause.

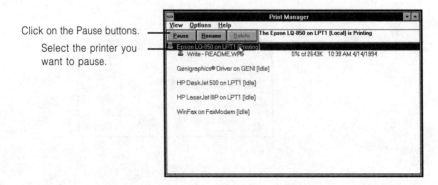

5. Click on the Pause button. A hand appears to the left of the printer, and [Paused] appears after it. The printer stops printing. (If your printer has lots of memory, it may continue to print for some time after you pause the printer.)

6. To resume printing, click on the Resume button. Print Manager continues sending information to your printer.

FasT printing = OpTions High Priority

You can use the Pause/Resume feature to print when you're at lunch or taking a break. Before you start printing, double-click on the Print Manager icon in the Main group window. Click on the printer you want to use, and then click on the Pause button. Minimize the Print Manager window, and then print your documents as you normally would. As you print, the documents are added to the print queue, but are not printed. Before you leave for lunch, go to Print Manager, and click on the Resume button. (Make sure you have enough paper loaded in the printer.)

Beyond Survival

Cancelling a Print Job

Sometimes, you may start printing an application by mistake, or something will get fouled up at the printer, and it will start printing strange text and symbols. If that happens, you'll want to cancel the print job and start over. Here's how you do it:

1. Press Ctrl+Esc. The Task List dialog box appears, displaying a list of the currently running applications.

2. Click on Print Manager.

Cancel all printing = View Exit

3. Click on the Switch To button. The Print Manager window appears.

4. Click on the print job you want to cancel. The print job appears highlighted. (You can select only one at a time.)

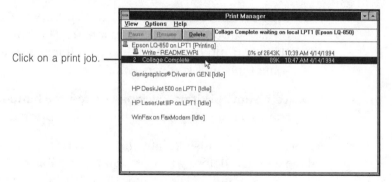

Click on a print job. ─

5. Click on the Delete button. Print Manager displays a message, asking you to confirm the deletion.

6. Click on the OK button. The selected print job is deleted from the queue.

Changing the Order of Print Jobs

If you print more than one document, the documents are added to the print queue in the order in which they were printed. You can rearrange the items in the list to print them in a different order. Here's what you do:

1. Double-click on the Print Manager application icon, if it is visible. (If you can't see it, press Ctrl+Esc, select it from the Task List, and click on Switch To.)

Pause before rearranging queue

2. Move the mouse pointer over the document whose position you want to change.

3. Hold down the mouse button while dragging the document to its new position in the queue.

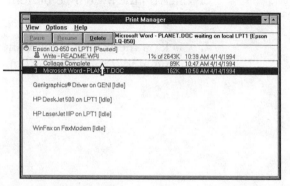

Drag a document up to print it sooner, or down to print it later. ─

4. Release the mouse button.

PART 6

Tricks and Traps

Are you starting to feel like a Windows expert yet? If so, this section contains some more advanced information that can help you solve problems and optimize Windows. You learn how to solve printer and modem problems, prevent conflicts between applications, and make Windows run faster (as well as more reliably). In addition, you learn some cool Windows tricks to wow your friends. Here's what you get:

- Reading and Editing System Files
- Editing PIFs for Stubborn DOS Applications
- Uncluttering Your Disk
- Speeding Up Windows
- Dealing with General Protection Faults
- Getting Your Mouse to Work in a DOS Window
- Solving Printer Problems
- Coping with "Out of Memory" Messages
- Ten Cool Tricks

Cheat Sheet

What Are System Files?

- System files include AUTOEXEC.BAT, CONFIG.SYS, SYSTEM.INI, and WIN.INI.
- AUTOEXEC.BAT contains commands that run when your computer starts; some of these can run the mouse driver and Windows.
- CONFIG.SYS has commands to run drivers for memory and hardware.
- SYSTEM.INI is like a CONFIG.SYS for Windows. When Windows starts, it reads this file and WIN.INI.
- WIN.INI is like an AUTOEXEC.BAT for Windows, containing information about colors, backgrounds, file associations, and more.

Making an Icon for the System Configuration Editor

1. Display the Program Manager window.
2. Open the group window in which you want the icon placed.
3. Open the Program Manager's File menu, and select New.
4. Click OK.
5. Type System Editor in the Description text box.
6. Tab to the Command Line text box.
7. Type **c:\windows\system\sysedit.exe**.
8. Press Enter.

Editing a System File

1. Double-click on the System Editor icon .
2. Click on the title bar for the file you want to edit.
3. Type your changes.
4. Open the File menu, and select Save.

49

Reading and Editing System Files

System files control overall computer operations.

Your computer has two system files (AUTOEXEC.BAT and CONFIG.SYS) that contain commands which are executed automatically whenever you start (boot) the computer. In addition, Windows has two files (SYSTEM.INI and WIN.INI) that Windows reads whenever you start Windows. All four files contain commands that tell your system how to run. In this chapter, you learn how to view the contents of these files, and how to edit the files. You also learn about some of the common instructions contained in these files.

Basic Survival

What Are System Files?

System files are files that your computer reads automatically to determine how to operate. Each system file contains commands and instructions that tell your computer, DOS, and Windows what to do on startup. In this chapter, you learn how to read and edit the following four system files:

- AUTOEXEC.BAT contains commands that run when you start your computer. Some of these may run the mouse driver; some may run Windows automatically. Others may tell the computer where to look for files, and how to display the DOS prompt.

- CONFIG.SYS has commands for running drivers that control the computer's memory and other hardware.

- SYSTEM.INI is like a CONFIG.SYS file for Windows. It contains the command for starting the Program Manager, and it loads the drivers for the keyboard, mouse, and monitor. It also contains settings you may have entered for options such as the Windows swap file. When it starts, Windows reads this file and WIN.INI.

- WIN.INI is sort of like the AUTOEXEC.BAT file for Windows. WIN.INI contains information about the Windows colors and backgrounds file associations, fonts, and much more.

You can edit these files to make your computer, or Windows, behave the way you want it to. For example, you add a command to the AUTOEXEC.BAT file to have Windows run automatically when you start your computer. Or, you can edit SYSTEM.INI so the File Manager runs instead of the Program Manager. In addition, you can delete several instructions or blank lines from WIN.INI to make your system run faster, as explained in Chapter 52, "Speeding Up Windows."

Playing It Safe

Copy files before editing

Before you edit *any* system file, make a copy of it (as explained in Chapter 31, "Copying and Moving Files and Directories"). Give the copy the same name, but a different file extension. For example, make a copy of AUTOEXEC.BAT called AUTOEXEC.OLD. If you run into problems after editing a file, you can then delete the edited AUTOEXEC.BAT file and rename the original file using the .BAT extension.

Making an Icon for the System Configuration Editor

Windows comes with an application that lets you edit your system files easily. Trouble is, you won't find the application in any of the group windows. You have to create an icon for it yourself. Here's how:

1. Display the Program Manager window.

2. Open the group window in which you want the icon placed. (The Main or Accessories group window is a good place.) For information, see Chapter 10, "Working with Group Windows."

3. Open the Program Manager's File menu, and select New. The New Program Object dialog box appears with Program Item selected.

4. Click OK. The New Program Item dialog box appears.

5. Type System Editor in the Description text box. This description will appear under the System Configuration Editor's program-item icon.

6. Tab to the Command Line text box.

7. Type **c:\windows\system\sysedit.exe**. If the Windows program files are on a different drive in your computer, replace C with the letter of the drive.

Here's the command that runs the System Configuration Editor.

Type a description of the application.

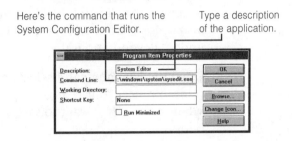

8. Press Enter. Windows creates a program-item icon for the System Configuration Editor, which you can use to start the application.

There's a quicker way to create a program-item icon for the System Configuration Editor. In File Manager, change to the \WINDOWS\SYSTEM directory. Resize or move the File Manager window, so SYSEDIT.EXE and the destination group window or group icon are both visible. Click on SYSEDIT.EXE, and then drag it to the desired group window or group icon. When you release the mouse button, an icon named Sysedit is created in the group window.

Editing a System File

Once you have an icon set up for the System Configuration Editor, editing a file is a snap:

1. Double-click on the System Editor icon 🖹 . The System Configuration Editor starts, and displays all four system files in separate windows.

All four system files are automatically opened.

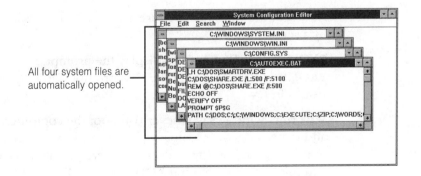

Ctrl + Tab To cycle Through windows

2. Click on the window that contains the system file you want to edit.

3. Type your changes in the file. (Edit the text just as you would in Notepad. See Chapter 20, "Editing Text with the Notepad.") For instructions about editing specific files, skip ahead to the sections under "Beyond Survival."

4. Open the File menu and select Save to save your changes. (If you want to cancel your changes, open the File menu and select Exit. When asked if you want to save your changes, click on the No button.)

Any changes you type in AUTOEXEC.BAT or CONFIG.SYS take effect the next time you boot your computer. Changes to SYSTEM.INI and WIN.INI take effect when you restart Windows.

Beyond Survival

Editing AUTOEXEC.BAT

I'm not going to tell you all the commands that you can possibly add to your AUTOEXEC.BAT file, but here's a list of common commands. Your AUTOEXEC.BAT file may already have several of these commands:

PATH tells your computer where to look for program files. If a drive and directory are in the PATH statement, you don't have to specify a drive or directory when you enter the command to run the program. You simply type the command, and DOS and Windows know where to look. A path command can be up to 127 characters. Here's an example:

PATH C:\;C:\DOS;C:\WINDOWS;D:\;D:\CARMEN

Note that the various drive/directory combinations are separated by a semicolon.

Make sure DOS and WINDOWS directories are on path

PROMPT tells DOS how to display the prompt. For example, **PROMPT PG** results in the **C:>** prompt. **PROMPT NQ** results in **C=**.

WIN runs Windows whenever you boot the computer. You can add switches to the command; for example, you can add a colon to prevent the Windows advertising screen from appearing. If you add this command to your AUTOEXEC.BAT file, add it to the end.

C:\DOS\MOUSE.COM tells DOS to run the mouse driver. Your mouse driver may be on a different drive or directory. Also, your computer may be set up to load the mouse driver from the CONFIG.SYS file instead.

ECHO tells DOS to display or not display the startup commands on-screen. **ECHO ON** displays the messages, and **ECHO OFF** turns them off.

VERIFY ON tells DOS to check data whenever it is written to disk, which takes time. Data-writing errors are rare; usually you need not turn on the verification option. If you do turn it on, you can enter the command **VERIFY OFF** to turn it off.

REM tells DOS to ignore the command. Instead of deleting a command from your AUTOEXEC.BAT file, you can type **REM** before the command to have DOS ignore it. That way, if you mess something up by removing the command, you can delete REM to return your system to normal.

PROMPT command ⎯

PATH command ⎯

REM tells
DOS to ignore ⎯
the command.

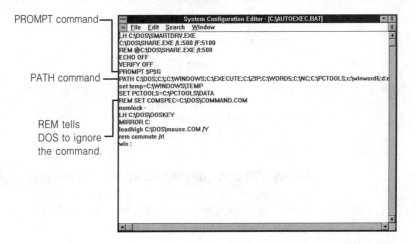

If you have DOS 6, and you run into problems after editing your AUTOEXEC.BAT file, you can step through or bypass the AUTOEXEC.BAT file commands to determine the cause of the problem. When booting, hold down F8 till you hear a beep, and then release the key. Now DOS will ask for your confirmation before executing each command.

To learn more about PATH, PROMPT, ECHO, VERIFY, or REM, go to the DOS prompt and type **HELP** followed by the command you want help with, and press Enter. For example, type **HELP PROMPT** and press Enter.

Editing CONFIG.SYS

The CONFIG.SYS file contains more complex commands than those included in AUTOEXEC.BAT; you shouldn't edit this file unless you really know what you're doing. If you delete a command by mistake, you may disable some of the memory-management drivers that Windows needs to operate. To understand some of the CONFIG.SYS commands, here's a list of the most common ones:

In DOS 5.0 and later, Type HELP and press Enter.

DEVICE tells DOS to load a device driver that controls a particular hardware device. For example, **DEVICE=C:\DOS\HIMEM.SYS** loads a DOS device driver that manages extended memory.

DEVICEHIGH is similar to DEVICE, but it loads drivers into an area of memory that is usually reserved, freeing memory for your applications. This command is available only in DOS 5.0 and later, and must be preceded by the following commands:

DEVICE=C:\DOS\HIMEM.SYS

DOS=HIGH,UMB

DEVICE=C:\DOS\EMM386.EXE NOEMS

If you have DOS 6.0 or later, exit Windows, type **memmaker**, and press Enter to have DOS make all these changes to your CONFIG.SYS file for you.

Set FILES=40

FILES tells DOS how many files it can have open at the same time (for example, FILES=30). If you get a message telling you that you have too many files opened, you may have to increase the number in this command. You probably shouldn't need to go past FILES=50.

BUFFERS tells DOS how many disk buffers to set aside in your computer's memory. DOS reads information from disk into the buffers, where DOS can get the information more quickly (than from disk). This speeds up the overall performance of your computer.

SHELL loads the command processor (COMMAND.COM), the program that interprets the commands you type and executes them.

REM tells DOS to ignore the command. Instead of deleting a command from your CONFIG.SYS file, you can type REM before the command to have DOS ignore it. That way, if you mess something up by removing the command, you can delete REM to return your system to normal.

DEVICE loads hardware device drivers.

FILES tells DOS how many files can be opened at one time.

SHELL tells DOS where COMMAND.COM is located.

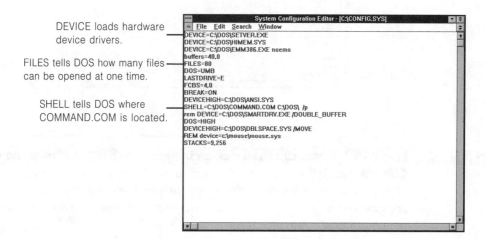

```
System Configuration Editor - [C:\CONFIG.SYS]
 File   Edit   Search   Window
DEVICE=C:\DOS\SETVER.EXE
DEVICE=C:\DOS\HIMEM.SYS
DEVICE=C:\DOS\EMM386.EXE noems
buffers=40,0
FILES=80
DOS=UMB
LASTDRIVE=E
FCBS=4,0
BREAK=ON
DEVICEHIGH=C:\DOS\ANSI.SYS
SHELL=C:\DOS\COMMAND.COM C:\DOS\ /p
rem DEVICE=C:\DOS\SMARTDRV.EXE /DOUBLE_BUFFER
DOS=HIGH
DEVICEHIGH=C:\DOS\DBLSPACE.SYS /MOVE
REM device=c:\mouse\mouse.sys
STACKS=9,256
```

Editing WIN.INI

You can usually avoid editing WIN.INI by using the Windows Control Panel to enter your preferences. For example, when you add or remove fonts (Chapter 41), enter mouse and keyboard settings (Chapter 42), or enter Desktop settings (Chapter 43), the changes are entered in WIN.INI.

However, if you install a Windows application, and then later remove it, it may leave all sorts of garbage in your WIN.INI, garbage that Windows has to read whenever it starts. You may want to go in and remove some of the superfluous items.

Installing applications adds instructions to WIN.INI

If you have some time, poke around in the WIN.INI file. You'll notice that commands are listed in logical groups. For example, Windows commands are in the [Windows] group, fonts are in [Fonts], Desktop settings are in [Desktop], and file associations are in [Extensions]. Most of the commands have descriptive names, but it's a good rule of thumb to not mess with any command you're unsure of.

The [Windows] group contains Windows startup commands.

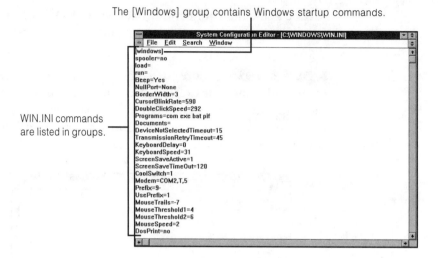

WIN.INI commands are listed in groups.

Editing SYSTEM.INI

Like WIN.INI, you can make some changes to SYSTEM.INI by using the Control Panel. For example, when you change the 386 Enhanced settings (Chapter 46) or add a device driver (Chapter 45), the changes are entered in SYSTEM.INI. Entering your preferences using the Control Panel is the safe way to go.

SHELL= WINFILE.EXE runs File Manager on startup.

There is, however, one command you may want to edit directly. For example, you can edit the SHELL command so it reads **SHELL=WINFILE.EXE** to have the File Manager, rather than Program Manager, start when you start Windows.

For more information about SYSTEM.INI or WIN.INI, open the Main group window, double-click on the Read Me icon, and then use the File Open command to open SYSINI.WRI or WININI.WRI. These are text files that explain many of the settings you'll see in those files.

You can edit SYSTEM.INI to run File Manager instead of Program Manager.

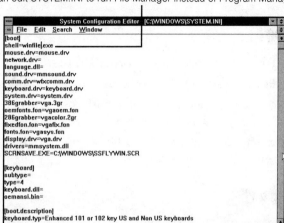

Cheat Sheet

About PIFs

- PIF stands for program information file.
- PIFs are used to help Windows run DOS applications.
- Most DOS applications come with their own PIFs, if the application needs a PIF, but you may have to create a PIF.
- You should create or edit a PIF if you are having trouble running the application under Windows.

Creating a PIF

1. Open the Main group window.

2. Double-click on the PIF Editor icon .

3. Open the Mode menu and select the mode in which you want to run the application.

4. Enter the desired PIF settings.

5. Select File Save.

6. Type a name for the file, and click OK.

Common PIF Settings

Program Filename   The drive, directory, and name of the file that runs the application. For example, c:\word5\word.exe.

Window Title   When the program runs in a window, this text appears in its title bar.

Optional Parameters   If you normally use switches to run the program, type them here. For example, /s or /e.

Video Memory   If you run a program in Text mode, choose Text; in CGA mode, choose Low Graphics; in EGA or VGA mode, choose High Graphics.

Display Usage   Normally, DOS applications are run in Full Screen mode. To start the application in a window, select Windowed.

50

Editing PIFs for Stubborn DOS Applications

In Chapter 9, "Setting Up Applications," you learned how to use Windows Setup to set up a DOS application to run in Windows. Windows Setup creates a PIF (program information file) and program-item icon for a DOS application. If you were successful in setting up a DOS application to run in Windows, and the application is running fine, you can safely skip this chapter. If Windows Setup was unable to create a PIF, however—or if you are having trouble running your DOS application—this chapter can teach you how to create and edit a PIF file to get the application up and running.

Basic Survival

What Is a PIF?

PIF stands for *program information file*. A PIF contains information that tells Windows how to run the application, including how much memory to give it, and what kind of graphics display the application requires. If the information in an application's PIF is incorrect, Windows may not be able to run the application (or run it properly).

Make custom PIFs for problem DOS apps

If you run a DOS application that does not have a customized PIF, Windows uses _DEFAULT.PIF or DOSPRMT.PIF when you try to run the application. These PIFs work for most applications, but if you are running into problems with a specific application, try creating a custom PIF that contains settings specifically for that application.

Your Application May Have a PIF

Before you go through the pain and agony of working with PIFs, check two things. First, check the application's documentation to find out if you can run it in Windows. Some applications (mostly games) cannot run in Windows. For example, Microsoft Flight Simulator requires most of your computer's conventional memory to run effectively; it runs poorly in Windows, if you can get it to run at all.

Second, check if the application already has a PIF. Many newer DOS applications come with their own customized PIFs that can do all the work for you. To check for a PIF, do the following:

1. Click on the application's program-item icon.

2. Open the File menu and select Properties.

Browse for a file

3. Click inside the Command Line text box, and click on the Browse button.

4. Change to the drive and directory that contain the application's files, and look in the File Name list for a file ending in .PIF. If you find one, click on it and skip to step 6.

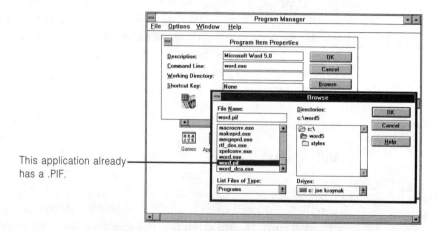

This application already has a .PIF.

5. Change to the \WINDOWS directory, and look for a file that has the same name as the file that runs the application but ends in .PIF. (For example, the file that runs Word 5.0 for DOS is WORD.EXE; its PIF is named WORD.PIF.) If you find the file, click on it.

6. Click on the OK button. You are returned to the Program Item Properties dialog box, and, if you selected a PIF, its name is inserted in the Command Line text box.

7. Click on the OK button.

If you found and selected a PIF, try running the application now. It should run okay, and you can skip the rest of this chapter. If you could not find a PIF, go on to the next section and create a PIF. If you found a PIF, but are still having problems running the application, skip ahead to the section called "Editing a PIF."

Creating a PIF

Once you've discovered that you don't have a PIF, you have no choice but to create one. It's actually fairly simple:

1. Go to the Main group window.

2. Double-click on the PIF Editor icon ⬚ PIF Editor . The PIF Editor starts and displays its default settings.

Usually don't change modes

3. Open the Mode menu and select the mode in which you want to run the application: Standard or 386 Enhanced. The currently displayed mode is usually the one you want. However, if you plan on running Windows in a different mode whenever you run this application, select the desired mode. (To learn more about modes, refer to Chapter 46.)

4. Enter the required information in the following text boxes:

Program Filename   Type the drive, directory, and name of the file that runs the application. For example, c:\word5\word.exe. The file that runs the program will end in .BAT, .EXE, or .COM.

Window Title   Type the text that you want to appear in the application window's title bar. If you leave this blank, the Program Filename entry will appear in the title bar.

Optional Parameters: Type ? for a Windows prompt

Optional Parameters   If you normally use switches to run the program, type them here. For example, in WordPerfect 5.1, you can use an /M *macroname* switch after the WP command to run a macro when you start WordPerfect. If you type a file name, that file will be opened whenever you run the program.

Start-up Directory   If an application needs access to files in a certain directory in order to run, type a path to the drive and directory here. Usually this is the drive and directory that contain the application's program files.

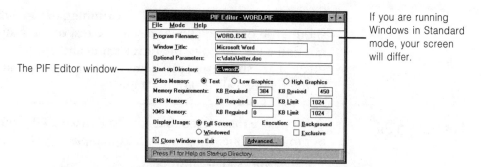

The PIF Editor window—

If you are running Windows in Standard mode, your screen will differ.

5. Enter your PIF settings for the mode you selected. If you selected 386 Enhanced, skip ahead to the section called "Entering PIF Settings for 386 Enhanced Mode." If you selected Standard mode, skip ahead to the section called "Entering PIF Settings for Standard Mode."

6. Open the File menu and select Save.

7. Type a name for the file, and click on OK.

8. Open the File menu and select Exit.

Beyond Survival

Editing a PIF

To edit a PIF, you simply open the PIF in the PIF Editor, and then enter your changes. Here's what you do:

1. Go to the Main group window.

2. Double-click on the PIF Editor icon ![PIF Editor icon] PIF Editor . The PIF Editor starts and displays its default settings.

3. Open the File menu and select Open. The Open dialog box appears, prompting you to select a PIF.

4. Change to the drive and directory that contain the PIF you want to edit. (This is usually the directory that contains the application's program files, or the \WINDOWS directory.)

5. Click on the PIF you want to edit in the File Name list.

6. Click on the OK button. The PIF is opened, and its settings appear.

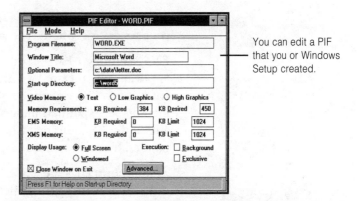

You can edit a PIF that you or Windows Setup created.

Remember To save changes!

7. Open the Mode menu and select the mode for which you want to edit the settings: Standard or 386 Enhanced. (To learn more about modes, refer to Chapter 46.)

8. Change any settings, as desired. If you selected 386 Enhanced, skip ahead to the section called "Entering PIF Settings for 386 Enhanced Mode." If you selected Standard mode, skip ahead to the section called "Entering PIF Settings for Standard Mode."

9. Open the File menu and select Save. The PIF Editor saves your changes.

10. Open the File menu and select Exit.

Entering PIF Settings for 386 Enhanced Mode

If you plan on running this application when you are running Windows in 386 Enhanced mode, you should enter PIF settings for that mode. With the PIF Editor displayed, enter the following settings:

Video Memory Check the application's documentation. If the application runs in Text mode, choose Text; in CGA mode, choose Low Graphics; in EGA or VGA mode, choose High Graphics.

Memory Requirements If the application specifies that it needs a minimum amount of RAM, enter the amount in the KB Required text box. This tells Windows not to run the application if that amount of memory is unavailable. In the KB Desired text box, enter the maximum amount of RAM the application can use. And entry of –1 gives the application all the memory that's available up to 640K. (Note: When setting memory requirements, don't use the RAM specified in the "system requirements" printed on the application's package. This number specifies the least amount of RAM your system must have. The application itself requires less RAM.)

EMS Memory   EMS stands for Expanded Memory System. If the application you want to run requires expanded memory, Windows (running in 386 Enhanced Mode) can use your system's extended memory as expanded memory. Leave the KB Required setting at 0, and in the KB Limit text box, type the maximum amount of Expanded memory you want to make available to this application.

XMS Memory Usage   XMS stands for eXtended Memory Specification. Very few DOS applications use extended memory, so you can usually leave these settings alone.

Display Usage   Choose Full Screen if you want the application to look as it does when you run it at the DOS prompt. Choose Windowed to run the application in a window.

Execution   Select Background if you want this application to continue to perform operations (such as printing or telecommunications) while you work in other programs. Select Exclusive if you want to suspend the operations of all other applications while you use this one. Exclusive gives this application more processor time and system resources when you are using it.

Close Window on Exit   If you have an application that runs and then quits itself, you may want to clear the X in this check box so the window will remain open when the application is finished. This allows you to see the application's output.

The Advanced button at the bottom of the dialog box allows you to enter additional settings. If you do not wish to enter advanced settings, Open the File menu and select Save to save your current settings.

[handwritten marginal note: Alt + Enter To switch from full screen To Window view]

Entering PIF Settings for Standard Mode

If you have a 386 computer with at least two megabytes of RAM, and you want to run DOS applications, you should run Windows in 386 Enhanced mode—and use the 386 Enhanced settings in your PIFs, as explained in the previous section. However, if you have a 286 computer (or a 386 with less than two megabytes of RAM), you should use the Standard mode settings for your PIFs. With the PIF Editor displayed, enter the following settings:

Video Mode   Choose Text if the application does not display graphics, and if you work in only one window in the application. Otherwise, choose Graphics Multiple Text.

Memory Requirements   In the KB Required text box, type the least amount of RAM the application needs to run. Check your application's documentation, but don't go by what is listed as system requirements. The system requirements number is usually too high.

XMS Memory   XMS stands for eXtended Memory Specification. Very few DOS applications use extended memory, so you can usually leave these settings alone. However, if you do have a DOS program (such as Lotus 1-2-3 version 3.1) that uses extended memory, you can enter settings here. Leave the KB Required setting at 0. In the KB Limit text box, type the maximum amount of extended memory you want this application to use. By limiting the amount of extended memory, you ensure that some is available for your other applications. An entry of –1 gives all available extended memory to this application.

Use 386 Enhanced unless you have no choice

Directly Modifies   Some applications refuse to share communications ports—or the keyboard—with other applications. If you have problems with this application and another application using the same COM port or keyboard, select each COM port (and the Keyboard option, if necessary) to prevent conflicts. This gives sole use of the COM ports and keyboard to this application, so they will be unavailable to other applications until you quit this application.

No Screen Exchange   When you press the Print Screen key, Windows dumps the currently displayed screen into the Clipboard, so you can paste it in another application. If you don't use this feature with this program, click on this option. This frees up a little memory for your other applications.

Close Window on Exit   If you have an application that runs and then quits itself, you may want to clear the X in this checkbox so the window will remain open when the application is finished. This allows you to see the application's output.

Prevent Program Switch   If you select this option, you have to quit the application to return to Windows or to switch to another application. This frees up a little memory, but you won't be able to use the Ctrl+Esc or Alt+Tab keys to switch applications.

No Save Screen   When you switch from an application to Windows, Windows saves the information that's currently displayed so it can "rebuild" the display when you switch back to that application. If the application can rebuild the display itself, select this option to turn it off. This frees up some memory and allows you to switch tasks faster.

Reserve Shortcut Keys   Windows uses some key combinations for specific tasks. For example, Alt+Tab lets you switch between tasks. If you want to use a key combination in this application, instead of giving it to Windows, click on the key combination you want to use. You can select more than one.

The PIF Editor in Standard mode.

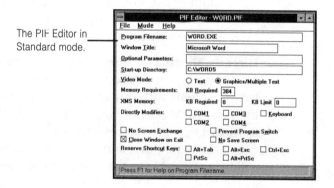

Cheat Sheet

Types of Files You Can Delete

- Windows comes with many files that it needs to run, plus two to three megabytes of additional files.

- The additional files include text files, accessories, screen savers, wallpapers, and games.

- You can delete additional files to free up disk space.

- You may also want to delete font files (see Chapter 41).

Removing Windows Files with Windows Setup

1. Open the Main program group.
2. Double-click on the Windows Setup icon Windows Setup.
3. Open the Options menu.
4. Select Add/Remove Windows Components.
5. Click on the Files button for the group that contains the file(s) you want to delete.
6. Click on each file you want to delete.
7. Click on the Remove button.
8. Click on OK.
9. Repeat steps 5–8 to delete additional files.
10. Click on OK.
11. Click on Yes or Yes to All.

Running ScanDisk or CHKDSK

- Run ScanDisk or CHKDSK to remove any lost file fragments from your hard disk.

- If you have DOS 6.2 or later, run ScanDisk; DOS 6.0 or earlier, run CHKDSK.

- To run ScanDisk, exit Windows, and change to the drive you want to scan. Type **scandisk** at the DOS prompt, and press Enter.

- To run CHKDSK, exit Windows, and change to the drive you want to check. Type **chkdsk /f** at the DOS prompt, and press Enter.

51

Uncluttering Your Disk

Don't use
Windows
Calendar?
Delete it!

Windows and Windows applications come with lots of files that consume lots of disk space. If you know what you're doing, you can use the File Manager to perform disk surgery—removing any unnecessary files. If you don't know what you're doing, that could be dangerous. In this chapter, you learn how you do some disk cleaning, even if you're not really comfortable about deleting Windows files.

Basic Survival

Types of Files You Can Delete

Windows consists of two types of files: files that are essential for Windows to run, and those that are not. If you're running out of disk space, you may have no choice but to delete some of the nonessential files:

- .TXT and .WRI (text) files that contain specific information about using Windows with some types of computers and printers.

- .BMP graphics files that are used as wallpaper. You may want to save one .BMP file to use as wallpaper.

- .HLP help files, if you never use the Windows Help system.

Delete
fonts you
don't use—
Chapter 41

- .EXE files for Windows applications you don't use. These include CLOCK.EXE, NOTEPAD.EXE, SOL.EXE, WINMINE.EXE, and PBRUSH.EXE. Be careful about deleting EXE files. Use the Windows Setup application (as explained in this chapter), to avoid deleting any of your executable system or application files. Also, keep in mind that if you delete an .EXE file, you won't be able to run the application.

- .FOT and .TTF TrueType font files for any fonts you do not use. For details about deleting font files, see Chapter 41.

Removing Windows Files with Windows Setup

The easiest and safest way to delete nonessential Windows files is to use Windows Setup. Windows Setup lets you delete groups of files or individual files.

Before deleting files, you may want to back up your WINDOWS directory. If you have DOS 6.0 or later, you may have a backup program. If you have the Windows installation disks, you can reinstall any of the Windows files you delete in this section.

Once you've backed up, here's what you do to delete files:

Back up files before deleting.

1. Open the Main program group.

2. Double-click on the Windows Setup icon . The Windows Setup window appears.

The Windows Setup window ——

| Windows Setup |
| Options Help |

Display:	VGA
Keyboard:	Enhanced 101 or 102 key US and Non US
Mouse:	Microsoft, or IBM PS/2
Network:	No Network Installed

3. Open the Options menu, and select Add/Remove Windows Components. The Windows Setup dialog box appears, showing the groups of nonessential Windows files.

The Windows Setup dialog box ——

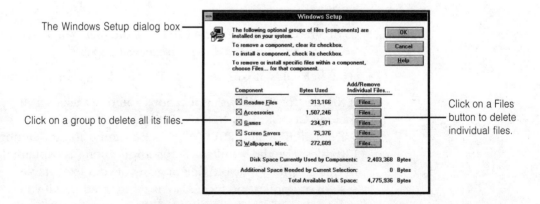

Click on a group to delete all its files. ——

Click on a Files button to delete individual files.

4. To delete an entire group of Windows files, click on the group to remove the **X** from its check box. To remove individual files from a group, perform steps 5–8.

5. To delete individual files, click on the Files button for the group that contains the file(s) you want to delete.

Click on group and Then Files

6. Click on each file you want to delete in the Install these files on the hard disk list. If you select a file by mistake, click on it again to deselect it.

7. Click on the Remove button. The selected files are moved to the Do not install these files list.

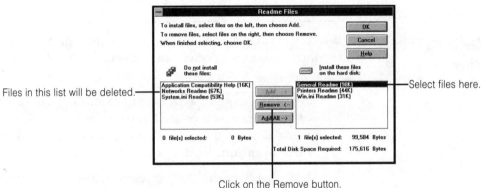

Files in this list will be deleted.   Select files here.

Click on the Remove button.

8. Click on the OK button. You are returned to the Windows Setup dialog box where you can choose to delete more files.

9. Repeat steps 5–8 to delete additional files.

10. Click on the OK button. A dialog box appears, asking you to confirm the deletions.

11. Click on Yes or Yes to All. The files are deleted.

Beyond Survival

Deleting Font Files

The easiest and safest way to delete fonts is to use the Fonts option in the Control Panel, as explained in Chapter 41 in the section "Removing Screen Fonts and TrueType Fonts." By using this method to remove fonts, font files are deleted from the disk, and font instructions are removed from the WIN.INI file.

Delete
fonts =
Chpt 41

Make sure this box has
an X in it to delete the ————
font files from disk.

Deleting Other Files

If you're really strapped for disk space, use File Manager to poke around in your other drives and directories. Look for any of the following files:

Delete
TMP files
in C:\WIN
DOWS
\TEMP

- **Files that have the .BAK or .BK! extension.** These are *backup files* of documents you created in your applications. You can copy these files to a floppy disk (if you want them), and then delete them from your hard disk.

- **Files that have the .TMP extension.** These are *temporary* files that Windows and applications create as you work on a document. If you quit the application the wrong way, or Windows crashes, these .TMP files get stuck in a directory somewhere, and can take up a lot of disk space. Use the File Manager's File Search command to find all the .TMP files, and then delete them.

- **Documents you no longer edit or refer to.** Copy these documents to a floppy disk, write-protect the disk, and store it in a safe location. Then, delete the document files from your hard disk.

- **Applications you no longer use.** Check around for directories that contain applications you no longer use. Some applications come with a Setup feature that lets you uninstall the application. If possible, use the Setup feature, because it edits your WIN.INI and SYSTEM.INI files to remove any instructions that relate to the application. If there is no Setup feature, use File Manager to delete the directories.

Running ScanDisk or CHKDSK

If your computer or Windows seems overly sluggish, or if you try to create a swap file (Chapter 46, "Changing the 386 Enhanced Settings") and you get a message telling you to perform disk maintenance, the problem might be that you have lost pieces of files on disk. To correct the problem, you can use the DOS ScanDisk utility or CHKDSK command.

If you have DOS 6.2 or later, it comes with both ScanDisk and CHKDSK. Because ScanDisk is more thorough, you should use it to fix any problems on your disk. Here's what you do:

ATT + F4
To exiT
Windows

1. Exit Windows. Running ScanDisk from Windows (if you can get it to run) may cause major problems.

2. Type **scandisk** and press Enter. ScanDisk checks the disk for lost pieces of files.

3. Follow the on-screen instructions to proceed.

If you have DOS 6.0 or earlier on your computer, you should use CHKDSK to clean up your disk:

1. Exit Windows. Running CHKDSK from Windows can cause major problems.

2. Type **CHKDSK /F** and press Enter. DOS checks the disk for lost pieces of files, and then displays a message telling you of any lost file fragments it found and asking if you want to save them.

3. To save the lost file fragments, press Y. To delete them, press N. The safe option is to type Y. The file fragments are then saved in files named FILExxxx.CHK in the root directory of the hard disk. You can open the files, see if they contain anything useful, and then delete them. Personally, I always press N to delete the files. I've never encountered one of these files that contained something I could do anything with.

Cheat Sheet

Five Ways to Speed Windows Startup

- Enter **win :** to start Windows.
- Remove blank lines from WIN.INI and SYSTEM.INI.
- Specify location of temporary swap file in SYSTEM.INI.
- Move mouse to COM1.
- Remove fonts you don't use.

Ten Ways to Speed Windows Overall

- Add RAM.
- Maximize the window you're using.
- Minimize windows you're not using.
- Run fewer applications at one time.
- Defragment your hard drive.
- Use a permanent swap file.
- Use solid wallpaper.
- Use solid windows colors.
- Add SMARTDRV.EXE to CONFIG.SYS or AUTOEXEC.BAT.
- Use a RAM drive for temporary files.

52

Speeding Up Windows

Windows can make even the quickest PC seem a little sluggish. A graphical interface is designed to make your computer easier to use; accordingly, it places much heavier demands on a computer than does a simple text-based interface. If you have a 386 25MHz computer or slower with only about 4 megabytes of RAM, you may find yourself waiting while Windows catches up with you. In this chapter, you learn about a few things you can do to speed up Windows.

Basic Survival

Five Ways to Speed Windows Startup

One of the slowest Windows activities is the startup. To speed it up, you can give Windows a few less actions to perform. Here are some tips:

Bypass apps in The StarTup group by holding down ShiET when sTarTing Windows

Bypass the advertising screen. To start Windows, type **win :** and press Enter. The colon tells Windows not to display the Windows advertising screen at startup.

Clean up your INI files. When Windows starts, it reads each and every line in WIN.INI and SYSTEM.INI. By removing blank lines, you give Windows less to read. Refer to Chapter 49, "Reading and Editing System Files" for details about editing these files.

Tell Windows where the temporary swap file is. Whenever Windows starts, it has to determine which drive to use for its temporary swap file. You can save Windows some time by specifying the location in the SYSTEM.INI file. Open the file as explained in Chapter 49. Under the section labeled [386Enh], type the line **PagingFile=c:\win386.swp** where c is the letter of the fastest drive with the most free space. Save SYSTEM.INI and restart Windows. (Better yet, create a permanent swap file, as explained in Chapter 46, "Changing the 386 Enhanced Settings.")

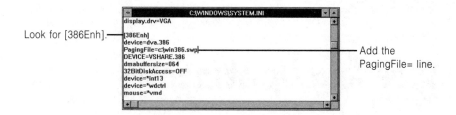

Look for [386Enh].

Add the PagingFile= line.

Move mouse to COM1. If you have another serial device (say, your modem), on COM1, and you have your mouse on COM2 or COM3, try moving the mouse to COM1. Whenever Windows starts, it stubbornly looks to COM1 for the mouse. By moving the mouse to COM1, you put it where Windows expects to find it.

Fonts Take Time To load

Reduce available fonts. Each font has a line in the WIN.INI file, which Windows must read at startup. Use the Control Panel's Fonts icon to remove fonts you don't use (see Chapter 41, "Working with Fonts"). You can remove the fonts without deleting the font files from disk. This removes the instructions from WIN.INI, but keeps the font files on disk so you can add them back in later.

Beyond Survival

Ten Ways to Speed Windows Overall

Once Windows starts, there are other areas you must focus on to increase its overall performance. The following list explains some obvious (and not-so-obvious) things you can do:

Add RAM. Windows likes RAM. Your computer should have at least 4 megabytes of RAM to run efficiently. The more RAM that's installed, the less often Windows has to use the hard disk, which is much slower than RAM.

Maximize the window you're using. When you have several application windows open at once, Windows has to keep checking all the open windows to find out which one is active. By maximizing the active window, you tell Windows that it can stop checking.

Keep screen clean and uncluttered

Minimize windows you're not using. Every open window requires screen space and system resources. By minimizing the window, you free up resources for the applications you are currently using.

Run fewer applications at one time. If you notice that Windows is becoming more and more sluggish, exit any applications you are not using.

Defragment your hard drive. The temporary swap files that Windows uses require disk space. By *defragmenting* your hard disk, you free up sections of the disk to use for these temporary swap files. You can use the DOS 6 Defrag program, or a third-party program such as PC Tools or The Norton Utilities. To use DOS 6 Defrag, exit Windows, and then enter **defrag** at the DOS prompt. Follow the on-screen instructions.

Defrag can open disk space.

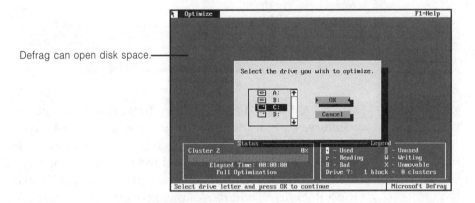

Permanent swap files are easter

Use a permanent swap file. With temporary swap files, Windows must create and manage files that may be scattered over the hard disk. With a permanent swap file, you give Windows a reserved portion of the disk that is in one set area on the disk. This makes disk-swaps much more efficient. See Chapter 46, "Changing the 386 Enhanced Settings," for details.

Use solid wallpaper. If you pick a fancy graphic image to display as your Windows wallpaper, the image may consume a great deal of RAM. Use no wallpaper or a solid background. (See Chapter 43, "Controlling Your Desktop.")

Use solid windows colors. Windows colors that are a mix of two or more colors, require more system resources than do solid colors. A monochrome configuration consumes even fewer resources. (See Chapter 40, "Changing the Screen Colors," for details.)

Add SMARTDRV.EXE to AUTOEXEC.BAT. When you installed Windows, the installation program added the SMARTDRV.EXE command to your AUTOEXEC.BAT file. Smart Drive is a disk-caching program that stores often-used data in memory so Windows can access the information more quickly (rather than having to read it from disk). To make sure the SMARTDRV.EXE command is in AUTOEXEC.BAT, open the AUTOEXEC.BAT file, as explained in Chapter 49, "Reading and Editing System Files."

Add the SMARTDRV.EXE
command to AUTOEXEC.BAT.

```
                         C:\AUTOEXEC.BAT
C:\DOS\SMARTDRV.EXE
C:\DOS\SHARE.EXE /L:500 /F:5100
REM @C:\DOS\SHARE.EXE /I:500
ECHO OFF
VERIFY OFF
PROMPT $P$G
PATH C:\DOS;C:\;C:\WINDOWS;C:\EXECUTE;C:\ZIP;C:\WORD5;C:\NC;C:\PC
set temp=C:\WINDOWS\TEMP
SET PCTOOLS=C:\PCTOOLS\DATA
REM SET COMSPEC=C:\DOS\COMMAND.COM
numlock -
```

Use a RAM drive for temporary files. If you have gobs of memory, say 8 or more megabytes, you may be able to increase system performance by setting some of the memory aside to use as a disk. You can then tell Windows to store temporary files on the RAM disk, which is much faster than a hard disk. To create and use a RAM drive, add the following command to your CONFIG.SYS file, after the HIMEM.SYS line:

device=c:\windows\ramdrive.sys 1024 /e

If Windows is on a different hard drive, type the drive letter in place of c. The number **1024** tells Smart Drive the size of the RAM drive. The **/e** switch tells Smart Drive to use extended memory. The RAM drive will be assigned the next drive letter; for example, if you have hard drive C and a CD-ROM drive D, the RAM drive will be drive E. Next, you have to add command lines that point temporary (swap) files to the RAM drive. For example, add these commands to AUTOEXEC.BAT:

set temp=e:

set tmp=e:

Very
advanced
stuff

In addition, if you used the PagingFile= command (as explained earlier) to tell Windows where to place temporary swap files, change the drive location to match that of the RAM drive. Exit Windows and reboot your computer after making all these changes.

Use
Windows'
accelerator
card to speed
Windows

One additional thing you can do to increase the performance of Windows is to buy a Windows accelerator or video accelerator card. Because Windows is so graphic, an accelerator card can take over much of the work that your system normally must perform just to create the graphic screens.

Another speed enhancement is to run Windows in Standard mode. However, do this only if your system has plenty of memory (6-10 megabytes) and if you run only Windows applications. If you try this and you keep getting Out of Memory messages, go back to running in Enhanced mode.

Cheat Sheet

What Is a General Protection Fault?

- A general protection fault (GPF) occurs when two applications attempt to use the same memory address.
- GPFs are usually caused by bugs in an application or device driver.
- When a GPF occurs, Windows usually displays the name of the culprit.

Taking Immediate Action

- When a GPF occurs, your system may lock up.
- If a message appears, write down the message, and perform any steps it tells you to perform.
- If no message appears, wait to see if your system will unlock itself.
- If the system is still locked, press Ctrl+Alt+Del to reboot. A message will appear, indicating the name of the application causing problems and asking you to make a decision.
- Press Esc to cancel the reboot, Enter to quit the application that is causing problems, or Ctrl+Alt+Del again to reboot.

General Protection Fault Protection

- Upgrade to the latest version of DOS.
- Disable any memory-resident applications.
- Reinstall the application.
- Call manufacturer for updated driver.

Dealing with General Protection Faults

GPF =
General
ProTecTion
FaulT

As you run applications in Windows, Windows keeps track of memory addresses (the location of each chunk of memory), and tries to resolve any conflicts. If an application attempts to store some data in an address that's already being used, the application will lock up, and Windows will usually display a message indicating that a *general protection fault* (*GPF*) has occurred, or your system may simply lock up. In this chapter, you learn what to do when a GPF occurs, and how to prevent GPFs from recurring.

Basic Survival

Taking Immediate Action

When a GPF occurs, you'll want to do two things: make a record of the problem, and get your system running again. When you first encounter a GPF, here's what you do:

1. Write down the GPF message (if there is one). This message usually indicates the name of the application that caused the fault, and the memory address where the fault occurred.

2. Write down exactly what you were doing when the fault occurred. Were you saving a file, printing, moving the mouse? Write down the names of the other applications you were running.

3. If no message is displayed, wait about a minute to see if your system will unlock itself. Sometimes (especially on slower computers), the system may be busy, not locked, and it will return control to you if you just wait.

4. If no message appears, and Windows is still locked, press Ctrl+Alt+Del. A message appears, indicating the name of the application causing problems and asking you to make a decision. This message may also indicate that the system is simply busy and you should wait longer.

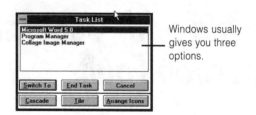

Windows usually gives you three options.

5. Perform one of the following steps:

Press Esc to cancel the reboot.

Press Enter to quit the current application and return to Windows.

Avoid rebooting

Press Ctrl+Alt+Del to reboot. *Avoid taking this option.* When you reboot Windows, you risk losing anything you were working on, and you may end up with lots of .TMP files scattered all over your hard disk.

Beyond Survival

General Protection Fault Protection

General protection faults are usually caused by a bug in an application or device driver. If you consistently encounter the same GPF in an application, try the following fixes:

- **Exit and restart Windows.** Sometimes a GPF will cause additional GPFs in the current work session. Exiting and restarting resets Windows and may prevent additional GPFs.

- **Upgrade to the latest version of DOS.** If you have a version of DOS written for a specific computer (say Compaq), run that DOS version only on the Compaq computer for which it was designed. If you run it on a different make or model of computer, you may encounter problems. Also, try using DOS 5 or DOS 6.x. Both versions of DOS come with advanced memory management tools that may help eliminate problems.

- **Disable any memory-resident applications.** If you have any memory-resident applications that run from your AUTOEXEC.BAT file, use the REM command to disable them, as explained in Chapter 49, "Reading and Editing System Files." Memory-resident programs include DOS screen savers and screen-capture programs. If you're not sure, copy CONFIG.SYS and AUTOEXEC.BAT (to CONFIG.OLD and AUTOEXEC.OLD), and then create the following "plain vanilla" versions to boot your computer:

AUTOEXEC.BAT
C:\WINDOWS\SMARTDRV.EXE
PROMPT PG
PATH C:\DOS;C:\;C:\WINDOWS
SET TEMP=C:\TMP

CONFIG.SYS
DEVICE=C:\DOS\SETVER.EXE
DEVICE=C:\WINDOWS\HIMEM.SYS
DOS=HIGH
BUFFERS=20
FILES=30
STACKS=9,256

Run only one disk-caching program

- **Use Smart Drive as your disk-caching program.** If you have a disk-caching program, such as QEMM or 386MAX, use the REM command in CONFIG.SYS and AUTOEXEC.BAT to remove any of its command lines, and then add the SMARTdrive command line to AUTOEXEC.BAT:

  C:\WINDOWS\SMARTDRV.EXE

- **Reinstall the application.** Sometimes reinstalling the application or device driver that is causing problems will correct the problem.

- **Call manufacturer for updated driver.** Manufacturers hear of problems that occur with their products. They may have the fix you need.

Cheat Sheet

Troubleshooting Mouse Problems

- Does the DOS application support a mouse?
- Does the mouse work if you run application from the DOS prompt instead of from Windows?
- Does the mouse work in Windows?
- Do CONFIG.SYS and AUTOEXEC.BAT run two mouse drivers?
- Are you using the latest version of the mouse driver?
- Are you using a special video driver?

Fixing Mouse Problems

- If the DOS application is in a window, press Alt+Enter to run it in full-screen mode.
- Check CONFIG.SYS and AUTOEXEC.BAT to make sure only MOUSE.COM or MOUSE.SYS is running (not both). If both are present, REM out the DEVICE=MOUSE.SYS command.
- Watch the screen when you boot your computer. Make sure you have a mouse driver version 8.20 or later for a Microsoft mouse.
- Check the [boot] section of SYSTEM.INI. It should have a command like this: **386grabber=VGA.3GR**.

Installing a Mouse Driver

1. Open the Main group window.
2. Double-click the Windows Setup icon.
3. Select Options Change System Settings.
4. Open the Mouse drop-down list and select the mouse driver for the mouse you have.
5. Click on OK.
6. Insert the mouse driver installation disk in drive A or B.
7. Type the drive letter, followed by a colon and backslash, and press Enter.
8. Click on OK.
9. Follow the on-screen instructions to complete the procedure.

54

Getting Your Mouse to Work in a DOS Window

Once a mouse is working, you shouldn't have any problems with it. The hard part is getting it to work in the first place. If you're having trouble getting your mouse to work in a DOS application that's running under Windows, this chapter helps you find and solve the problem.

Basic Survival

Troubleshooting Mouse Problems

Mouse driver must start at boot

Before you can solve a problem, you should try to determine the cause of the problem. The following questions should help you trace the problem to its cause:

- **Did you install a mouse driver?** Plugging a mouse into your computer's serial or mouse port isn't enough. You must run the setup program for the mouse. The setup program copies a mouse driver to your hard disk, and edits the AUTOEXEC.BAT or CONFIG.SYS file so the mouse driver will run whenever you boot your computer. If your computer came with a mouse, the driver is probably installed. If you bought a mouse, you must install the driver.

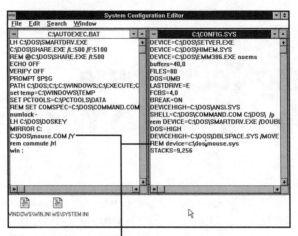

A mouse command must be in
CONFIG.SYS or AUTOEXEC.BAT.

- **Does the DOS application support a mouse?** Some old DOS applications do not allow you to use a mouse. If you can't get the mouse to work in the DOS application, it won't work if you run the DOS application from Windows. Try exiting Windows and running the application from the DOS prompt. If the mouse works, you know you have a problem in Windows.

- **Does the mouse work in Windows?** If you can't get the mouse to work in Windows, the mouse driver may not be installed, you may have two mouse drivers installed, or you may have the wrong mouse driver installed. To check which Windows mouse driver is installed, open the Main program group, double-click on Windows Setup, and then open the Options menu and select Change System Settings. Look in the Mouse box to figure out which mouse driver Windows is set up to use.

Run only one
mouse driver

- **Do CONFIG.SYS and AUTOEXEC.BAT run two mouse drivers?** Running two mouse drivers can be just as bad as running no mouse driver. Check CONFIG.SYS for a line such as **DEVICE=C:\WINDOWS\MOUSE.SYS** and check AUTOEXEC.BAT for a line such as **MOUSE.COM**. Skip ahead to the next section to figure out what to do.

- **Are you using the latest version of the mouse driver?** Old mouse drivers can cause problems. When you boot your computer, look for information about the mouse. The screen should display the version number of the mouse driver. If you are using a Microsoft mouse, the driver should be version 8.20 or later.

- **Are you using a special video driver?** Windows 3.1 comes with the video drivers that are capable of displaying the mouse pointer in a DOS application window. However, if you installed a special video card, the driver that came with it may be causing problems.

Beyond Survival

Fixing Mouse Problems

Alt + Enter runs DOS app in full screen

Once you've discovered the problem with the mouse, you'll want to take some action to correct the problem. The following list tells you what to do to correct most common problems:

- **If DOS application is in a window, press Alt+Enter to run it in full-screen mode.** If you can use the mouse in full-screen mode, try adding the following command to the [NonWindowsApp] section of your SYSTEM.INI file:

  MouseInDosBox=1

  See Chapter 49, "Reading and Editing System Files," to learn how to edit SYSTEM.INI. You'll have to restart Windows for the change to take effect.

- **Make sure the correct mouse is selected in Windows.** Open the Main group window, double-click on the Windows Setup icon, open the Options menu, and select Change System Settings. Open the Mouse drop-down list, and select the mouse you're using.

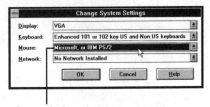

Windows Setup displays the name
of the selected mouse driver.

- **Make sure only one mouse driver is running.** If AUTOEXEC.BAT and CONFIG.SYS both contain a mouse command, use the **REM** command to disable the **DEVICE=MOUSE.SYS** command in **CONFIG.SYS**. Usually, MOUSE.COM works better. (See Chapter 49, "Reading and Editing System Files," to learn how to edit these files.)

- **Use the latest version of the mouse driver.** If you have an old mouse driver (pre version 8.20), contact the mouse manufacturer and ask for an updated driver. If you upgrade to the latest DOS version, you might already have the driver you need. Check the C:\DOS directory for a file called MOUSE.COM. Add the command **C:\DOS\MOUSE.COM** to your AUTOEXEC.BAT file, and remove all other references to mouse drivers in AUTOEXEC.BAT and CONFIG.SYS.

- **Make sure there is only one MOUSE.INI file on your hard drive.** Use the File Manager's Search feature (Chapter 29, "Searching for a File") to find the MOUSE.INI files. Delete all the MOUSE.INI files except the one in the \WINDOWS directory.

- **Use the VGA driver that came with Windows.** Make a copy of your SYSTEM.INI file. Check the [boot] section of SYSTEM.INI. It should have a command like this: **386grabber=VGA.3GR**. Add the command or edit the existing command so it matches the one here. If that doesn't work, contact the manufacturer of your video card and ask about getting an updated driver.

Problem may be video driver, nōt mouse driver

Installing a Mouse Driver

If the wrong mouse driver is installed for your mouse, or if you get an updated driver from the manufacturer, you can install it by performing the following steps:

1. Open the Main group window.

2. Double-click on the Windows Setup icon. The Windows Setup dialog box appears.

3. Open the Options menu and select Change System Settings. The Change System Settings dialog box appears, showing the Display, Keyboard, and Mouse drivers set up in Windows.

4. Open the Mouse drop-down list and select the mouse driver for the mouse you have. If the mouse driver is not on the list, select Other mouse.

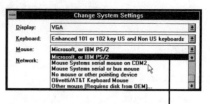

Select the correct mouse driver.

5. Click on the OK button. A dialog box appears, telling you to insert the disk that has the mouse driver into drive A.

6. Insert the mouse driver installation disk in drive A or B, and close the drive door, if necessary.

7. Type the drive letter, followed by a colon and backslash, and press Enter.

8. Click on the OK button. Windows copies the selected mouse driver to the hard disk.

9. Follow the on-screen instructions to complete the procedure.

Procedure may noT work for some drivers

If you get a message that says the OEMSETUP.INF file is missing, you may have to follow a different procedure. First, check the disk to see if it has a SETUP or INSTALL file, and use the Program Manager's File Run command to try to run it. If that doesn't work, exit Windows, and try running **SETUP** or **INSTALL** from the DOS prompt.

If there is no SETUP or INSTALL file on the floppy disk, try copying the .COM or .SYS file from the floppy disk to the \WINDOWS directory. Then, edit your AUTOEXEC.BAT or CONFIG.SYS file to run the mouse driver. If you have a .COM file, add a command such as **C:\WINDOWS*driver*.COM** to the AUTOEXEC.BAT FILE. In place of *driver* type the name of the driver file, usually **MOUSE**. If you have a .SYS file, add a command such as **DEVICE=C:\WINDOWS*mouse*.SYS** to the CONFIG.SYS file. In place of *mouse* type the name of the driver file, usually **MOUSE**. Exit Windows and reboot your computer when you are done.

Cheat Sheet

Checking the Obvious

- Is the printer turned on?
- Does the printer have paper?
- Is the printer on-line indicator lit?
- Is the printer plugged in?
- Is the printer connected to the system unit?

Checking Print Manager's Print Queue

1. Press Ctrl+Esc.
2. Click on Print Manager.
3. Click on Switch To.

Possible Print Queue Problems

Printer stalled   Make sure the printer is on, and has paper. Click on your print job; click on Resume.

Print job paused   Click on your print job; click on Resume.

Printer not selected or online   Turn the printer on, make sure printer is selected in the application. Click on your print job, and then click on Resume.

Checking Your Printer Setup

1. Open the Main group window.
2. Double-click on the Control Panel icon .
3. Double-click on the Printers icon .
4. Click on the printer in the Installed Printers list.
5. Click on the Set As Default Printer button.
6. Click on the Close button.

55

Solving Printer Problems

See Chapters 47 and 48 for details

If you followed the instructions in Chapter 47 ("Setting Up and Selecting a Printer") to select the correct printer driver and port for your printer, printing should proceed without a glitch. Even with the proper setup, however, you may run into problems when you attempt to print a document. In this chapter, you learn how to trace the problem back to its cause, and get on with your printing.

Basic Survival

Checking the Obvious

If you have successfully printed in Windows before, and are just now encountering problems, the cause of the problem may be very simple. Ask yourself the following questions:

- **Is the Print Manager dialog box displayed?** If it is, make sure your printer has paper, turn the printer on, and press its On-line button so the indicator lights. Click on the Retry button.

Check for problems, then click on Retry.

- **Is the printer turned on?** If the printer is turned off, turn it on.

- **Does the printer have paper?** A printer won't even go through the motions unless it has paper.

Check printer's on-line indicator

- **Is the printer on-line indicator lit?** Most printers have an on line indicator that lights when the printer is ready to print. If the indicator is not lit, press the on-line button.

- **Is the printer plugged in?** If you can't get the printer to turn on, check to make sure it is plugged into a power source.

- **Is the printer connected to the system unit?** Sometimes the cable that connects the printer to the system unit will wiggle loose from the system unit or printer. Exit Windows, turn off your computer, and check the connections at both ends.

Resuming Your Print Jobs

Once you've solved the mystery, you can continue printing. If the Print Manager dialog box is displayed, click on the Resume button to continue printing. If the Print Manager dialog box is not visible, take the following steps:

1. Press Ctrl+Esc.

2. Click on Print Manager.

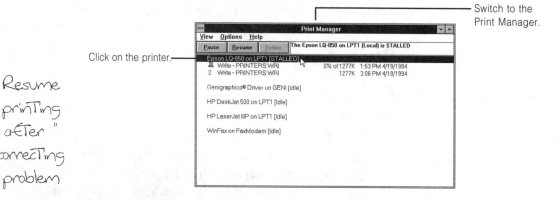

Switch to the Print Manager.

Click on the printer.

Resume printing after "correcting problem

3. Click on Switch To.

4. Click on the printer you're using. It should be marked [Stalled].

5. Click on the Resume button. Printing should start.

Beyond Survival

Checking the Print Manager's Print Queue

The Print Manager (described in Chapter 48, "Using the Windows Print Manager") is great for managing your printing "behind the scenes," while you work in other applications. If a problem occurs during printing, however, all remaining print jobs get backed up at the Print Manager.

Print jobs might get bottled up at Program Manager

What do you do? The natural inclination is to try the File Print command again. All this does is send another document to Print Manager, where it will wait hopelessly behind the others. Instead, check the print queue to see what's going on. Here's how:

1. **Press Ctrl+Esc.** The Task List appears, showing the names of all the applications. If Print Manager is enabled, it should appear in the list.

2. **Click on Print Manager.**

3. **Click on Switch To.** The Print Manager window appears, showing a list of files waiting in the print queue.

Files waiting hopelessly to be printed.

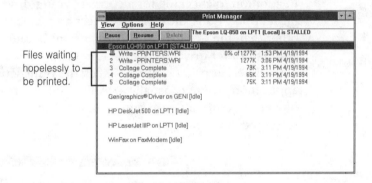

Two common problems may reveal themselves in the Print Manager queue:

Document may have gone to wrong printer

- **Sent print job to wrong printer.** If you set up two or more printers in Windows, you may have selected the wrong printer when you printed the document. The document is waiting for the other printer to get online, while you're trying to get the wrong printer online. Exit Print Manager (to cancel all print jobs), and then try printing the document again. This time, use the Print Setup command to choose the correct printer.

- **Printer is stalled.** A printer usually stalls because it is not turned on, connected, or online. Check the obvious solutions described earlier. Then, click on the printer and click on the Resume button to start printing.

Checking Your Printer Setup

If none of the obvious solutions work, go back to Chapter 47, "Setting Up and Selecting a Printer," and check your printer setup. You need to check for two things:

- **Correct printer driver.** Open the Main group window, double-click on the Control Panel icon, double-click on the Printers icon, and make sure the printer driver for the printer you're using is selected as the default.

- **Correct printer port.** If your printer is on port LPT2, and LPT1 is selected, the printed document will never reach the correct destination.

Check printer setup from application

In addition to checking for a correct printer driver, keep in mind that most applications allow you to select a specific printer driver (a driver other than the default). This is important because even if you select the correct printer driver as the default, the application may be set up to use a different printer driver. Check the print setup from inside the application. There is usually a Print Setup command on the File menu, or a Print Setup or Setup button in the Print dialog box when you select the File Print command.

Default printer ——

Specific printer ——
is chosen for
this application.

Hints and Tips for Stubborn Printing Problems

If you tried all the solutions up to this point, and are still unable to print, here are some hints for tracking down the cause:

- **Problems in only one application?** If you can print from other applications, the problem is with the printer setup in the problem application.

- **Problems in all Windows applications?** Try printing from DOS. Go to the DOS prompt, type the command **dir > LPT1** and press Enter. This prints the current directory list. If it prints okay, the problem is in the Windows printer setup. Use the Printers icon on the Control Panel.

- **Don't print from DOS apps and Windows apps at the same time.** DOS applications come with their own print drivers that may try to print to the same printer that the Windows print driver is using. This usually results in a garbled printout. Cancel the printing in the DOS application, exit Print Manager, turn your printer off, wait 30 seconds, and turn it back on.

- **Disable Fast Printing to Port.** The dialog box that lets you select a printer port (Chapter 47) has an option Fast Printing Direct to Port. This tells Windows to disregard any DOS interrupts. Try turning this option off.

Turn this option off.

- **Disable Print Manager.** This may slow your printing operations and prevent you from working in other applications during printing. However, it does bypass the middleman.

- **Increase the size of your temporary swap file.** If you get general printer errors, try increasing the size of your temporary swap file, as explained in Chapter 46, "Changing the 386 Enhanced Settings." This gives Print Manager more storage space for the files that are waiting to be printed.

Speedy
printing =
PrinT
Manager
OpTions
High PrioriTy

- **Do you get Time Out messages on long print jobs?** The dialog box that lets you select a printer port (Chapter 47) has a Transmission Retry option that specifies how much time Print Manager will wait before notifying you that your printer cannot accept new information. Try entering a value of **90**. This usually corrects problems for PostScript printers.

Cheat Sheet

Checking Available Memory

1. Switch to Program Manager.
2. Open the Help menu.
3. Select About Program Manager.

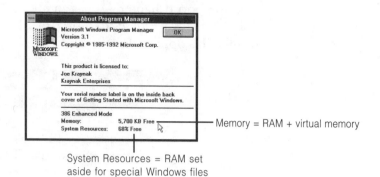

Memory = RAM + virtual memory

System Resources = RAM set aside for special Windows files

Quick Solutions

- Delete the Clipboard contents.
- If Memory drops below 30K, shut down applications.
- If System Resources dips below 30%, exit applications, and minimize group windows.
- Run Windows in 386 Enhanced mode.
- Increase the size of the swap file used as virtual memory.

Meeting Your Long-Term Needs

- Install more RAM.
- Use a permanent swap file.
- Upgrade to DOS 5 or later, and use their advanced memory managers.

56

Coping with "Out of Memory" Messages

Windows—and Windows applications—require a great deal of memory (RAM) to run. Although most recent computers have the 2 to 4 megabytes of RAM required for Windows, problems may result if you test the system limits of your computer. If you run too many applications, or have lots of group windows and icons displayed, Windows may greet you with an Out of Memory or Insufficient Memory message. In this chapter, you learn how to reclaim memory and avoid these messages.

Basic Survival

Checking Available Memory

Most applications have an About command on the Help menu

If your system starts to act sluggish, or you get an Out of Memory message, check the available memory:

1. Switch to Program Manager.

2. Open the Help menu.

3. Select About Program Manager. The About Program Manager dialog box appears, showing the available memory and system resources. The next section explains how to interpret this information.

Available memory

Available system resources

Understanding Memory and System Resources

If you get an Out of Memory message, it means that your system is running out of one (or both) of the elements it needs to run applications:

Memory is RAM (chips) plus virtual memory (disk space that Windows uses as RAM when running in 386 Enhanced mode). Applications use memory directly for their program files. If the amount of available memory dips below 30K (kilobytes), you may start getting Out of Memory messages.

System Resources consist of portions of RAM that are reserved for Windows system files: KERNEL.EXE, USER.EXE, and GDL.EXE. KERNEL.EXE is the Windows manager in charge of managing memory and launching applications. USER.EXE is in charge of the keyboard, mouse, sounds, and COM ports. GDL.EXE controls printing and graphics. Each application that's running uses part of the system resources reserved for each of the system files. The problem is that each file gets only 64 kilobytes of RAM. If the running applications approach this limit (leaving 30% or less of System Resources free), you can have plenty of free memory and still get Out of Memory messages.

Memory or System Resources < 30—close applications and minimize

Quick Solutions

Once you know whether your problem is caused by low memory or low system resources (or both), you can take some immediate action to correct the problem:

- **Run Windows in 386 Enhanced mode.** Check the About Program Manager dialog box to see if you are running Windows in Standard or 386 Enhanced mode. If you are running in Standard mode, exit Windows, and then use the win /3 command to restart Windows.

- **Increase the size of the swap file used as virtual memory.** If you are running Windows in 386 Enhanced mode, you can create a swap file that uses disk space as memory. See Chapter 46, "Changing the 386 Enhanced Settings," for details on how to create the swap file and increase its size.

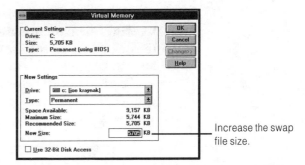

Increase the swap file size.

Copy a single character To replace The Clipboard conTenTs

- **Delete the Clipboard contents.** If you have a graphic image on the Clipboard (say you pressed the Print Screen key), it can consume lots of memory. Open the Main group window, double-click on the Clipboard Viewer icon, and press the Del key.

ShuT down apps

- **Minimize, minimize, minimize.** If System Resources dip below 30%, exit applications and minimize group windows. To reclaim large percentages of system resources, exit applications. Minimizing group windows reclaim tiny amounts of system resources, but it be enough to bring you within the limits.

Minimize groups

- **Turn off backgrounds and use solid window colors.** See Chapters 40, "Changing the Screen Colors," and 43, "Controlling Your Desktop," for details.

- **If Memory drops below 30K, shut down applications.** Exit any applications that you are not currently using. If you're not sure which applications you are running, press Ctrl+Esc to view the Task List.

Increase swap file size

Beyond Survival

Meeting Your Long-Term Needs

The immediate action you took can free up a little memory to get you out of trouble. Probably, however, you'll still have memory problems over the long haul. For more permanent cures, try these tactics:

Add RAM for real performance gain

- **Install more RAM.** The required 2 megabytes of RAM is simply not enough. Your computer will do much better with 4 to 6 megabytes of RAM, more if you can afford it.

- **Use a permanent swap file.** A permanent swap file is faster than a temporary swap file, making it more like RAM. See Chapter 46 for details.

- **Run DOS 6's Memmaker.** If you have DOS 6.0 or later, exit Windows, type **memmaker** at the DOS prompt, and then follow the on-screen instructions to perform an Express Setup. MemMaker edits your CONFIG.SYS and AUTOEXEC.BAT files to load certain device drivers into a normally reserved portion of your computer's memory. This frees some memory for use by Windows.

MemMaker can configure memory for you.

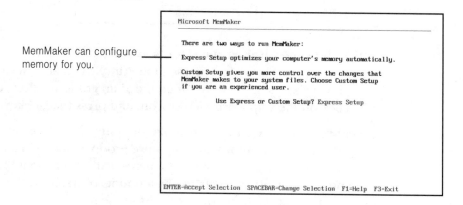

```
Microsoft MemMaker

There are two ways to run MemMaker:

Express Setup optimizes your computer's memory automatically.

Custom Setup gives you more control over the changes that
MemMaker makes to your system files. Choose Custom Setup
if you are an experienced user.

        Use Express or Custom Setup? Express Setup




ENTER=Accept Selection  SPACEBAR=Change Selection  F1=Help  F3=Exit
```

- **Use DOS 5's advanced memory tools.** If you don't have DOS 6.0 (but you do have DOS 5.0), you can do manually what MemMaker does automatically. First, use the System Editor (Chapter 49, "Reading and Editing System Files") to add the following lines to your CONFIG.SYS file in the order given here:

  DEVICE=HIMEM.SYS

  DEVICE=EMM386.EXE NOEMS

  DOS=HIGH,UMB

The DEVICE=EMM386.EXE NOEMS line frees the reserved portion of memory (upper memory), so other device drivers can use it. DOS=HIGH,UMB loads DOS into upper memory. You can edit DEVICE= lines that come later in CONFIG.SYS to load device drivers into upper memory. Change DEVICE= to **DEVICEHIGH=** (for example, **DEVICEHIGH=C:\DOS\ANSI.SYS**).

If you load a driver from your AUTOEXEC.BAT file, you can use the **LOADHIGH** or **LH** command to load the driver into upper memory. For example, if you use MOUSE.COM, you can add the LH command before the MOUSE.COM line (**LH C:\DOS\MOUSE.COM**).

Use DEVICEHIGH and LOADHIGH only for device drivers, noT for applicaTions

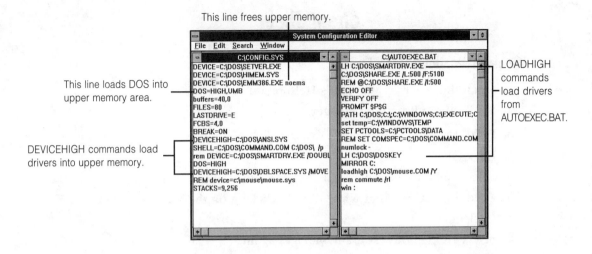

This line frees upper memory.

This line loads DOS into upper memory area.

DEVICEHIGH commands load drivers into upper memory.

LOADHIGH commands load drivers from AUTOEXEC.BAT.

640 kilobytes conventional + 384 kilobytes upper = 1 megabyte

A Note About Memory

If all this talk about memory is making your head spin, just remember that there are four types of memory at work:

Conventional   Directly-usable memory that comes with all computers. Programs use conventional memory to run. The maximum amount a computer can have is 640 kilobytes.

Upper   Memory that is reserved for system use, such as controlling a disk drive. Of a computer's first 1 megabyte of memory, upper memory is the 384K left over after conventional memory has been allocated. DOS 5 and later versions allow you to free this portion of memory for use by device drivers that would otherwise use conventional memory.

Extended   Additional memory that Windows and Windows applications can use. When you install additional RAM, you should install extended memory chips.

Expanded   Additional memory that some applications can use. This memory swaps information into and out of conventional memory (640K RAM) at high speeds, giving the user the impression that the computer has more random-access memory (RAM) than the conventional 640K. Some programs are written to use expanded memory, allowing larger programs to run under DOS. You can use expanded memory for a swap file, as explained in Chapter 52, "Speeding Up Windows."

347

Cheat Sheet

Viewing a Windows Gang Screen

1. Open the Program Manager's Help menu.
2. Select About Program Manager.
3. Hold down Ctrl+Shift while double-clicking on the Windows icon .
4. Click OK.
5. Select Help About Program Manager again.
6. Hold down Ctrl+Shift while double-clicking on the Windows icon.
7. Click OK.
8. Select Help About Program Manager again.
9. Hold down Ctrl+Shift while double-clicking on the Windows icon.

Making Your Own Wallpaper

1. Make a picture using Paintbrush.
2. Save picture in \WINDOWS directory as a .BMP file.
3. Open the Main group window.
4. Double-click on the Desktop icon.
5. Open the Wallpaper File drop-down list.
6. Click on the name of the file you created in Paintbrush.
7. Click OK.

Drag-and-Drop Printing

1. Open the Main group window.
2. Double-click on the Print Manager icon.
3. Click on the Print Manager's Minimize button.
4. Double-click on the File Manager button.
5. Change to the drive and directory that contains the file you want to print.
6. Drag the file's icon over the Print Manager icon.
7. Release the mouse button.
8. Click OK.

57

Ten Cool Tricks

Time to play. In this chapter, you learn about ten cool, fun, mean things you can do with Windows.

Basic Survival

#1: Viewing a Windows Gang Screen

Windows and some Windows applications have undocumented on-screen animations called *gang screens*. To view a gang screen, you must perform a series of actions that no normal person would ever think of doing. Windows 3.1 comes with its very own gang screen. To view it, here's what you do:

1. Open the Help menu in Program Manager, or in any of the Windows Accessories.

2. Select the About command. (In Program Manager, you select the About Program Manager command.) The About dialog box appears.

Alt + H
Then press
A

3. Hold down Ctrl+Shift while double-clicking on the Windows icon .

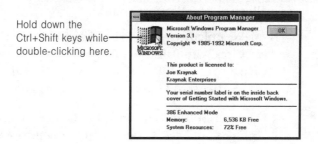

Hold down the Ctrl+Shift keys while double-clicking here.

4. Click on the OK button. The dialog box closes, and nothing really happens till you perform the next few steps.

5. Select Help About again. The About dialog box appears again.

6. Hold down Ctrl+Shift while double-clicking on the Windows icon. A waving flag and a dedication message appear. There's more—keep reading.

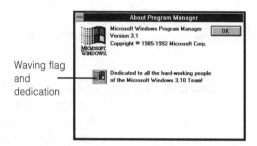

Waving flag
and
dedication

7. Click on the OK button. The dialog box disappears.

8. Select Help About again. The About dialog box reappears.

9. Hold down Ctrl+Shift while double-clicking on the Windows icon. This time, a figure appears, and the names of the Windows developers and marketing team scroll past. (You'll get a different figure each time you run this.)

#2: Making Your Own Wallpaper

Use PaintBrush To make a wallpaper picture

In Chapter 43,"Controlling Your Desktop," you learned how to select the wallpaper design that you want to appear as a backdrop for Windows. You can use Paintbrush to create your own graphic image to use as wallpaper. Here's what you do:

1. Make a picture using Paintbrush. Refer to Chapter 14, "Making Pictures with Paintbrush" for details. To fill the entire screen, make sure you fill the entire "page" in Paintbrush. You may have to use the scroll bars to bring blank parts of the page into view.

Another option is to open the Options menu, select Image Attributes, and set the width and height to smaller values (for example 1 inch by 1 inch). Then, when you select the image as wallpaper, specify that it be Tiled instead of Centered.

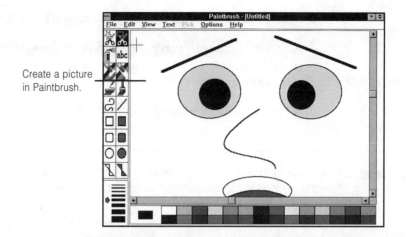

Create a picture in Paintbrush.

2. Use the File Save command to save the picture in \WINDOWS directory as a .BMP file. If the file is saved in any other directory or in any other format (say .PCX), it will not appear in the list of Wallpaper options.

3. Open the Main group window, and double-click on the Control Panel icon.

4. Double-click on the Desktop icon . The Desktop dialog box appears.

5. Open the Wallpaper File drop-down list. A list of graphic files appears. You may have to use the scroll bar to bring your graphic file into view.

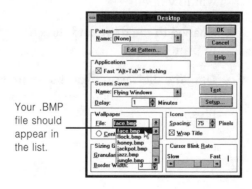

Your .BMP file should appear in the list.

6. Click on the name of the file you created in Paintbrush.

7. Click on Center to place the graphic in the middle of the screen (if it is big enough, it will cover the entire screen), or click on Tile to fill the screen with several copies of the image.

Fill screen by Tiling small pictures

8. Click on the OK button. You may have to minimize some windows to see your wallpaper in action.

#3: Drag & Drop Printing

You can use File Manager and Print Manager together to print files without opening them in an application. The only stipulation is that you must first have created file associations for the files you want to print. See Chapter 37, "Running Applications from File Manager," for details. Once you have your file associations set up, here's how you drag-and-drop print:

1. Open the Main group window.

2. Double-click on the Print Manager icon ![Print Manager]. The Print Manager window appears.

3. Click on the Print Manager's Minimize button. If the Print Manager application icon gets buried under a stack of windows, you may have to minimize or resize some windows to bring it into view. For drag-and-drop printing to work, you need both the File Manager window and Print Manager icon visible.

4. Double-click on the File Manager icon ![File Manager]. The File Manager window opens.

5. Change to the drive and directory that contains the file you want to print.

6. Drag the file's icon over the minimized Print Manager icon. (You can select more than one file before dragging to print several files.)

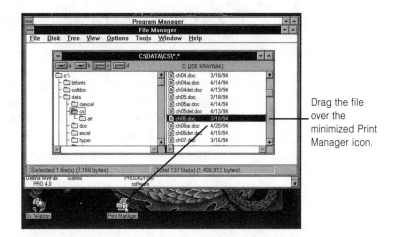

Drag the file over the minimized Print Manager icon.

Use File Manager's File Print command To bypass Print Manager icon

7. Release the mouse button. Print Manager runs the associated application, loads the document file into it, and enters the File Print command. The Print dialog box appears, asking you to enter your printing preferences.

8. Enter any printing preferences, and then click on the OK button.

Trying to get the minimized Print Manager icon and the File Manager on-screen at the same time can take some time and patience. An easier way to print files is to select the file(s) in File Manager, and then open the File menu and select Print.

#4: Load Specific Files with Icons

Use more Than one version of an icon

Most applications allow you to specify a document file you want to open when you run the application. For example, the command WINWORD.EXE runs Word for Windows. You can type a document's file name after the command to have Word for Windows open that document automatically on startup. If you commonly work with a document, you might want to create an icon specifically for that document. Here's how you do it:

1. Copy the icon for the application you use to edit the document. (To copy an icon, you hold down the Ctrl key while dragging the icon. You can copy the icon to the same group window or a different one.)

2. Open the File menu and select Properties. The Program-Item Properties dialog box appears for the copied icon.

3. Click inside the Command Line text box, right after the command used to run the application (for example, right after WINWORD.EXE).

4. Press the spacebar, and then type the drive, directory, and name of the document file you want to open at startup. (For example, type C:\DATA\SALEREP.DOC.) Most applications let you open more than one document at a time. You can separate document names by spaces to open more than one document file on startup.

   Also, instead of specifying a drive and directory on the Command Line, you can type the drive and directory name in the Working Directory text box.

Command that runs the application.

Path and name of file to load.

5. To change the icon for this application/document combo, click on the Change Icon button, and select an icon. If there aren't many icons available, click on the Browse button, and select the MORICONS.DLL file from the Windows directory. This file is packed with icons.

6. Click on the OK button when you're done.

You can make icons for more than one document file. However, keep in mind that you can run more than one copy of most applications, which can consume lots of system resources.

#5: Bypassing the Screen Saver Password

In Chapter 43, "Controlling Your Desktop," you learned how to add a password to the Windows screen saver to prevent meddlesome fellow workers from messing with your system. I hope you didn't rely on that method to protect your *supersecret* secrets. Here's how easy it is to get around the screen saver password:

• Reboot and start Windows. Before the screen saver has a chance to kick in, open the Main group window, double-click on the Control

Panel icon, and double-click on the Desktop icon. Open the Screen Saver Name drop-down list, and select None. Click on OK. The Screen Saver won't even come on, let alone demand a password.

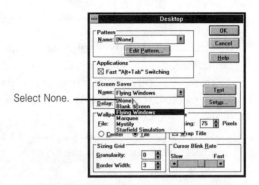

Select None.

- **Remove password protection.** Reboot, restart Windows, get the Desktop dialog box on-screen, and click on the Screen Saver Setup button. Click on Password Protected (removing the X), and click on OK. Click on OK again.

- **Delete the password from CONTROL.INI.** Open the CONTROL.INI file (it's in the \WINDOWS directory) in a text editor (Windows Notepad works). Look in the [ScreenSaver] section for Password= and then delete everything after the equal sign. When you restart Windows, the screen saver won't ask for a password. This is the best of the three options, because it allows you to enter a new password if you forgot your old one. If you just turn password protection off, you'll have to type the old password to enter a new one.

#6: Additional Cheap Security Tricks

Swap leFT/ righT mouse buTTon for securiTy

As you learned in the last section, anyone with any experience in Windows can get past the screen saver password trick, and that's probably the first thing they'll look for. I have some other cheap security tricks that they may not think of:

- **Swap the left/right mouse buttons.** Chapter 42, "Controlling Your Mouse and Keyboard," explains how to set your mouse for left-handed use. If you swap the mouse buttons, a user can left-click on a menu until he gets Carpal Tunnel Syndrome, and nothing will happen.

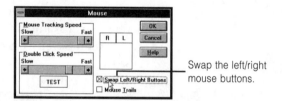

Swap the left/right mouse buttons.

- **Create a dummy Program Manager window.** Get your Program Manager on-screen, and then press the Print Screen key. This dumps a copy of the Program Manager screen onto the Windows Clipboard. Go to the Main group and double-click on the Clipboard Viewer icon. Click on the Clipboard window's Maximize button. Except for the Clipboard title bar at the top of the screen, this looks exactly like Program Manager—but clicking on an icon does nothing.

- **Make everything white.** Edit your screen colors (Chapter 40, "Changing the Screen Colors") to make the Menu Bar and Menu Text white. This hides the names of all menus.

- **Rename group windows and program-item icons.** If you created an icon that runs your word-processing program and loads your diary, don't name the icon Diary. Name it something really boring like Sales Rpt or Budget.

Beyond Survival

#7: Preventing Changes to Your Desktop

Specify what can/cannot be changed on DeskTop

If you share your computer with meddlesome co-workers, or with inexperienced users who like to foul up your carefully-constructed Windows desktop, you can lock your desktop. Here's how you do it:

1. Run Notepad from the Accessories group.

2. Open PROGMAN.INI. It's in the \WINDOWS directory.

3. At the end of the file, type **[restrictions]** and press Enter.

4. Type one or more of the following restrictions. Type each command on a separate line:

   NoSaveSettings=1 prevents any changes to the desktop from being saved when you exit Windows.

EditLevel=1 prevents anyone from creating, deleting, or renaming your program group windows. EditLevel=2 prevents all those changes plus any changes to program-item icons. EditLevel=3 prevents changes to the Command Line entry. EditLevel=4 prevents all changes to groups or icons.

5. Open the File menu and select Save.

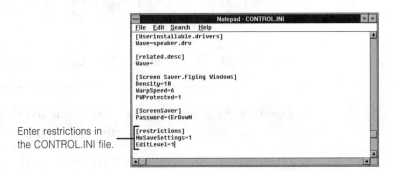

Enter restrictions in the CONTROL.INI file.

These changes will not take effect until you exit and restart Windows. If you want to change your desktop later, open CONTROL.INI, delete these lines, save the file, and then exit and restart Windows.

An even easier way to prevent changes is to open the Program Manager's Options menu and select Save Settings on Exit to turn it off. (However, this is easier to disable as well.)

#8: Creating Icons for Macros

Use icons To run macros

In Chapter 24, "Automating Windows with the Recorder," you learned how to create macros for automating tasks. However, macros are not the easiest kind of program to run in Windows. You have to assign a hot key to the macro, and then remember the hot-key combination, or you have to run the Recorder, open your macro file, select the macro, and then open the File menu and select Run. Hardly a timesaver. For often-used macros, consider creating a macro icon. Here's how:

1. Use the Recorder to record a macro, and assign it a shortcut key. The macro must have a shortcut key assigned to it, or you cannot create an icon for it. (Refer to Chapter 24 for details about creating macros and assigning them shortcut keys.)

2. Hold down the Ctrl key while dragging the Recorder icon inside the Accessories group or to another group window. (This copies the Recorder icon.)

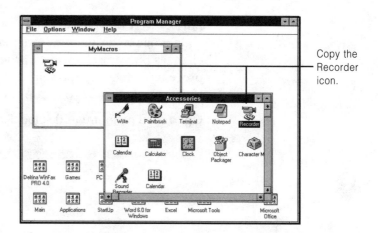

Copy the Recorder icon.

3. Open the Program Manager's File menu and choose Properties. The Program-Item Properties dialog box appears.

4. (Optional) To change the Recorder icon's title, type a new title in the Description text box.

5. Inside the Command Line text box, move the insertion point after the RECORDER.EXE line, and press the spacebar.

6. Type the command line required to run the macro. This is the tricky part. Here's an example: Say you saved your macro file in the WINDOWS directory and named it MYMACROS.REC. You assigned the macro the shortcut key Ctrl+Shift+F11. The command line would read:

RECORDER.EXE -H ^ +F11 c:\windows\mymacros.rec

(It's important that the -H be uppercase.) Here's a rundown of the command: RECORDER.EXE runs the Recorder application. -H tells the recorder to run a macro. ^ stands for the Ctrl key, while + stands for the Shift key. (If you used the Alt key for a hot key, you would use % to represent it.) c:\windows\mymacros.rec specifies the location and name of the macro file that contains the macro you want to run.

^ = Ctrl

+ = Shift

% = Alt

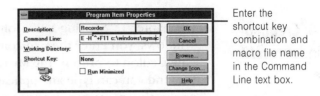

Enter the
shortcut key
combination and
macro file name
in the Command
Line text box.

Drag icon into
Startup
window To
have IT run on
Windows
startup

7. (Optional) To change the icon for this macro, click on the Change
Icon button, and then click on the Browse button. Select the
MORICONS.DLL file or PROGMAN.EXE (both in the \WINDOWS
directory) or select some other file that contains icons. Click on
the OK button. Then select the icon you want to use, and click on
the OK button.

8. Click on the OK button. You can now double-click on this icon to
run the macro.

#9: Read Any .HLP File

Sometimes, you'll get an application that comes with one or more .HLP
files. These files are designed to display help screens if you open the
application's Help menu and select a topic. However, you may not
even be able to get to the application to view its help system. In such a
case, you can use WINHELP.EXE to view the .HLP file. To run Windows
Help, here's what you do:

1. Open the Program Manager's File menu and select Run.

2. Type **c:\windows\winhelp.exe** and press Enter.

The Windows
Help screen

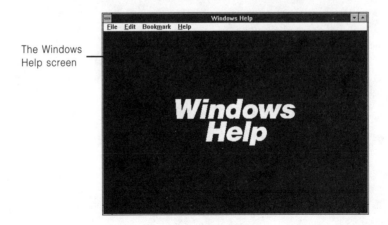

3. Use the File Open command to open the .HLP file you want to
view.

#10: Creating Windows .BAT Files

Create several batch files with different names

In Chapter 1, "Starting Microsoft Windows," you learned that to run Windows, you enter the win command. You also learned that you can type a colon to prevent the Microsoft advertising screen from appearing, and you can type an application name to have Windows load the application at startup. If you commonly start Windows a certain way, consider creating a batch file to enter all your preferences. Name the file W.BAT and store it in the root directory of drive C. That way, all you have to do is press W and then Enter to run Windows. Following are a couple sample .BAT files:

win : (Starts Windows without the advertising screen.)

win : c:\winword\winword (Starts Windows without the advertising screen, and loads Word for Windows.)

win : c:\excel\excel c:\data\excel\salesrep.xls (Starts Windows without the advertising screen, loads Excel, and opens the file SALESREP.XLS.)

Use Notepad, as explained in Chapter 20, to create your batch files. Run Notepad, type the desired command, and then use the File Save command to save the batch file. Type a name for the batch file, and add the .BAT extension. To be able to run the batch file from any directory, use the Drives and Directories options to select the root directory of drive C.

Cheat Sheet

What You Need to Run Windows 3.1

- IBM PC or compatible with an 80286 or better processor.
- 1 megabyte or more of RAM for a 286, or 2 megabytes or more for a 386 or better. 4 megabytes or more is recommended.
- EGA or VGA graphics adapter or better.
- A hard disk with 5 megabytes free space (if you are installing over an existing version of Windows) or 10 megabytes if installing Windows for the first time.
- At least one 1.2M or 1.44M diskette drive.
- MS-DOS 3.1 or higher. MS-DOS 5.0 or higher is recommended.
- A Microsoft (or compatible) mouse.

Windows Setup Options

- Windows Setup gives you two setup choices: Express or Custom.
- Express Setup does a lot for you: it copies the files to the \WINDOWS directory, edits CONFIG.SYS and AUTOEXEC.BAT, and sets up your hardware to work with Windows.
- Custom Setup requires you to know about your system's hardware; it lets you choose which parts of Windows to install. Choose this option only if you are an experienced Windows user.

Performing an Express Setup

1. Write-protect your Windows Setup diskettes.
2. Insert Windows Setup Disk 1 in drive A or B.
3. Type **a:setup** or **b:setup** and press Enter.
4. Press Enter.
5. Press Enter to choose Express Setup.
6. Follow the on-screen instructions, and swap disks when instructed to do so.

Installing Windows 3.1

Most PCs nowadays come with Windows installed on the computer's hard disk. You simply enter the command to run Windows (see Chapter 1, "Starting Microsoft Windows"), and you're up and running. If you just bought Windows 3.1, however, this chapter will show you how easy it is to install it.

Basic Survival

What You Need to Run Windows 3.1

Need IBM PC, 386 or better, 4 megs or more of RAM

If you just bought a new PC, it is probably Windows-ready. Most new PCs come with a 386 or better processor (486 or Pentium), large hard disks, VGA or better monitors, and a workable version of DOS. However, if you have an older PC, check the documentation to make sure it meets the minimum requirements for running Windows 3.1:

- IBM PC or compatible with an 80286 or better processor. To run Windows 3.1, you should really have a 386 or better that runs at least at 25MHz. Otherwise, your system will appear slow.

- 1 megabyte or more of RAM for a 286 or 2 megabytes or more for a 386 or better. 4 megabytes or more is recommended. To check for memory, type **mem** at the DOS prompt, and press Enter.

- EGA or VGA graphics adapter or better. If your system has a graphics accelerator or Windows accelerator card, it will run Windows much faster.

- A hard disk with 5 megabytes free space (if installing over an existing version of Windows) or 10 megabytes (if installing Windows for the first time). This is free—that is, available—disk space. To check free disk space, type **chkdsk** at the DOS prompt, and press Enter.

- At least one 1.2M or 1.44M disk drive. A floppy drive is required to copy the Windows files from the disks you purchased to your hard disk.

- **MS-DOS 3.1 or higher.** MS-DOS 5.0 or higher is recommended.

- **A Microsoft (or compatible) mouse.** You may be able to work without a mouse, but the process could drive you insane.

Windows Setup Options

Express Setup = best choice in most cases

Before installing Windows, you should be aware that Windows gives you two setup options:

Express Setup asks you for your name and prompts you to select the type of printer that's installed. The Setup program takes care of the rest. It creates a \WINDOWS directory on your hard disk, and copies the Windows files to the directory. It edits your CONFIG.SYS and AUTOEXEC.BAT files for optimal Windows performance, and sets up your hardware to work with Windows. It even searches your hard disk for non-Windows applications, and creates icons for them so you can run those applications easily from Windows.

Custom Setup requires you to know about the hardware installed on your system. This option also lets you choose which Windows features and applications you want to install. You'll be asked to specify the type of computer you're using, the monitor type, and which changes you want to make to AUTOEXEC.BAT and CONFIG.SYS. Choose this option only if you are an experienced Windows user.

When Setup starts, it gives you two Setup options.

```
Windows Setup

    Windows provides two Setup methods:

    Express Setup (Recommended)
    Express Setup relies on Setup to make decisions,
    so setting up Windows is quick and easy.

        To use Express Setup, press ENTER.

    Custom Setup
    Custom Setup is for experienced computer users who
    want to control how Windows is set up. To use this Setup method,
    you should know how to use a mouse with Windows.

        To use Custom Setup, press C.

    For details about both Setup methods, press F1.

  ENTER=Express Setup   C=Custom Setup   F1=Help   F3=Exit
```

Performing an Express Setup

The Express Setup option is the easiest, fastest, safest way to install Windows 3.1. Here's what you do:

1. Write-protect your Windows Setup disks. For 3.5-inch disks, slide the write-protect tab so you can see through the "window." For

5.25-inch disks, place a write-protect sticker over the notch in the side of the disk.

2. Insert Windows Setup Disk 1 in drive A or B, and close the drive door if necessary.

3. Type **a:setup** if the setup disk is in drive A, or **b:setup** if the disk is in drive B, and press Enter. A welcome screen appears, allowing you to continue, get help, or exit.

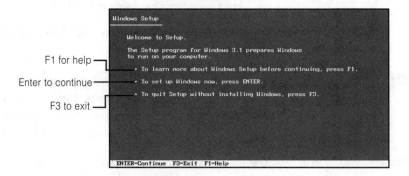

F1 for help

Enter to continue

F3 to exit

Press Fl at any Time for help

4. Press Enter to continue. Setup displays a dialog box asking if you want to perform an Express or Custom setup.

5. Press Enter to choose Express Setup.

6. If you have a previous version of Windows on your computer, Setup displays a message asking if you want to upgrade that version of Windows. It provides a box that shows the directory in which the existing version is stored. Press Enter to install Windows 3.1 over the existing version. (If you type a different drive or directory name, Setup will copy the files there, but this may cause problems when you try to run Windows.)

7. Setup displays a message telling you to wait while it checks your system. Then Setup starts copying the files from Disk 1 to the specified hard drive and directory (usually C:\WINDOWS). When Setup is done with Disk 1, it displays a message telling you to insert Disk 2.

It is recommended
that you install over
the previous
version.

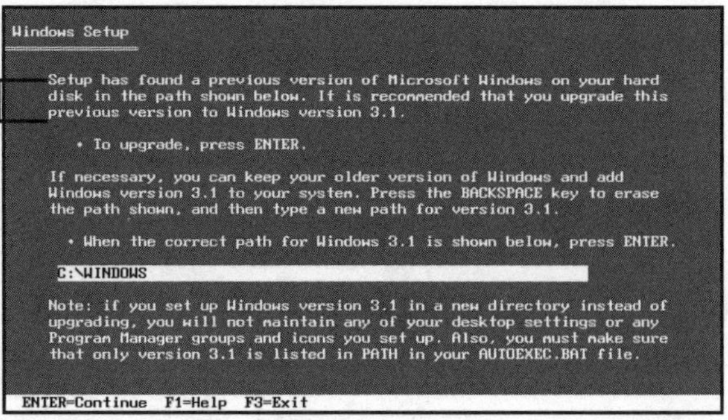

```
Windows Setup

Setup has found a previous version of Microsoft Windows on your hard
disk in the path shown below. It is recommended that you upgrade this
previous version to Windows version 3.1.

     • To upgrade, press ENTER.

If necessary, you can keep your older version of Windows and add
Windows version 3.1 to your system. Press the BACKSPACE key to erase
the path shown, and then type a new path for version 3.1.

     • When the correct path for Windows 3.1 is shown below, press ENTER.

C:\WINDOWS

Note: if you set up Windows version 3.1 in a new directory instead of
upgrading, you will not maintain any of your desktop settings or any
Program Manager groups and icons you set up. Also, you must make sure
that only version 3.1 is listed in PATH in your AUTOEXEC.BAT file.

ENTER=Continue   F1=Help   F3=Exit
```

8. Remove the disk from the drive, insert the next disk, and press the
Enter key.

9. Repeat step 8, swapping disks when told, until Setup displays a
screen indicating that it must start Windows to complete the
installation process. The Windows Setup screen then appears,
asking you to type your name and company name.

*Reboot
when asked*

10. Follow the on-screen instructions. You'll have to pick a printer
and swap one or two more disks in and out of the drive. When
Setup is done installing Windows, it asks if you want to reboot.
Choose the reboot option to activate any changes.

Beyond Survival

**Custom Setup:
Why Bother?**

If you're strapped for disk space and you don't want Setup deciding
which features and applications to install, you can run the Custom
Setup. You might also want to run Custom Setup if your computer has
hardware that requires special treatment. However, I don't recommend
it, unless you're a computer expert.

*Use Control
Panel To
change
options later*

My recommendation is to go with the Express Setup and then use the
Control Panel, as explained in Part 5 of this book, to change any system
settings. If you're strapped for disk space, see Chapter 51,
"Uncluttering Your Disk," for details on how to delete the Windows
files that you don't use. If Setup makes unwanted changes to your
CONFIG.SYS and AUTOEXEC.BAT files, see Chapter 49, "Reading and
Editing System Files," to learn how to edit those changes.

In short, let Setup do its thing to ensure a thorough and correct installation, and *then* you can go back and tweak it when you know what
you're doing.

Index

X-Y-Z

Who cares what you think? WE DO!

We take our customers' opinions very personally. After all, you're the reason we publish these books. If you're not happy, we're doing something wrong.

We'd appreciate it if you would take the time to drop us a note or fax us a fax. A real person—not a computer—reads every letter we get, and makes sure that your comments get relayed to the appropriate people.

Not sure what to say? Here are some details we'd like to know:

- Who you are (age, occupation, hobbies, etc.)
- Where you bought the book
- Why you picked this book instead of a different one
- What you liked best about the book
- What could have been done better
- Your overall opinion of the book
- What other topics you would purchase a book on

Mail, e-mail, or fax it to:

Faithe Wempen
Product Development Manager

Alpha Books
201 West 103rd Street
Indianapolis, IN 46290

FAX: (317) 581-4669
CIS: 75430,174

Special Offer!

Alpha Books needs people like you to give opinions about new and existing books. Product testers receive free books in exchange for providing their opinions about them. If you would like to be a product tester, please mention it in your letter, and make sure you include your full name, address, and daytime phone.

Starting and Exiting Windows

Starting Windows

1. At DOS prompt, type **c:** and press Enter.
2. Type **cd\windows** and press Enter.
3. Type one of the following, then press Enter:

   win starts Windows

   win : bypasses Windows advertising screen

   win /s forces Windows to run in Standard mode

   win /3 forces Windows to run in 386 Enhanced mode

Getting Help

- Open the Help menu and select the desired type of help, or press the F1 key for Help Contents.
- Press F1 again for help on how to use Help.

Use buttons to go forward or back.

Click on dotted underlined term to see definition.

Click on solid underlined term for more help.

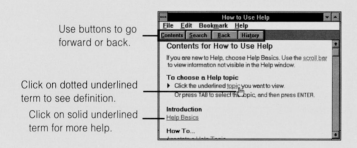

Running the Windows Tutorial

Open Program Manager's Help menu

Click on Windows Tutorial

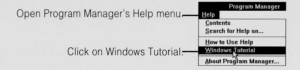

Exiting Windows

- Open Program Manager's File menu, and select Exit.
- Press Alt+F4.
- Double-click on the Control-menu box ⬒ in the upper left corner of the Program Manager window.

Windows Anatomy

Windows Parts

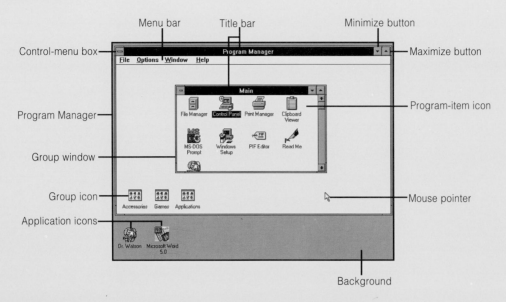

Program Manager allows you to run other applications in Windows.

The **title bar** tells the name of the application and sometimes the name of the open document.

Click on the **Control-menu box** to open a menu that lets you close, resize, or move a window.

Click on a **Minimize button** to shrink a window to icon size.

Click on a **Maximize button** to make a window full-screen.

The **menu bar** contains the names of pull-down menus; click on a menu name to open a menu.

Double-click on a **group icon** to see its contents.

Group windows contain program-item icons for running applications.

Double-click on a **program-item icon** to run an application.

Application icons represent running applications whose Minimize buttons were clicked.

The **background** is the backdrop for Windows.

The **mouse pointer** lets you point to and select menus, commands, and objects on-screen.

Basic Windows Tasks

Using a Mouse

- **Point**   Roll the mouse on your desk until the tip of the mouse pointer touches the desired object on your screen.
- **Click**   Press and release the left mouse button once, without moving the mouse.
- **Double-click**   Press and release the left mouse button twice quickly, without moving the mouse.
- **Drag**   Hold down the left mouse button while moving the mouse.

Opening Group Windows

- Double-click on the group icon ![Games icon] Games.
- Open the Program Manager's Windows menu, and select the group window.

Running Windows Applications

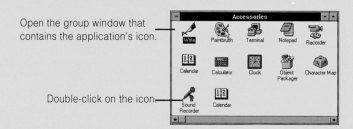

Open the group window that contains the application's icon.

Double-click on the icon.

Switching Between Applications

- Press Ctrl+Esc, select the application, click on the Switch To button.
- Hold down the Alt key while pressing the Tab key until the name of the application is displayed. Release the Alt key.
- Click anywhere inside desired application window.

Moving and Sizing Windows

Drag the title bar to move the window.

Drag the border to size the window.

Entering Commands in Windows

Selecting a Menu Command

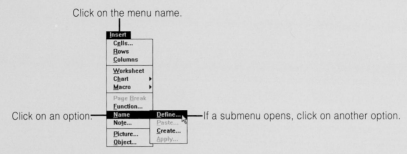

Click on the menu name.

Click on an option. —— If a submenu opens, click on another option.

Types of Menu Commands

Light gray options are unavailable for what you are currently doing.

Options with an arrow open a *submenu* that requires you to select another option.

Options with a check mark indicate that an option is currently active. To turn the option off, select it.

Options followed by a series of dots (...) open a *dialog box* that requests additional information.

Working with Dialog Boxes

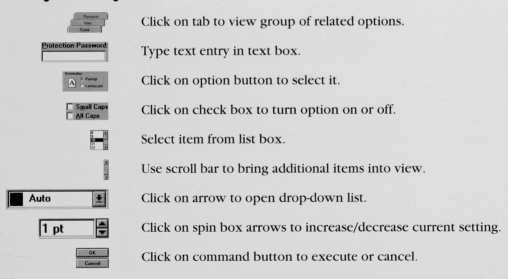

Click on tab to view group of related options.

Type text entry in text box.

Click on option button to select it.

Click on check box to turn option on or off.

Select item from list box.

Use scroll bar to bring additional items into view.

Click on arrow to open drop-down list.

Click on spin box arrows to increase/decrease current setting.

Click on command button to execute or cancel.

Using Shortcut Keys to Bypass Menus

- To learn of available menu shortcut keys, open the menus; shortcut keys are usually listed next to options.
- Press shortcut key to bypass menu.

Using the File Manager

Starting File Manager

1. Open the Main group window.

2. Double-click on the File Manager icon .

Changing Drives and Directories

Click on a drive icon to activate the drive.

Shift+click on a drive icon to see all the directories on the drive.

Click on directory name to select it.

Click on file name to select it.

Selecting Files

- To select one file, click on it.
- To select a group of neighboring files, click on the first file, and then Shift+click on the last file.
- To select non-neighboring files, Ctrl+click on each file.

Copying and Moving Files

Select the files or directory to move.

Drag one of the selected files over a drive or directory icon. Hold down the Shift key to move or Ctrl to copy.

Common Windows Application Tasks

Saving a File

1. Click on File in the application's menu bar.
2. Click on Save.

Double-click here to move up the directory tree.

Type a name (up to eight characters).

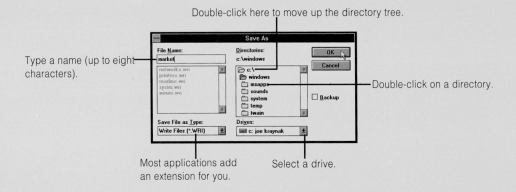

Double-click on a directory.

Most applications add an extension for you.

Select a drive.

Opening a File

1. Click on File in the application's menu bar.
2. Click on Open.

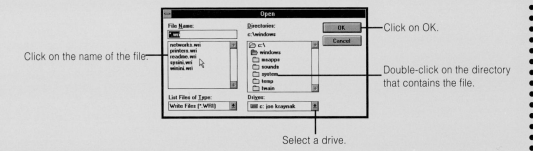

Click on OK.

Click on the name of the file.

Double-click on the directory that contains the file.

Select a drive.

Printing a Document

1. Create or open the file you want to print.
2. Click on File in the menu bar.
3. Click on Print.
4. Click on the OK button.

Cutting, Copying, and Pasting Selections

1. Open the document that contains the item you want to cut or copy.
2. Select the text, graphic, or other object to copy.
3. Open the Edit menu and select Cut or Copy.
4. Go to where you want the copied or cut selection pasted.
5. Open the Edit menu and select Paste.